A Day in the Life

A Day in the Life

*one family, the beautiful people,
and the end of the sixties*

Robert Greenfield

DA CAPO PRESS
A Member of the Perseus Books Group

Designed by Trish Wilkinson
Set in 11 point Minion

Library of Congress Cataloging-in-Publication Data

Greenfield, Robert.
  A day in the life : one family, the beautiful people, and the end of the sixties / Robert Greenfield. — 1st Da Capo Press ed.
     p.   cm.
Includes bibliographical references.
ISBN 978-0-306-81622-2 (alk. paper)
  1. Weber, Thomas Evelyn, 1938–2006. 2. Weber, Thomas Evelyn, 1938–2006—Marriage. 3. Weber, Thomas Evelyn, 1938-2006—Family.
4. Upper class—England—Biography. 5. Married people—England—Biography. 6. Socialites—England—Biography. 7. England—Biography.
8. Denmark—Biography. 9. Social history—1960–1970. 10. Problem families—Case studies. I. Title.
CT788.W396G74 2009
942.085'60922—dc22   2009004146

First Da Capo Press edition 2009
ISBN 978-0-306-81622-2
Published by Da Capo Press
A Member of the Perseus Books Group
www.dacapopress.com

Da Capo Press books are available at special discounts for bulk purchases in the U.S. by corporations, institutions, and other organizations. For more information, please contact the Special Markets Department at the Perseus Books Group, 2300 Chestnut Street, Suite 200, Philadelphia, PA 19103, or call (800) 810-4145, ext. 5000, or e-mail special.markets@perseusbooks.com.

10 9 8 7 6 5 4 3 2 1

For Jake, Charley, Buddy, Beau,
and Waylon Weber, and Gabriel Bailey

"Beauty is truth, truth beauty,"—that is all
Ye know on earth, and all ye need to know.
—JOHN KEATS, "ODE ON A GRECIAN URN"

She fell for all that peace and love and it worked to a certain extent and then it became an excuse for the worst people to get involved with the best people and they were brought down to that level.
—TOMMY WEBER, ON HIS WIFE, PUSS

Funnily enough, I've often thought, "I wonder what happened to Tom."
—HUGH RAMSBOTHAM, TOMMY WEBER'S CLASSMATE

contents

prologue: a day in the life, villa nellcote, june 1971

The boys have had a fantastic day. Beneath a canopy of endless blue sky filled with so much sunshine that the world itself seems to have been spun from liquid gold, they have been out and about and having fun on the French Riviera, the playground of choice for those with enough time and money to afford only the best that life can offer. Now they have returned to the great house where for the past month, they have been staying with their father as honored guests.

Although the boys are brothers and both beautiful in their own way, they do not look at all like one another. The older one, eight years old, has a small, fine-boned face framed by long, straight, blond hair that any girl his age would envy. Having grown up among adults, he is finely attuned to their changing moods. By far the more independent and self-reliant of the two, his six-year-old brother sports a wild unruly mane of thick brown hair that makes him look like a young knight of the realm in training.

As they both rush toward the front door of the house, eager to tell their father about all they have done and seen today, the air is rich and thick with the scent of flowers in full, riotous bloom.

Surrounded by exotic trees brought from all over the world that have grown wild into a tangled jungle through which the boys make their way each day like explorers in darkest Africa, this house has become for them a veritable Garden of Eden, where life is an endless party and nothing bad can ever happen.

Their father, a shockingly handsome man of regal bearing who has long since become accustomed to staying in such houses, has always felt very much at home on the French Riviera. Nine years ago, he brought his beautiful young bride, then already three months pregnant with their first son, here on their honeymoon. More recently, he and his two sons spent several weeks on the Côte d'Azur accompanying the beautiful actress with whom he was living as she made her latest film. That relationship is now over. For the past month, he has been waiting for his former wife, who has not been well but whom he still loves, to join him so they can begin putting their family back together again.

As the older boy enters the house, he sees the utterly stricken look on his father's face. Immediately, he knows something bad has happened. Without any preamble, the father tells his sons that he has terrible news. Their mother has died. The older boy's reaction is instantaneous. Uncontrollable hysteria. As if on cue, his younger brother begins to weep as well. Finding it hard to breathe, the boy tries to steady himself, but it does no good. As one, both brothers begin wailing at the top of their voices.

Although the father goes on talking, explaining that this was an accident, the older boy can no longer hear a word he says. For him, everything has gone white, like at the end of a movie, when the final credits disappear and the screen is suddenly filled with harsh, brilliant light as the projector burns through empty, flapping frames of film stock. In his head, he can hear only a whirling, symphonic cacophony of noise much like the one created by the Beatles at the end of one of their most iconic songs. It is as though he has been placed into an isolation chamber from which there is no escape. For both boys, the days that follow become a blank and empty period about which they will later remember nothing whatsoever.

If this were a movie, it would track the effect of this disastrous event on their lives. Because it is a moment in time, replete with all the messy complications that occur in real life, the father and his boys know only that the woman who was always at the center of their lives is now gone and that what for them was just a day in the life has suddenly become something else again.

1
hald hovedgaard

Right from the start, nothing about him was ordinary. Thomas Evelyn Weber, born Thomas Ejnar Arkner on December 1, 1938, was raised in a great house on a twenty-five-hundred-acre estate where those with wealth and power had lived in baronial splendor since the start of the Middle Ages. Located in the Dollerup Hills not far from Viborg, the seat of Denmark's Jutland Peninsula, the sprawling manor house that was the fifth and final incarnation of Hald Hovedgaard (the ruins of four castles also bearing the name can still be found on the land) was built in 1787 by a high-court judge known as "the mad magistrate of Hald." The estate then passed through the hands of fourteen owners before being given in 1936 as an incredibly extravagant wedding gift to Poul Christian Arkner and his brand-new bride, the former Pamela Joyce Weber.

Blonde and good-looking, she was the daughter of a wealthy, well-educated English businessman named Reginald Evelyn Weber, who by dint of his great success in trade and close ties to the royal family claimed to be a baron. Although both Pamela, a talented painter and pianist, and her older sister Ann, could have referred to themselves as baronesses, they never did so, in part because their parents divorced when both girls were still quite young.

1

Renounced by her family for her part in the divorce, Pamela's mother, the former Joyce Warner, set off with her daughters to make a new life for herself in Africa. In 1925, when Pamela was eight years old, Joyce married a fifty-year-old retired British army brigadier general named Lionel Boyd, who had been awarded the Distinguished Service Order and the Croix d'Officier of the Legion of Honor for his service during World War I. Much like Karen Blixen and her husband, Bror, in nearby Kenya, the couple established a coffee plantation in a forest not far from the city of Arusha near Kilimanjaro in the northern region of what is now called Tanzania.

Unlike Karen Blixen, Joyce Boyd viewed the natives who worked for her as lazy, shiftless children who had little or no ambition. She complained bitterly about trying to live a truly civilized life in a land still so untamed that she would sometimes step out onto her veranda only to find a leopard playing with the household cat. Becoming a dedicated and fearless hunter, she spent her days stalking through the bush in a cloche hat and a long dress with a rifle in her hand, intent on killing anything wild that moved. She also welcomed Edward, Prince of Wales, to her farm, which was renowned for its gardens.

In 1933, four years before *Out of Africa* by Isak Dinesen (Karen Blixen's pen name) was published, Joyce Boyd wrote a book titled *My Farm in Lion Country*. A classical colonial text, her memoir has none of the deeply felt love for the land and those who lived on it that makes *Out of Africa* an enduring classic. Nonetheless, whenever Joyce Boyd went on safari in Kenya, she stayed with Karen Blixen on her farm at the foot of the Ngong Hills.

It was there that sixteen-year-old Pamela, who along with her sister had become one of the most eligible and attractive young women in the territory, met the legendary English aesthete and jungle guide Denys Finch Hatton. Pamela also caught the eye of Karen Blixen's husband, Bror, a Swedish baron who was a big-game hunter and a well-known serial philanderer. Pointedly, Joyce

Boyd once told "Blix," as he was known to his many friends, "There are two girls in Africa you'll never get your hands on, and those are my two daughters."

Although she managed to keep her girls out of Blixen's clutches, Joyce Boyd could not prevent Pamela from falling in love with the handsome Danish former soldier who was nearly twice her age and who managed a nearby sisal farm. From an early age, Poul Arkner, born Poul Christian Anderson in March 1902, seems to have suffered from what his older son would later call delusions of grandeur. Hoping to discover royalty in his ancestry, Poul Arkner once hired someone to trace his ancestry, only to discover that although his family had lived in Denmark since the eleventh century, he was in fact the direct descendant of a casual relationship between a Spanish soldier and a Danish prostitute. He changed his last name to Arkner to avoid being confused with a Danish printer named Poul Anderson, who became a well-known resistance leader during World War II.

After graduating from the Royal Danish Military Institute, Poul Arkner, whose father had served with distinction as a lieutenant colonel in the Royal Danish Army, began what should have been a lifelong career of service to his country. Deciding to look elsewhere for advancement and adventure, Poul Arkner persuaded a cousin who was a medical doctor to certify that he suffered from a heart condition. After being discharged from the army, he joined the French Foreign Legion.

Stationed for five years at Sidi bel Abbès, the notorious desert hellhole that served as legion headquarters in Algeria, Poul Arkner became one of the few foreign enlistees to rise up through the ranks and be commissioned as an officer. Fluent in French, German, Danish, Swedish, and Norwegian, he learned to speak Swahili in Tanganyika. His older son would later describe him as someone who "just used people all his life and when he had used them up, then he would discard them." Poul Arkner, who as a young man looked much like Errol Flynn in his heyday, had little trouble persuading Pamela Weber that he was the man with whom she was meant to spend her life.

In 1936, Pamela defied her mother's wishes and eloped with Poul Arkner to Denmark. The newlyweds were on a boat headed for their new home when Pamela learned that her mother had died of typhoid, which meant that her father was now her sole protector. Fearing that fortune-hunting young men might try to marry his daughters solely for their money, Reginald Weber had already established large trust funds in both their names to safeguard their wealth.

Any doubts Poul Arkner may have had as to the size of the dowry that Pamela would bring to their marriage were immediately dispelled by her father's lavish wedding gift. In 1936, when the British pound was still worth five American dollars, the estate known as Hald Hovedgaard was valued at a million pounds. It is difficult to come up with a modern equivalent for this sum. In terms of buying power, fifty million dollars might be a more accurate estimate than five. The title to the estate, first registered in Reginald Weber's name, was soon transferred to Poul Arkner.

In November of the year she was married, Pamela gave birth to her first son, Anders Reginald Arkner. That Poul Arkner chose to name the boy after his own father rather than the man whose incredible largesse had enabled him to live like a lord at Hald and whom he treated with great respect, always addressing him as "Sir," says a good deal about the man. So does the fact that when his second son was born two years later, Poul Arkner chose "Ejnar" as his middle name. In Danish, the name is synonymous with *dristig*, meaning "bold, audacious, daring, frank, or outspoken." It also corresponds with the Icelandic term for "the one who fights alone."

At the age of twenty-one, Pamela found herself living with two young sons and her husband on a great estate with a lake, ancient earthworks, moats, battlements, barns, roundhouses, and depots. For a while, life at Hald was good. Thanks to Pamela's trust fund, money was not a problem. As soon as her first son was old enough to sit at the keyboard, she began teaching him to play the piano. Poul Arkner bought his own plane and began growing potatoes for export to Britain. Becoming part of a social set composed of the local nobility as well as those who had attained some degree of celebrity in Denmark, the couple entertained constantly.

On August 24, 1939, the Soviet Union and Nazi Germany signed a nonaggression pact that included a secret protocol ceding Finland to Russia as a Soviet sphere of influence. Three months later, on November 30, 1939, Russian troops invaded Finland and the Winter War began. A staunch patriot who had always hated the Bolsheviks, Poul Arkner flew off in his own plane to help the Finns defend their land.

Years later, Tommy Weber could still remember watching his father take off for war from Hald, his plane so heavily laden with sides of pork and crates of schnapps that it barely cleared the trees along the lakeshore. "That was the last I saw of him for a long while," he said. "I assumed he was fighting the Germans." Becoming a captain in the Finnish army, Poul Arkner helped battle the invading Red Army to a standstill. When the war ended in March 1940, he returned to Hald.

A month later, on April 9, 1940, Denmark was overrun by the Nazis. Because most Danes could trace the purity of their blood line back to the Vikings and many of them looked like the race of true Aryan supermen Adolf Hitler hoped would soon take over the world (and because Nazi troops were needed to fight on other fronts), the Third Reich offered the king of Denmark a deal. As long as there was no organized resistance within the nation's borders, Germany would respect Danish independence.

Knowing that his nation stood no chance against the overwhelming power of the Nazi military juggernaut, King Christian X quickly capitulated and the five-year German occupation of Denmark began. Although it is a myth that the king wore a yellow Star of David when the Jews in his country were ordered to do so, the Danes as a people did such a good job of protecting their Jews that when the Nazis finally began rounding up Danish Jews in 1943, most were already gone.

Although the Nazi occupation put an abrupt end to Poul Arkner's potato export business to Great Britain, a nation the Luftwaffe had already begun bombing on a nightly basis, he had little trouble accommodating himself to the new state of affairs. On a regular basis at Hald, he began entertaining high-ranking Nazi officers, all of whom would have looked on him with favor for several reasons. Poul Arkner could trace his own lineage back through several generations (though not with the results he had expected). A wealthy land owner of pure blood as well as a highly trained soldier, he had already demonstrated his courage and military expertise by serving as an officer in the Royal Danish Army and the French Foreign Legion.

That he had also fought against the Communists in Finland was yet another feather in his cap. When the Nazis abrogated their nonaggression pact with the Soviet Union by invading Russia on June 22, 1941, Poul Arkner's stock rose even higher. And then there was the way he felt about the Jews. "I wouldn't say he was anti-Semitic," his older son would later say, "but when my father spoke about the Jews, it was as though he was speaking about a lesser people."

On June 25, 1941, Finland declared war on Russia, beginning the Continuation War, which went on until September 1944. Although many Danish Nazis went off to fight the Soviets, Poul Arkner refused to serve with them and instead joined a Swedish-speaking unit of the Finnish army. At Hald, he left behind his two young sons and Pamela, whom the Nazis considered an enemy subject.

Clearly identifying themselves with their mother and the land of her birth, both boys began riding around the vast estate with Union Jack flags affixed to their bicycles while wearing caps bearing the red, white, and blue roundel of the British Royal Air Force. Six months after the Continuation War began, Great Britain, now an ally of the Soviet Union, declared war on Finland. Technically, Poul Arkner was now fighting against his wife's homeland. Returning to Hald after his term of service ended, he resumed his position as the lord of the manor.

By then, Pamela had realized that, much like the armed conflict raging throughout Europe, her marriage had now also become a long and bitter war. A lifelong alcoholic who became angry and violent whenever he was drunk and his wife dared to confront him about his behavior, Poul Arkner once beat his young wife so badly that she ended up in the hospital. Fearing for her life, she left him three times, only to return to Hald to care for her sons.

The marriage finally ended after a rancorous argument at the breakfast table in front of both boys on Easter Sunday 1943. "I don't blame her for leaving the man," her older son said, "because he was a vicious bugger. He was a bully and he struck me. It's horrible for a son to say about a father who's been dead for twenty years, but he was a sod. The truth is that neither my mother or my father had the slightest conception of what it meant to be a parent."

Moving to Copenhagen, Pamela went underground and began working as a cipher officer for the British navy. In return for being allowed to hide out in an attic, she played boogie-woogie piano in a nightclub for a well-known swing band. At Hald, where Poul Arkner was now in control of his sons, neither boy could escape his wrath for long. Uncontrollable even as a child, Tommy later remembered that his father regularly kept him tethered to a ring mounted on a post in the yard outside the manor house.

One night, during a big dinner party attended by several drunken Nazi officers and their lady friends, Anders dared Tommy to crawl under the table and urinate in the officers' boots. Instead, the boy relieved himself in his father's shoes: "I pissed in his pumps, and Pa recognized this little tinkle in his boots and he looked down, and there I was, laughing at him. He picked me up by the scuff of my neck like a rabbit in front of all these people and said, 'This is an Englander and he has just pissed in my boots.'"

After he had been given a "frightful beating" for somehow managing to flood his father's office on another occasion, Tommy ran to one of the henhouses on the estate. In a fit of anger, he emptied all the laying boxes and threw the eggs against the wall. As he later said, "I'm sure I got another beating for that." Subconsciously, Tommy may have also been sticking up for his mother, with whom he now had contact only via the radio. Avidly, he would listen to her play piano whenever she performed. Saying "I'm playing this one for my son," Pamela would launch into her own rendition of the Andrews Sisters' worldwide hit, "Boogie Woogie Bugle Boy," a song she knew that he loved.

As she neared the end of her life more than sixty years later, Pamela would often sit down to play the piano, only to begin looking nervously over her shoulder. Abruptly, she would then put an end to her performance. It was a habit she had picked up during the war while performing in nightclubs where Nazi officers came to be entertained. Living underground while working for the British navy, she was by then firmly convinced that her husband had denounced her to the SS, thereby giving her good reason to fear for her safety.

By 1943, the Nazis, whom Tommy would later remember as being "very easy-going" when they first occupied Denmark, had ratcheted up their own activities throughout the county. Three years earlier, they had seized the large tuberculosis sanatorium that had been built near Hald because the climate was considered beneficial. Scouring Denmark, Norway, and Finland for itinerant gypsies, whom the Danes called *zigeuners*, the Nazis converted the sanatorium into a large holding facility for the Romany.

Coming home from school one day, Anders heard a loud commotion at Baekkelund, the railway station nearest Hald. As the seven-year-old drew nearer the railway siding, he saw two Nazi officers, one with a monocle in his eye, standing side by side. Wearing tailor-made uniforms with long great coats, riding breeches, and high leather boots, they were chain-smoking cigarettes from long holders as they engaged in a very intense discussion, quite possibly about what they planned to have for dinner. Neither paid any attention to the noncommissioned officers who were using Alsatian dogs to herd hundreds of gypsies, some playing violins, into transport trucks for a journey to Auschwitz from which few would return. The scene made such an indelible impression on the young boy that to this day, his attitude toward "the Germans as a nation is one I still can't repeat."

In 1945, as the war in Europe began winding down, Pamela was sent with Wing Commander Hamish Mackenzie-Kerr to find the graves of British pilots who had been shot down over Denmark. The two fell in love and planned to be married when they returned to England. Before they could leave Denmark, Pamela had to reclaim her sons from Poul Arkner, who was now facing charges for having fought with the Germans, which he had in fact never done.

When Pamela returned to Hald for the first time since leaving her husband, she was accompanied by a crew of technicians so she could play the piano there for a live radio broadcast. Hearing the thrilling sound of Chopin's *Fantasie Impromptu* coursing through the house, seven-year-old Tommy ran into the music room only to realize that his mother, whom he had not seen for two years, was home again. Turning from the keyboard, Pamela saw her son and said, "Ah . . . *Tommy!*" Forsaking Chopin, she launched into "Boogie Woogie Bugle Boy." "I had this smile on my face that I couldn't wipe off," he recalled. "She stopped in the middle and played my song, a boogie. It was a wonderful, wonderful reunion. Then came the legal battles over the estate and who it belonged to, and Pa was on criminal charges for fighting with the Germans. They were going to drop all the charges if he gave up both me and my older brother and he said yes."

Fairlie Mackenzie-Kerr, one of Pamela's two daughters by Hamish Mackenzie-Kerr, tells a slightly different version of the story. After Pamela hired a lawyer who sent Poul Arkner a letter stating that Pamela was going to sue him for three manslaughter attempts at Hald, Arkner contacted Pamela and said, "No, no, no, don't do that. I'll meet you and give you the children. You can have the children and we'll forget about all that. And you can go."

A meeting for the transfer of the children was arranged. As Poul Arkner drove there with his sons, Anders sensed something was about to happen and kept a tight hold on his younger brother. After handing over Tommy, Poul Arkner drove off with his older son, leaving Pamela screaming hysterically in his wake. "We were a pair, the two of us," Anders remembered. "We were inseparable, like a pair of twins. We even shared a bicycle because we could not get two sets of tires during the war. I would go to school in the morning on the bicycle and meet him halfway in the afternoon, and he would bicycle to school and then back again in the afternoon. And that is why, when we were separated, I can still see it in front of my eyes. The car. The open door. My mother. My father. And me, struggling and holding on to Tommy. I wouldn't let him go. I will never forget that."

With help from Pamela's uncle, Sir Edward Neville Syfret, lord commissioner of the Admiralty and vice chief of the British Naval Staff, two British navy officers flew Tommy from Jutland to his mother's cottage by a fjord in Halbeck. To the end of his days, he would remember being "literally captured and kidnapped, screaming with a broken arm in a cast, by two British navy officers." Quickly, the boy was then transported with his mother to England on a Royal Air Force Dakota C-47 commanded by a British army general who let Tommy sit on his lap during the flight while Pamela made polite conversation with an admiral.

Far too young to understand what was happening, Tommy could not have known he was now leaving the vast estate where he had been free to roam wherever he pleased on land that belonged to his family in every direction as far as he could see. Nor could he know that he would never again have significant contact with the older brother to whom he had always been so close.

Quite clearly the product of a marriage that should never have taken place and most certainly a casualty of the greatest war the world had ever known, Thomas Ejnar Arkner, seven years old and unable to speak a word of English, was on his way to the country where he would spend the rest of his life. Although nothing about it had been ordinary, his childhood was now over.

2
twatley manor

They called her Puss because even as a child, she looked like the cat who had swallowed the cream. With her lustrous, thick black hair, enormous almond-shaped eyes, and perfect complexion, she was the great beauty of a family whose own history was as tortured and complex as that of the man she would eventually marry.

Born on December 3, 1943, Susan Ann Caroline Coriat was the daughter of Priscilla Chrystal Frances Blundell Weigall, an extravagant heiress of great wealth, and Harold Isaac Coriat, the former land agent for her first husband, Viscount Edward Richard Assheton Curzon. A direct descendant of Admiral Richard Howe and General William Howe, the two brothers who commanded the British forces during the American Revolution, Richard Curzon would in time himself become the sixth Earl Howe.

Priscilla's great wealth came from her grandfather, John Blundell Maple, the most successful entrepreneur of the Victorian era. In 1871, at the age of sixteen, he began working in his father's modest furniture store on Tottenham Court Road in London. In ten years, he transformed it into the world's largest luxury furniture empire. Employing a huge workforce in a manufacturing complex so large that it occupied an area where two hundred houses had once stood,

Maple furnished Czar Nicholas' Winter Palace in Russia, the Hof-burg Imperial Palace in Vienna, most of the great houses and grand hotels in England and Europe, as well as virtually every British em-bassy throughout the world, "even if it meant carrying the grand pi-ano up the Khyber Pass on packhorses."

After he was elected as the Conservative MP for Dulwich in 1887, Maple was knighted. Ten years later, he became a baronet. A successful racehorse owner and breeder who regularly entertained royalty at Childwickbury, his huge estate near St. Alban's in Hert-fordshire where film director Stanley Kubrick would later live, Sir John Blundell Maple helped rebuild University College Hospital in London and provided St. Albans with Sisters Hospital, named after two of his daughters who died in successive years.

When Sir John died in 1903 at the age of fifty-eight, he left an es-tate valued at more than £2.1 million (about $10.5 million then, but an incalculable fortune in terms of what could then be bought for a pound or a dollar) in trust for Grace, his only surviving daughter. Establishing a family pattern that would be repeated throughout the years, the money came with certain conditions attached.

Seven years earlier, Grace had married Baron Hermann von Eckardstein, a Prussian nobleman who served for ten years as first secretary of the German delegation to the Court of St. James. After giving birth to a daughter named Kit, Grace divorced her husband for cruelty, a decree rarely granted at the time. Sorely disappointed by the failure of his daughter's marriage, Sir John left her an in-come of thirty thousand pounds a year from the family trust. If Grace lived in the United Kingdom for 240 days a year, the sum would double to sixty thousand pounds a year, thereby providing her with a healthy incentive to make her life in England.

On August 16, 1910, Grace fulfilled her father's wishes by mar-rying Lieutenant Colonel William Ernest George Archibald Wei-gall. A tall, balding gentleman with a moustache, Weigall had served with distinction in the British army during the Second Boer War in South Africa. Described by his granddaughter Jenny Ponte,

Puss' older sister, as "a complete charmer and a lovely man" to whom Grace "was absolutely not faithful at all," Archibald Weigall was elected to the House of Commons as the representative from Horncastle. He then served for two years as the governor of South Australia. Returning to England, Weigall went into business only to lose all his money in the stock market crash of 1929. Knighted for his service to the crown, he lived for the rest of his life on his wife's considerable wealth.

By far the dominant partner in the marriage, Grace always did just as she pleased. A woman who so loved being the center of attention that she once carefully arranged herself at the bottom of the stairs in her home and then cried out for help while claiming that she had fallen, Grace wore her dyed blonde hair done up in curls like a teenager to the very end of her days. After she died, Grace left money in her will for several of her former lovers to be dug up and reinterred around her in a great walled garden beneath tombstones that identified them as either a "Dear" or a "True Friend of Family." As her granddaughter Jenny Ponte said, "She was an absolute old tart. She really was."

Grace and Archibald Weigall had only one child. Born in 1914, Priscilla was four years old when her beloved half-sister, Kit, died during an operation, thereby making Priscilla the sole heir to the entire Maple family fortune. From then on, Priscilla received the kind of unrelenting public attention reserved for what had already become a media archetype—the richest little girl in the world.

The parabola of Priscilla's life can be traced in the extensive coverage she received in the society pages of London's newspapers. On the day of her elaborate christening on May 19, 1914, the crypt of the House of Commons was decorated for the occasion with arches of pink and white Dorothy Perkin roses hung with little doves. Banks of flowers surrounded the baptismal font. The ceremony was attended by, among others, Princess Helena Victoria, Queen Victoria's granddaughter, who stood in for her sister Princess Marie Louise as Priscilla's godmother. In an era before professionals were hired to perform such tasks, all the publicity Priscilla received was generated by her mother.

An accomplished public speaker who led various social and philanthropic campaigns, Grace entertained constantly at Petwood, the oversized Tudor cottage she had built on her estate in Woodhall Spa. She also worked tirelessly to keep her daughter's name in the news. At the age of eleven, Priscilla, who had been given a brown Dartmoor pony by the Prince of Wales, was selected to appear at a high-society gala dressed in a riding kit, even though, as one London society reporter noted, "the soiree may be too grown up a function for her."

When Priscilla turned eighteen in 1932, Grace pulled out all the stops to ensure that her daughter would be recognized as the debutante of the year. "Who will be the prettiest debutante of 1932?" an unnamed *Daily Mail* correspondent asked on January 11, 1932. "My own choice is Miss Priscilla Weigall, who will be 18 in April. She is radiantly lovely, with dark brown hair, the most attractive brown eyes, and a complexion which a woman described to me as 'the most perfect natural complexion I have ever seen.' She is a fine dancer and swimmer and equally popular with her men and women friends."

Three months later, another reporter visited Priscilla, who was then residing with her mother and father at Englemere, an imposing white mansion on twelve acres of wooded land in Berkshire where Princess Helena Victoria and Princess Marie Louise had lived during World War I. "The lovely young Weigall daughter has her own suite at Englemere, bedroom, boudoir, and guest's bedroom, all painted an exquisite shade of palest water lily green." Surrounded by famous sporting pictures and photos of her favorite horses, Priscilla, who also had her own piano, was described as a passionate lover of animals and someone who enjoyed spending time with the family's sixteen dogs "of nearly as many breeds. Riding is part of the daily routine."

On June 23, 1932, Priscilla was formally presented at court. Because her mother used a wheelchair after having suffered a knee injury in an accident some years earlier, Sir Archibald was allowed to rehearse with his daughter so he could wheel Grace in during the ceremony, thereby making Priscilla the only girl to have both of her parents present when she curtsied to the king and queen. Although the practice ended in 1958, the two-hundred-year old ritual of presenting debutantes at court each year, "marked the beginning of the 'Season,' the annual round of balls, parties and sporting events that for debutantes doubled as a four-month hunt for a husband with prospects and, preferably, a title."

In a remarkable photograph taken by Cecil Beaton, the royal family portraitist, Priscilla stands with arms akimbo inside an ornate wrought-iron floral trellis. She wears a loose-fitting white evening jacket with a beaded collar and wide, flaring sleeves brocaded halfway to the elbow over a white dress with three large semiprecious stones at the neckline. Similar stones set in gold form her earrings. Her jet-black hair has been marcelled to within an inch of its life. Three strands of perfectly matched pearls hang around her neck.

Against her pale skin, her thickly drawn eyebrows and lipstick-covered, bee-stung mouth stand out like exclamation points. Looking incredibly stylish and quite bored at the same time, she stares directly into the camera with what her oldest daughter, Mary, later described as "that fashionably kind of shot-at-dawn gloomy expression." Priscilla's body language suggests that there is somewhere else she would much rather be and that she is only putting up with all this for the sake of her mother, who was then just beginning what would become an arduous campaign to find a suitable match for her daughter.

On July 12, 1932, Grace gave a ball for Priscilla at Lady Cunard's house at Number 7 Grosvenor Square. By all accounts, it was the event of the season. "In the small hours of the morning, immense dark gleaming cars filled the roadway and between the cars, laughing young men and radiant girls threaded their way to take the cool night air." In June of the following year, Grace announced yet another ball for Priscilla at Englemere that featured "midnight bathing in the swimming pool or the lake as part of the fun."

Six months later, Priscilla left with her parents to spend the winter in Australia. On the occasion of her twenty-first birthday in April 1935, she was feted with a tea and a party for the staff and tenants at Petwood followed by the appearance of her godmother Princess Marie Louise, who laid the foundation stone of a new Jubilee Baths House and opened a new Jubilee Park, both of which had been paid for by Grace. Having by then already gone through about six hundred thousand pounds of the money left her, Grace also established a trust fund of a million pounds in her daughter's name. From this trust, Priscilla would receive seven to ten thousand pounds a year for the rest of her life.

In May 1935, Priscilla announced her engagement to Viscount Richard Curzon, the twenty-seven-year-old son of the fifth Earl Howe, Francis Richard Henry Penn Curzon. A former Conservative MP from South Battersea, the senior Curzon had taken up the sport of motor racing at the age of forty-four at the suggestion of a magistrate after having been fined several times for speeding.

After a difficult and protracted struggle to find the perfect husband for her daughter, Grace had at last achieved her goal. The victory had not come easily. "David Niven was quite in love with my mother," Jenny Ponte said. "But my grandmother gave him a thousand pounds and told him to go to Hollywood. So I suppose in some way she was responsible for his career. But she was a terrible old snob. She really was. There was no consideration of romance. None at all. Mummy absolutely loathed her."

On July 12, 1935, in an area of St. Paul's Cathedral cordoned off to form a large church, one thousand guests attended the wedding of Priscilla Weigall to Viscount Curzon. The event was so massive in scale that Grace had been forced to rent a flat in Porchester Terrace to serve as an office from which to coordinate the affair. Given away by her father, the bride carried a prayer book and wore a close-fitting gown of white brocade with long tight sleeves, a square neckline, and a long train shaped at the end like a three-pointed ivy leaf so the children carrying it would not be huddled together. Her wedding ring was made of platinum with a guard ring of diamonds. To accompany the ceremony, Priscilla chose her favorite children's hymn, "All Things Bright and Beautiful."

The extensive guest list included King George II of Greece; Lord Athlone and his wife, Princess Alice of Albany; Prince and Princess Arthur of Connaught; Princess Marie Louise; Princess Helen Victoria; Lady Iris Mountbatten; the ambassadors from Italy and Germany; the ministers of Czechoslovakia, Switzerland, and Finland; the high commissioners of Canada and India; and the admiral of the fleet of the Royal Navy; as well as far too many dukes, duchesses, counts, and countesses to name or number. Although Priscilla's honeymoon plans had to be curtailed when she was operated on for appendicitis two weeks after the wedding ceremony, she was soon on her way with her parents to Urie in Scotland for the shooting season.

Although Richard Curzon had planned to move with his bride into Gopsall Hall, a beautiful house on a family estate in South Leicestershire, where Handel had written part of his *Messiah*, Priscilla wanted to be nearer to London and her mother. And so used her own money to establish a country residence in Ascot while also acquiring a London pied-à-terre at 3 Porchester Close in Bayswater. By all accounts, the flat was a minor work of art, with various tints of apricot, peach, and buff employed throughout. In the study Priscilla designed for her husband, all the woodwork, including the piano and radio gramophone, was made of oak pickled to a pale shade of gray. Paintings of ships from her husband's extensive collection of naval art hung on the cream-colored walls.

Assuming the role her mother had once played in London society, Priscilla was soon gathering together "some of the year's most interesting young-marrieds and debutantes" for her first major social function, the Crocus Ball on St. George's Day on April 23, 1935. Identified as the "Ideal New Hostess" in the *Daily Mail*, she organized a film premiere for a hospital, opened a YWCA bazaar in Westminster, and sent out more than a thousand letters to raise money for social work.

When Richard Curzon decided to stand for a seat on the London City Council from South Battersea, Priscilla worked alongside her husband in the district his father had once represented in the House of Commons. Speaking to crowds and canvassing the neighborhoods, she contributed to his successful campaign for office on a platform of municipal reform. As the *Daily Sun* noted on February 27, 1937: "Fortunately, speaking comes easily to her for even in her childhood, Lady Weigall used to let her open bazaars."

Two years later, the fifth Earl Howe, now reportedly spending most of his time abroad, decided to hand over Penn House, the family seat in the village of Penn Street near Beaconsfield in Buckinghamshire, to his son and daughter-in-law. In truth, the gift was less generous than it seemed. The house, which had five principal staircases, a baronial hall with mullioned windows, stone-flagged floors, steps, and carved pillars, was by then so run-down that only Priscilla could afford to restore it. Using her own money, she filled it with richly colored Persian rugs and old, carved oak seats and chests as well as priceless eighteenth-century, Louis Seize, Chippendale, and Hepplewhite furniture.

Behind the brilliant public facade that Richard and Priscilla Curzon presented to the world, a different reality prevailed. The union, which had been arranged by her mother so Priscilla would gain a title in return for the Maple family fortune, was strictly one of convenience. As Priscilla herself would later confirm, the marriage was never consummated. (Curzon did, however, father two daughters with his second wife.)

Five years into what had been a childless marriage, Priscilla gave birth to two daughters, Lady Priscilla Mary Rose Curzon and Lady

Jennifer Jane Curzon, within the relatively short space of fifteen months. By then, a man calling himself Robert Coryat was already working as the land agent at Penn House. Charged with running the estate on a daily basis, he seemed the very picture of a perfect English gentleman. Having attended the very prestigious Perse School in Cambridge, he could trace his family lineage all the way back to Thomas Coryate, a noted sixteenth-century travel writer and eccentric who had walked overland from Great Britain to India and is credited with having introduced the fork to England.

While no one seems to have delved too deeply into the subject at the time, Thomas Coryate himself never married. Nor did he have any siblings, thereby making it impossible for the land agent at Penn House to have been related to him in any way except through his own need to claim that his family had lived on English soil for nearly four hundred years.

Robert Coryat's real name was Harold Isaac Coriat. Born on February 13, 1904, in the port city of Mogador on the Atlantic coast of Morocco, he was the second son of a wealthy Sephardic Jewish trader named Abraham Coriat. Now called Essaouira, Mogador had been built as a center for maritime trade with Europe in the eighteenth century by King Mohammed III, who encouraged foreign traders to settle there. By 1780, the Jewish population in the city numbered around a thousand.

Among them were the Coriats. Over the course of the next century, they became one of the most prominent, learned, and wealthy Sephardic families in North Africa. In successive generations, five rabbis bearing the Coriat name wrote commentaries on the Talmud and other codes of Jewish behavior that are still read today. Unlike his father, Abraham Coriat dedicated his life to business, becoming so wealthy and powerful that he welcomed visiting foreign dignitaries to his home in Mogador while also maintaining a large farm forty kilometers outside the city.

In keeping with the long-standing tradition of intermarriage among Sephardic families, all of whom traced their lineage to

Spain before the Inquisition in 1478, Abraham married his maternal aunt's daughter. Donna Florence Cazes, known as "Flora," was an English citizen born in London in 1871. On February 28, 1898, Flora gave birth to a son named Percy. Six years later, she died one week after giving birth to her second son, Harold. Two years after her death, Abraham married Flora's younger sister Evelyne, who had been born in London in 1874. They then had three more children.

In 1910, when Harold was six years old, his aunt Aida came from London to visit the family in Morocco. When she returned to England, she took Harold with her so he could be with his older brother, Percy, who was then entering the Perse School. Harold remained in England until his aunt took him back to Morocco in 1914 just before the start of World War I.

In 1919, at the age of fifteen, Harold returned on a French passport to England, where he also attended the Perse School for a while. Both Harold and Percy (called "Cory" at school, he then went on to a long and distinguished career in the British army), were sent to Perse by their grandmother. Dr. W. H. D. Rouse, the headmaster at Perse, openly encouraged Jewish boys to attend the school. In 1911, he had established a separate boardinghouse, known as Hillel House, for them.

Even as a young man, Harold Coriat was constantly in trouble with the law. An inveterate womanizer throughout his life, he was named at the age of twenty in 1924 as the co-respondent in a divorce suit filed by Adney Richard Preece against his wife, Florence. In February of that year, Harold Coriat was fined for failing to produce a driver's license. In August, his license was endorsed for his failure to stop at the request of the police and to produce his license on demand. One year later, he was fined five pounds at the Marlborough Street Police Court for obtaining credit through fraud. A year later, he claimed to have lost his alien registration book for the second time and was issued a new one.

On April 8, 1926, Robert Coryat, as Harold was now calling himself, was charged by the same court for obtaining credit by fraud, failing to produce a registration document on demand, and using a name other than the one by which he was ordinarily known. The first charge was dropped, and he paid a fine of twenty pounds on the other two.

Leaving England, he went off to seek his fortune in New Zealand. On June 6, 1928, Colin Coryton, as Harold was now calling himself, was sentenced by the Napier Supreme Court to nine months of hard labor for false pretenses, which in English law is defined as "the obtaining from any other person by any false pretence any chattel, money or valuable security, with intent to defraud . . . The broad distinction between this offence and larceny is that in the former the owner intends to part with his property, in the latter he does not." Based on his lifelong interests, he had most likely acquired property, livestock, farm machinery, or an automobile on credit for which he was then unable to pay.

Two years later, Colin Coryton was sentenced in the Dunedin Magistrate's Court to ten months of hard labor on three charges of false pretenses and two charges of obtaining credit by fraud. Leaving New Zealand, he moved to Australia, where on April 3, 1933, Colin Powell, as Harold was now calling himself, was sentenced by a court in Melbourne to fifteen months in prison on five counts of false pretenses.

Nine months after being released from jail, he married a twenty-nine-year-old English woman named Muriel on May 29, 1935, in Melbourne. Returning with her to England, he appeared at the Oxford City Police Court on a perjury charge that was dismissed. Arrested again, he was conveyed to Liverpool for removal from the United Kingdom under Article 3 of the Aliens Order of 1920. After obtaining a French passport in London in September 1935, he left for Tangiers, only to return to England a month later. Claiming he had again lost his alien certificate, he was issued a new one that specifically prohibited him from seeking employment in the United Kingdom.

Using the name Robert Coryat, Harold Coriat then went back and forth between England and Dublin in what was then the Irish Free State until the Home Office issued a circular on July 6, 1937, denying him permission to land in the United Kingdom. Turned back at Folkestone on July 31, 1937, he told the immigration officer that he was making arrangements to reside in the Irish Free State and would soon have an Irish passport.

By 1939, Robert Coryat was working as the land agent at Penn, a position he had obtained by falsely stating he had attended public school at Winchester College from 1919 through 1924 and then gone to Trinity College, Cambridge, where during his second year he had passed his "little go" examination, which enabled him to continue his studies for a degree in rural economy. In May of that year, the British Parliament adopted a Conscription Act, establishing a system of peacetime military training. In September, conscription for all males between the ages of nineteen and forty-one into the military was instituted.

Two months later, Robert Coryat joined an officer candidate training program as a cadet. Discharged from it in April 1940, just three months after Priscilla's daughter Mary was born, he applied for a commission in the Royal Air Force Volunteer Reserve. Knowing that his record as a former convict would have made him ineligible to serve in the RAF, he stated on his application that his name was Robert Coryat and that he had been born on February 12, 1907, at Bideford, Devon. He also claimed that his father, Robert Coryat of Dunster, Somerset, a man of "independent means," was British, as was his mother, Evelyn Daunay of Waterford, Ireland.

Expressing a desire to become a commissioned air gunner, he listed his hobbies as squash and hunting while noting he was "a good shot" and had been an "ex-Master of Hounds." He also stated that he could speak French, English, and Arabic and was qualified to fly all types of planes. As one of his two character references,

Priscilla stated she had known the applicant for twelve years, which cannot possibly have been true.

Six weeks after his application was forwarded to the selection board, Robert Coryat was posted as an acting pilot officer on probation in the Royal Air Force. As a gunner, he participated in combat during multiple operational flights over Germany and northern France in either the twin-engine Vickers Wellington or the new four-engine Halifax or Lancaster bombers, all of which were subjected to heavy fire during nightly bombing runs as the Battle of Britain raged.

After returning from one such mission about two months after Priscilla's daughter Jenny was born, Robert Coryat was arrested at a British military airfield and taken to London, where he was informed by the chief inspector of Scotland Yard that he would be charged with false registration. "Yes, I understand," he replied. "I will be quite frank. I do not want to give the authorities any trouble. I want to get the matter over as soon as possible." With France (and by extension, the French colony of Morocco as well) having by then fallen to the Nazis, Harold Coriat was now technically an enemy alien and so could have been interned under the rules of Defence Regulation 18-B.

On July 15, 1941, the trial of *Rex v. Harold Isaac Coriat alias Robert Coryat* was held at London's Bow Street Police Court. Through his counsel, whom Priscilla had hired to defend him, Harold Coriat pleaded guilty "subject to circumstances of strong mitigation which will be developed at the proper time" to one count of misrepresentation under the Defence Regulations Act of 1939. He then served about eight months in prison, most likely in London's notorious Wormwood Scrubs.

Precisely how much Priscilla actually knew about Harold Coriat's background at the time is impossible to say. As the Viscountess Curzon, with a husband who was then serving in the Royal Navy, she could not have attended their former land agent's trial without attracting undue attention to herself and creating a scandal. Considering her nature, she may have just decided to turn a blind eye to his past, choosing instead to believe whatever story he concocted to explain his difficulties as simply the result of governmental confusion about his origins.

To the day she died, Priscilla never told any of her children the true circumstances of Harold Coriat's imprisonment, allowing them to believe he had been unjustly interned as a foreign national. Concerning his own military service, Harold Coriat would later tell his son Christopher that he had trained with a special forces unit during the Winter War and then served as a fighter pilot in the RAF, eventually attaining the rank of captain. Although Puss herself never knew the truth about her father, she would eventually marry a man who seemed to be his direct opposite but was quite like him in many ways.

After Harold Coriat was released from prison, Priscilla visited his wife, Muriel, at her home in Berkshire. Priscilla informed Muriel that she had engaged in misconduct with her husband at an address in Oxfordshire, thereby providing her with grounds for divorce. The decree was granted on April 18, 1942. Less than three months later, Royal Navy Lieutenant Viscount Richard Curzon was granted a divorce from Priscilla on grounds of adultery in a suit that was undefended.

Seven years after the couple had been married in St. Paul's Cathedral before a throng of nobles and high-ranking dignitaries, their final parting was less than amicable. After Priscilla left the house where both her daughters had been born, her former husband burned everything she had left behind. Neither daughter ever saw Richard Curzon again. Nor did Priscilla ever speak to them about him.

In a ceremony that received no newspaper coverage, Priscilla, who may have been pregnant at the time, married Harold Coriat in 1943. Although they both desperately wanted a son, the long line of daughters in successive generations on the Maple side of the family remained unbroken when Puss was born at Englemere, her grandmother's stately home in Berkshire. Using a large sum of money from her trust fund, Priscilla then bought the three-hundred-year-old manor house on 250 acres of beautiful open countryside in Wiltshire, where Puss would spend her childhood.

By any standard, Twatley Manor, as it was then known (an abbreviation of "to the wet lea," a lea being a grassland or a meadow), was a spectacular place to live. Hand-tinted color photographs of the estate from that era show lilies growing in great profusion beside a running stream as sheep graze in a lush, verdant meadow. Violets line the top of high gray stone walls framing an expansive, formal garden of perfectly ordered plots in which flowers of every hue grow surrounded by low green hedges. At a bend in the Sherston, a branch of the River Avon running through the property, daffodils sprout beneath ancient oak trees draped with vines. In the stables, attached to the house by a vaulted archway into which an ornate clock was set in stone, there were ten "boxes" or stalls where horses specially trained for hunting were kept.

During the lean, cash-poor years of the Depression, or "the Great Slump," as it was known in England, H. C. Cox, the self-made Canadian life insurance millionaire who then owned Twatley Manor, had poured money into the Beaufort Hunt. Through his efforts, its members were able to continue riding out in pursuit of the fox across more than 750 square miles of privately owned land four days a week from October to May.

Like Cox, Harold Coriat was a passionate hunter. "He used to hunt six days a week," Jenny Ponte said. "He was a master of the Vale of the White Horse Hunt, which is a sister pack of hounds to the Beaufort. That was what he did. He was an absolute fanatic about it." In large part, the family's decision to move to Wiltshire was based on the fact that the area was then the center of the hunting world in England.

As much a ritualistic social gathering of landed aristocrats as a recreational pursuit, the Beaufort Hunt, founded in 1682 by the first Duke of Beaufort, began early each morning during the season. The master of the hunt, clad in a scarlet hunting jacket and a black riding hat, would set a course that would then be followed by a large pack of baying hounds herded together by the "whippers-in." The pack was followed by men and women in formal hunting attire astride field hunters who would continue the chase until the fox had been run to ground by the hounds and then killed by terriers specially bred to follow the prey into its lair.

Any doubt that Harold Coriat was in fact the English gentleman he claimed to be would have been quickly dispelled by the enthusiasm with which he threw himself into the hunt as well as the elaborate balls and social gatherings associated with it. Any questions about his financial status would have been answered just as quickly by his very expensive hunting attire, the crew of five stable girls he employed to care for his horses, the staff of sixteen who maintained the grounds of his manor and surrounding farmland, and the nine household servants, a butler, a chauffeur, and a nanny among them, who worked in the main house.

Made of weathered gray stone with six great chimneys, Twatley Manor had twenty-nine rooms, each with a coal or wood-burning fireplace. A set of wide wooden steps with a wide flat banister, each hand-turned baluster thicker at the end than in the middle, led up to the bedrooms and children's nursery on the second floor, where dormer windows looked out over open fields to the river. "It was absolutely incredible," Jenny Ponte recalled. "The landing had blue silk on the walls interspersed with mock wood painted by hand with a feather by an Austrian who lived in the house for a year. It was very opulent, and growing up there was very much a formative influence for Puss and I."

Beyond its undeniable beauty, Twatley Manor was also the physical embodiment of a way of life that even in England has now largely disappeared except in films based on the works of Jane Austen. What should have been the ideal environment for three young girls soon became something else again. In part, this was because Harold Coriat thoroughly embraced the values of the Victorian era when daughters did not count for much and the object of every upper-class marriage was to produce a son and heir. Consumed with their own lives, Priscilla and her husband inhabited a completely separate world from their daughters.

"We barely saw them as children," Priscilla's daughter Mary would later say of her parents. "We came downstairs in smart clothes and hung about at tea time and then went up to bed. I might see my mother for an hour a day, if that. I remember her coming to the nursery one day when I was eight or nine and teaching us 'Racing Demon,' a card game her friends played. We enjoyed it and were rather good at it and she said, 'Oh, darlings, I never knew it could be such fun playing with you!' It was the way the upper classes then brought up their children."

After going through a series of nannies toward whom both older girls acted, in Mary's words, "really foul," Priscilla found "this heavenly girl called Valerie Smith who looked after us. She had been with the Duchess of Kent and had looked after Princess Alexandra. So I used to get all of Princess Alexandra's cast-off clothes. Val was young, very pretty, and wonderful. And she played with us."

At Twatley Manor, Priscilla's daughters assumed roles they would play for the rest of their lives. Brilliant and cerebral, Mary was also, in the words of Reg Wood, then a garden boy at the manor, "a bit snooty. One of the jobs I had to do was keep the log box full of logs every morning. And I spoke to her one morning and she was having a bit of a mood and I said to her, 'Morning, Miss Mary.' And she never answered. During the afternoon, I was working down by the river. She came down and said, 'I've come down to say, 'Sorry.' And I said, 'Whatever for?' And she said, "I was very rude this morning and Daddy sent me down to apologize because you spoke to me civil and you called me my proper name and I didn't answer. And he said that was very rude so I've come down to apologize.' That was the way they were brought up."

Jenny, an ardent horsewoman who hunted from an early age and became a member of the Junior Olympic equestrian team, was bold, brash, and utterly fearless. "Jennifer was in all the mischief," recalled Reg Wood. "If you left the tractor with the keys in it, she would be gone with it. And you had to come home to the front door in the afternoon to get it. She'd go off in it."

Closer to Jenny than Mary, Puss seems to have always been the odd girl out. "We had sort of a horse governess who taught us to ride," her sister Mary said, "and Jenny and I loved it and did lots of competing, but I don't remember Puss riding at all. I don't think she liked it." Described by both of her sisters as "very naughty" as a child, Puss may have simply been playing out the only role available to her as the third daughter of parents who had desperately wanted a son. A poem written by Puss when she was eight years old says a good deal about her day-to-day life at the manor:

> There is nothing to do, and nothing to see
> Except for the lawn and the laurel tree
>
> Down by the stream where the daffodils grow
> There is nothing there but snow and snow.
> The dreary winter goes on and on for three
> whole days the sun has not shone.
>
> Silence has fallen on meadow and wood,
> If the sun would shine, oh' if only it could.
>
> There is nothing to do and nothing to see
> Except for the lawn and the laurel tree.

By this time, both Mary and Jenny had already been sent off to an exclusive boarding school in Worcestershire, leaving Puss alone at the manor to be driven back and forth each day to a local school. Far too young to fully understand what had already become a fairly complicated family dynamic, she must have known that neither of her sisters had taken very kindly to the man whom they all now called father.

"My mother did love him," Mary said, "but they had the most appalling rows when we were children. He was constantly threatening to kill himself. He used to shut himself in the bathroom with the revolver and say he was going to shoot himself or when we were all in the car, he would say, 'I'm going to drive the car off the road and kill us all.' It was terrifying."

And then there was his nickname. Harold Coriat was called "Camel," a name he may have acquired from "How the Camel Got His Hump," one of Rudyard Kipling's *Just So Stories* in which the best solution for having "the cameelious hump" (i.e., being depressed) is to find something to do. "That's a romantic thing that his name 'Camel' comes from the Kipling poem," Jenny Ponte said. "I think it came from when he went to prep school. He must have looked like or behaved quite Moroccan. And so they nicknamed him Camel. And the name stuck. He was totally, absolutely self-invented, a figment of his own imagination. When he was seven, his father handed him a gun and said, 'Shoot yourself.' Which isn't a very stable background."

Puss' younger brother Christopher tells yet another version of the story. While at prep school, his father was put in a laundry hamper and unceremoniously tossed out a window, developing a hump in his back. Whatever the real source of his nickname may have been, both Mary and Jenny were, in Mary's words, "very, very amused" when they discovered that the very proper Harold Coriat's middle name was Isaac. "We called him 'Isaac' for a bit," Mary said, "which made him absolutely hopping."

What none of Priscilla's daughters understood was the social position in which their mother now found herself. After losing her title in the divorce, Priscilla had married a man whose own background was dubious, and so she was not nearly so welcome as she had once been in London high society. Thanks to her trust fund,

Priscilla was, however, still able to indulge her every whim. At a time when England was deeply in debt and food everywhere was in short supply, she continued to live in what can only be called the royal manner.

After falling in love with a brand-new Rolls Royce while attending the first motor show in London after the war, Priscilla decided to buy the car. Told that the first model had been made for the royal family and that this particular vehicle was headed for the showroom in New York so it could be sold for American dollars, she said, "Oh, it doesn't matter. I can still have it." Paying for the car in dollars, Priscilla had it shipped to New York. The vehicle was then shipped back to England at her expense and sent to Derby so it could be equipped with left-hand drive, thereby making Priscilla Coriat the first "ordinary person" in England to be driven about by her chauffeur in a brand new Rolls Royce after the war. She also bought her husband a Bentley in which to tool around the countryside.

Although she was no longer asked to chair gala film premieres or open charity bazaars in London, Priscilla entertained regularly at Twatley Manor. Whenever she gave a formal ball, her daughters would hang over the banister to watch elegantly dressed adults file into the great ballroom, where all the food and champagne was provided by caterers Priscilla had hired to drive down from London to Wiltshire for the occasion.

After deciding one day that she wanted fresh salmon for that night's dinner party, Priscilla rang the local fishmonger, who explained that although he had none to sell her, he could ring up a wholesaler in London to put some on the train so it could be collected at the station. Unfortunately, the last train of the day from London to Wiltshire had already gone. "Oh, I know that," Priscilla said. "Ring them up, tell them to go out and grab a taxi, and have it sent."

Long before the first motorway was built in England, the journey from London to Wiltshire, a distance of one hundred miles, could be made only on narrow, twisting country lanes lined with high green hedges. Hours later, a London black cab pulled up the front drive at Twatley Manor. "Blimey," the driver said after he had made his delivery. "I hope she wants some bleedin' fish tomorrow. She paid me what was on the clock and gave me a ten-pound tip."

Sixty years later, as he sat in what had been the great ballroom at the manor, Reg Wood still could not get over the grand manner in which Priscilla had lived. "Can you imagine what that salmon must have cost? You couldn't believe Mrs. Coriat's extravagance. The Christmas parties alone she used to give here for the staff, each person taking home a bag of food when it was still scarce, must have cost thousands of pounds. She couldn't do anything by halves. That was not her style."

Through her newfound social connection with the Duke and Duchess of Norfolk, who had moved to Wiltshire during the war, Priscilla began buying racehorses just as her grandfather had done before her. Returning one day from the thoroughbred sales at Doncaster racecourse in South Yorkshire, she turned to her husband in the back seat of the Rolls Royce and said, "Now, how much did we spend today, dear?" Carefully, he wrote down the cost of each horse they had bought. It was an enormous sum by any standard but Priscilla had never bothered to wonder about the amount until that moment. As Reg Wood noted, "She didn't seem to have any comprehension about money at all."

Convinced that Harold Coriat could make a go of raising corn, wheat, and barley at Twatley Manor, Priscilla bought two local farms while renting a third in addition to the farmland she had already purchased in Berkshire after the war. She also gave her husband large sums of money to buy herds of very expensive show cattle.

Nor did she seem to mind that the man she adored was not spending all his time in the stables with his horses. "He was an absolutely appalling womanizer," Jenny Ponte remembered. "There was a glass roof on the tack room, and I was sort of the tomboy of the family, and I could climb up on this glass roof and watch him shagging all the stable girls. Then we used to get the stable girls to take us out for rides. We used to blackmail them. We made a very healthy living out of it." To his credit, Harold Coriat seems to have always treated all those who worked for him (with the possible exception of the stable girls) with great respect, often putting an extra pound in their pay packet at the end of the week if they had performed some special task for him.

After suffering several miscarriages, Priscilla finally gave birth to a son named Christopher Archibald Coriat on September 13, 1954. When his proud father returned from the hospital to the manor, he joyfully tossed away his hat, threw his arms in the air, and, with tears rolling down his face, proclaimed, "We've got a son! We've got a son! We've got a son!" Without ever going back for his hat, he invited his workers into the house to celebrate his good fortune. They all then proceeded to drink up every last crate of the continental beer that Harold Coriat favored. Family friends jokingly began referring to the boy as "the crown prince" because, as Christopher Coriat himself later explained, "Everybody was like, 'Thank God Camel finally has a son. Now he can shut up and get on with life.'"

When Christopher was christened a month later, Priscilla brought a leading flower arranger and her team down from London to decorate the church. That morning, Harold Coriat reminded his workers that since this was a special day, he expected to see them all in church for the ceremony. When they told him that the large crop of oats in his fields needed to be harvested before they spoiled, he said, "You can grow some more next year. But you'll never have another day like this." As Reg Wood would later say, "My God, did we have a party!"

As everyone soon discovered, the never-ending party that had been life at Twatley Manor was about to end. Not long after Christopher, who within the family was known as "Archie," was born, farm workers had to send two fat cattle to Swindon market on a Monday so there would be enough money to pay the staff on Friday. In December 1954, the man who raised turkeys at the manor brought to the house two hundred picked and dressed birds ready to be sold, only to have Priscilla give them all away as Christmas presents. By February, the bill for the turkey feed had still not been paid and the staff was forced to sell barley from the manor store to cover the cost. After one of the staff was given a check that bounced, some of those who worked at the farm, Reg Wood among them, began looking elsewhere for employment.

In August 1956, ten years after Priscilla and Harold Coriat had taken possession of Twatley Manor, Priscilla's name was back in the newspapers, albeit in a manner she had never anticipated. The richest little girl in England, who at the age of twenty-one had been given a million pounds in trust by her mother, was served with a receiving order for bankruptcy. As Priscilla told a reporter from the *Daily Express*, her troubles were "due to two things. First I had to meet very considerable death duties following the death six years ago of my mother, Lady Weigall. . . . The other reason for my difficulties is that I have tried to help my husband with his farming and cattle breeding activities."

Just as Sir John Blundell Maple had attached stringent conditions to the money he had left his only daughter, Grace Weigall had agreed to establish trust funds for Priscilla's children on the condition that her daughter pay all the death duties on the Weigall estate if Grace died within five years of the agreement. In no position to bargain, Priscilla accepted her mother's offer. Eighteen months later, in 1950, Lady Weigall died unexpectedly of a heart attack at the age of seventy-two. Unable to pay £40,000 in death duties, Priscilla secured the debt with the manor and went right on spending money as she always had before.

"When my mother was making settlements," Priscilla told the *Evening Standard*, "she wanted to leave my children free of any burden, and I agreed—on legal advice—to pay any death duties. My mother was hale and hearty at the time, but as events turned out my gesture was a foolish one for she collapsed and died of a heart attack soon afterwards. For more than a year now we have been trying to sell our 250-acre farm with 15 cottages together with our house of 16 rooms, eight bathrooms, and five reception rooms but without success. I bought it ten years ago but the market for big houses has dropped since then." Although the estate was valued at £75,000, the government refused to accept it in lieu of the death duties Priscilla owed. Wistfully, she told another reporter, "Sometimes I wonder where all the money has gone."

Two weeks after she had been served with the bankruptcy notice, Priscilla attended a meeting of her creditors in Bristol. Although only one moneylender appeared in person to present his claim, it was revealed that Priscilla owed more than £28,000 to forty-four unsecured creditors as well as about £36,000 in death duties on her mother's estate. Her own assets at the time amounted to about £6,800.

In October 1956, Priscilla, clad in a sensible suit jacket and matching skirt, and her husband attended a formal hearing in bankruptcy court. Referring to the money put in trust for Priscilla when she had turned twenty-one, the official receiver said, "That is the thing we have to find the answer to—where has the million pounds gone?" The answer was not long in coming.

Over the past twenty-one years, Priscilla had withdrawn £357,000 from her trust fund. Of this, £235,000 had gone into her husband's farming ventures. As the official receiver pointed out, this meant that about £120,000 had gone into private affairs, such as running racehorses. "I agree," Priscilla answered, "and I admit extravagance."

To help her husband, Priscilla had also guaranteed a bank overdraft, which at one point had reached £100,000, and then obtained further loans for him from moneylenders. Harold Coriat's own debts ran to more than £81,000. When the official receiver said that had it not been for Mr. Coriat's losses, Priscilla would never have been in court, she replied, "No, I could have paid my debts." While Priscilla may not have known this, Harold Coriat had done all this before in both Australia and New Zealand. Because he had used his real name to secure the loans at Twatley Manor and his incredibly loyal wife was willing to cover his debts, he would not be sent to jail for a crime he had already committed many times before.

During the hearing, it was also revealed that when payments from her trust fund had ceased three years earlier, Priscilla had begun living on the £5,000 paid each year by the trust to her children. All told, there was still £250,000 left in trust for them. Over the course of twenty-one years, Priscilla and her mother, both of whom had obtained court permission to make multiple withdrawals from the capital forming the basis of the trust, had somehow managed to go through the astonishing sum of about £1.2 million.

Under a headline that read "Let My Children Pay, Says Woman Who Spent A Million," the *Daily Mail* quoted Priscilla: "I hope the law will allow my children to pay my creditors. I feel it is in their best interests that their parents should be clear of debt." As Harold Coriat got into his car after the hearing to drive Priscilla back to Twatley Manor, where they were now living in the servants' quarters, he said, "My wife was jolly well off. Now we are finished."

Insofar as the newspapers were concerned, the entire affair was not just a scandal of major proportions but also the perfect ending to the story of the woman who had once been the richest little girl in England. In a nation where great estates everywhere were being shuttered because of prohibitive death duties, Priscilla's precipitous fall from grace seemed to prove beyond all doubt that the very rich were not only different from everyone else but also sometimes completely hopeless when it came to keeping their money. As Priscilla herself noted at the time, "I was brought up in a very extravagant way but I have learned a bitter lesson."

Whether or not this was true, the fabulous lifestyle she had enjoyed with her equally profligate husband at Twatley Manor was now done. The estate, the manor house, and all its contents were soon sold at auction. Harold and Priscilla Coriat, who by court order were no longer even allowed to have a bank account, moved with their four children to a rented house in Alveston, about thirteen miles north of Bristol in South Gloucestershire.

Although her family had undergone a financial disaster of major proportions, it seemed that Puss, who was then just ten years old, would be all right. Thanks to her grandmother, she had a generous trust fund of her own. The bad news was that, much like the heirs to the Jarndyce fortune in Charles Dickens' *Bleak House*, she was now a ward of the court, entirely dependent on decisions made by trustees assigned to safeguard her welfare by a legal decision in which she had played no part.

The good news was that just like her mother and her grandmother before her, Susan Ann Caroline Coriat would have enough money to live on for the rest of her life. Even if all else failed, it was something on which she could always rely.

3
new barn farm and haileybury

Knowing only that he had been taken from the land of his birth and that the older brother who had always been his protector was no longer by his side, Tommy arrived in England with his mother in 1945. Because Pamela had always spoken to her son in her native language at Hald, he picked up English quickly and was able to speak it reasonably well within three weeks' time.

In May 1946, at the age of seven-and-a-half, Tommy was sent by his mother to a boarding school about twenty miles from where they were then living in Surrey. In the St. Edmund's School uniform of a blue shirt, a pair of gray trousers, a V-neck pullover, and a blue-and-silver horizontally striped tie, he attended class each day in the sprawling, gabled, red brick country mansion where George Bernard Shaw had once lived and that now housed 150 boys of various ages during the school year.

Although Tommy could speak English perfectly when he entered St. Edmund's, it was not until he was nine years old that he could read a page of text without difficulty. What would now be recognized as dyslexia was then seen as part of his rebellious attitude to the English boarding school system that he hated "because it was so awful and so cruel. Every time I couldn't read, I got beaten."

And then there was the question of his nationality. Although school officials at St. Edmund's knew Tommy was Danish, this distinction was lost on his fellow classmates, all of whom had been born and raised in England. "I was considered a Nazi when I came in there," Tommy would later say, "because in England in 1945, that was how they thought of anyone foreign. I had gone from living on land owned by my family as far as the eye could see to being stuck in an English prep school with a bunch of kids who were real fascists."

For the next six years at St. Edmund's, where Christopher Isherwood and W. H. Auden had been students before him, Tommy boxed without much success, appeared once as a member of the rugby team, and spent most of his free time on the school's private nine-hole golf course. He also won three prizes for good work and conduct, a copy of Robert Louis Stevenson's *Treasure Island* and Rudyard Kipling's *Sixty Poems* among them.

By the time Tommy left St. Edmund's in March 1952, at the age of 13½, his mother; her second husband, Hamish Mackenzie-Kerr; and their two young daughters, Pamela Jane and Fairlie, known as "Baba" and "Lulu," were living in a large manor house in Bromley. It was located not far from Down House, where Charles Darwin had resided for forty years after returning from his epic voyage on HMS *Beagle* in 1836.

Just sixteen miles from the center of London, New Barn Farm was entirely removed from the hustle and bustle of the city. Surrounded by rolling open meadows in which horses grazed and wildflowers bloomed each spring, the farm was, as Tommy's half-sister Lulu later described it, "absolutely gorgeous. We had our own milking cows, massive flower gardens, a donkey, Whinny the cat, and two spaniels named Potty and Sandy. Although it's been fifty years since I was there, I still dream about it. Such a fantastic place."

Not surprisingly, New Barn Farm had been yet another lavish wedding present from Pamela's father, Reginald Evelyn (R. E.)

Weber. Having learned a lesson from the dissolution of his daughter's first marriage, Weber put New Barn Farm in trust for Pamela with the provision that it would become part of his estate when he died. A frequent visitor to the farm who had his own room at the top of the stairs, R. E. Weber soon forged a close bond with his grandson. Because he had no son of his own, Weber decided to adopt Tommy and give him his own last name, which in England was pronounced "Weeber."

For Tommy, being adopted by his wealthy and powerful grandfather was the kind of stroke of good fortune most often found in the pages of English penny fiction. Abandoned by his own father in the most dramatic manner imaginable, Tommy had never gotten on particularly well with his stepfather, Hamish Mackenzie-Kerr. As Lulu recalled, "My dad shot at Tommy one day for playing the drums in Mum's studio at New Barn Farm. Fortunately, the shotgun pellets went right over his head." Despite all that he had already suffered as a child, Tommy now had a most impressive upper-class British gentleman upon whom he could pattern his life.

A fabulous character of the first order, R. E. Weber owned four extraordinarily expensive indigo blue Armstrong Siddeley Sapphire saloon cars that to the untrained automotive eye looked much like Rolls Royce limousines. After wrapping one around a lamppost, he stalked angrily from the scene while insisting the lamppost should never have been there in the first place. He also possessed what was then considered the largest and most valuable stamp collection in the world, a hobby he shared with his good friend King George VI. Although Tommy's grandfather maintained a lavish country estate, called The Grange, in Surrey; a house near the sea in Sandwich, Kent; and an apartment on Pall Mall near St. James Palace in London, he spent most of his time in a flat above his club. The flat was not far from 94 Baker Street, where the Beatles' clothing store, the Apple boutique, would later be located.

After attending Haileybury College in Hertfordshire, where he had been a close personal friend of Clement Atlee, the future prime minister of England, R. E. Weber graduated from Pembroke College, Cambridge, with a second in history. When World War I began, he enlisted in the British army at the age of thirty-one. While serving as a major in the Royal Artillery, he was awarded the Military Cross for bravery after being wounded during an attack on Bourlon Wood near Cambrai in France. When the war ended, he rejoined his father, Edward, at the family firm, Weber, Smith & Hoare Ltd., at 7 Mincing Lane in London.

As a wharfinger, Edward Weber owned and maintained the wharves as well as the great warehouses in which coffee, tea, and spices shipped from all over the world were stored along the Thames from the Tower of London to the famed Prospect of Whitby pub in Wapping. The firm, which had been founded by Edward Weber after the all-powerful East India Company was dissolved by Parliament in 1874, maintained similar facilities in Rotterdam, Antwerp, and other vital port cities throughout Europe.

Succeeding his father as director of the firm, R. E. Weber served on the boards of several large corporations, British Petroleum among them. Although there is no record of this honor having been conferred upon him by his good friend King George VI, and no listing of it in the register of nobility in Austria, where R. E. Weber's grandfather, Dr. Fredric Weber, had been born, Tommy's grandfather laid claim to the title of "Baron von Weber und Scher" (or possibly von Weber und Scheckt) and was called "the Baron" by all who knew him. Married twice, he had numerous mistresses, all of whom he provided for generously in his will.

During school holidays, Tommy often stayed with his grandfather in London. At one point, Tommy decided he too should be called a baron, a concept he was forced to abandon when, as Lulu later explained, "My grandfather's sister Audrey, my great auntie, was absolutely furious he could think he had the title as he had behaved like a scoundrel. She was horrified by his dealings, and in her eyes, he did not live up to the standards of a baron."

Because both R. E. Weber and his younger brother Harold had gone there before him, Tommy was sent to Haileybury and Imperial Service College in the spring of 1952. Although Tommy had made his way through St. Edmund's without great difficulty, Haileybury was a quantum leap from anything he had ever known before. The sheer scale of the school was daunting. Designed by William Wilkins, who also built the National Gallery in London, the great classical Greek buildings at Haileybury framed what was then the largest open academic quadrangle in Europe. The great green dome of the school's chapel made the building resemble St. Paul's Cathedral in London.

Directly across from the chapel in the great dining hall, where boys sat twenty-four to a table, the walnut-paneled walls were covered with large oil portraits of former headmasters and pupils (or "old boys," as they are known in England) who had gone on to achieve great honors in their lives. Among them were Field Marshall Viscount Allen, the conqueror of Syria and liberator of the Holy Land; Sir Thomas Wentworth "Pasha" Russell (depicted in a red fez), who had curtailed the drug trade in Afghanistan during the Opium Wars; and Lord Trevithin and Oaksey, formerly Geoffrey Lawrence, who had served as the presiding judge at the Nuremberg war trials.

At Haileybury, the past was always present. In the school library, two panels of honor listed the seventeen old boys and one member of the staff who had been awarded the Victoria Cross, England's highest military honor for valor in combat as well as those who had been given the George Medal for bravery. The names of all the old boys who had given their lives for king and country were etched on a graven stone cross by the playing field, where each year on November 11, Remembrance Day, a solemn ceremony was held to honor their memory. The abiding spirit and underlying purpose of the school were best embodied by a campus landmark known as "the Lightning Oak," a majestic tree that had continued to grow after having been struck by a thunderbolt on June 2, 1898.

Like his grandfather and great-uncle before him, Tommy was placed in Melvill House, named after the Reverend Henry Melvill, a former pupil who had become the most celebrated preacher in England during the mid-nineteenth century. "Haileybury then was a very hard place," recalled Richard Rhodes James. After graduating from Queen's College, Oxford, Rhodes James spent thirty-four years teaching at Haileybury, twenty-one of them as the master of Melvill House. A seasoned war veteran like many of those who taught at the school, he had parachuted behind Japanese lines in Burma in 1944 as a cipher offer with a British army special forces unit known as the Chindits. "There was quite a lot of bullying. Not so much in Tom's house, but England had barely recovered from the war and it was a rough time. The boys were from an upper-class background. Almost all had come up from private schools, and I never heard a dropped *h* in the whole time I was there."

In his memoirs, Royal Air Force Group Captain Peter Townshend, a decorated war hero who attended the school during the 1920s and then became the great love of Princess Margaret's life, wrote of the school: "At Haileybury, where life for us young ones was hard and sometimes cruel, there was no one to help us but ourselves. Yet, for all the cruelty, the callousness, and the unloveliness, it did no good to cry out for pity. On the contrary, the grim conditions made me clench my teeth; I felt within me a growing determination to resist. Without knowing it I was being inoculated with the serum of survival. Survive your first two years at Haileybury and you could survive anything."

During Tommy's time at Haileybury, Melvill House itself looked much like a British army barracks or a detention camp for youthful offenders. In a huge, stark, completely antiseptic room, forty-seven boys ranging in age from thirteen to eighteen slept in identical iron-frame beds side by side on a spotless wood plank floor beneath a high ceiling supported by large wooden arches. Each bed was covered with the striped school woolen blanket and separated from the one beside it by a low wooden wall, over which the white school towel was draped beneath a curved iron railing from which coats were hung. Barely wider than the bed itself, the compartments, or "comparts," as they were called at Haileybury, afforded no privacy whatsoever, an arrangement entirely in keeping with the philosophy of the school.

Awakened by a bell each morning at half past seven in a room that was always cold, Tommy would leap from his bed along with forty-six other boys and make a mad dash to the bathroom to wash before putting on his school tweed jacket and gray flannel trousers so he could be in the dining hall for breakfast by eight o'clock. "It was cold baths every morning," he said. "Grandpa kept up the habit and had one every day until he died. Every morning, you had to make this run out of the barracks room. If you're healthy at that age, you wake up with an erection. I must have been slightly better endowed than most people, so every morning for about three years, I had to bend this thing down and tuck it in, and it was agony. I'm sure it must have done something awful to me."

After breakfast, Tommy attended classes from nine until one. Along with all the other boys, he then played compulsory games— rugby in the winter and cricket in the summer (football was then still considered strictly for the lower classes). On Wednesdays, there were no games. In full military uniform, Tommy marched and drilled with the school's Combined Cadet Force. On his head, he wore a beret bearing the badge of the East Anglican Brigade, the local regiment in which his grandfather had served with distinction during World War I.

Three days a week, there were evening classes from five to seven. After supper, it was study or "prep" time, as it was known in England. The younger boys in Melvill House went to sleep at nine o'clock. The older boys went to bed an hour later. "The prefects could go to sleep when they liked," Richard Rhodes James said.

"This sometimes imposed discipline problems, but the prefects were a critical part of the house setup. They were the elite and they carried out the orders of the housemaster. You relied absolutely on the prefects to monitor what was going on. If you had good prefects, that was great. If you had bad prefects, it was a nightmare."

At Haileybury, the prefects were also in charge of corporal punishment administered for what Hugh Ramsbotham, Tom's classmate at Melvill House, would later call "consistent anti-social behavior—major misdemeanors being dealt with by the House Master. Over the four and a bit years of my time there, I can remember the occasional regime when beatings might take place every other week." While the practice was no longer so common as it had been, "Tom had certainly been beaten in his time by prefects."

Although the prefects no longer ran in one at a time to administer a single swipe of the cane to the bottom of a boy kneeling on one chair while his head rested on another chair beside it, the ritual still retained its intended function. In Peter Townshend's words: "For the victim, a caning from prefects was a test of behaviour." After the victim was told that he could go, "you rose with all the dignity you could summon and, head held high, left the room—with the certainty, if you had not flinched, that you had successfully accomplished yet another exercise in survival."

While there were occasional weekends when boys could be taken out by their parents, there was very little visiting. Classes were held on Saturday mornings. In the afternoon, the boys would go to the games field to watch the Haileybury rugby XV or the Haileybury cricket XI compete against other schools. On Sunday evenings, at the chime of the bell from the Porter's Lodge, the boys attended services in the school chapel just as they did each morning from Tuesday to Friday and then again at night.

Tommy's journey through Haileybury can be traced in a series of group photographs taken before the four great classical Greek stone columns and ornate iron barred gates that form the entrance to the school. In the first photograph, taken in 1952 not long after he had entered Melvill House, Tommy sits on the ground in the front row squinting into the sunshine in the requisite school tweed suit, white shirt, dark tie, dress stockings, and black shoes. With his neatly combed, bright blond hair parted on the side and his arms crossed before him like all the other boys in his row, Tommy looks completely innocent and far younger than his age.

One boy to Tommy's right, Hugh Ramsbotham, sits directly in front of his older brother, David John Ramsbotham, who as a British army general in Northern Ireland would come to be known as "Rambo" and then served as the chief inspector of Her Majesty's Prisons before becoming a baron who now sits in the House of Lords. "Tom and I went to Haileybury the same term and we left the same term," said Hugh Ramsbotham, who went on to teach at Peterhouse College, Cambridge. "We were close to begin with because young boys going to school together, you're against the world. He was different in a way, but I'd hate to say how. He was unusual. Certainly more sophisticated, and he didn't have a close family. There was a grandfather very much in the background. A towering figure indeed and obviously very important in Tom's life. I remember the Baron coming to visit him but only when we were young and going out for Sunday lunch and Tom very kindly used to invite me."

Tommy was never much of a student at Haileybury, because, as he later explained, "Being dyslexic, I couldn't get through all the reading and so I didn't bother to do any work." Tommy only paid attention in class when he was interested in the subject under discussion. The decidedly mixed reviews he received from his masters over the years are recorded in longhand in a bound ledger book preserved in the school archive. Accurately, their observations portray how he spent his time at Haileybury.

According to his masters, Tommy was "really sensible, but casual." He was "capable, but sometimes hides it," and "should get rid of casual manner." Variously described as "clumsy," "lively," and "erratic," he demonstrated an "ignorance of French" and was "idle" in Latin. His failure to pass the O-level exam in Latin was also duly noted. The most telling comments are those noted on September 12, 1953: "color blindness diagnosed—wanted RAF but color defective (unfit for pilot)," and, as noted during the Easter term in 1955: "immature and undignified."

Because he loved going fast and there seemed no more dashing and romantic a career for a boy at Haileybury, Tommy joined the Royal Air Force section of the Combined Cadet Force when he was fifteen and set his sights on flying the single-seater British-made de Havilland Vampire jet fighter. With a top speed of more than five hundred miles an hour, the Vampire was the first jet to fly nonstop across the Atlantic Ocean.

Knowing he would never be allowed to become a pilot if his color blindness were discovered, Tommy cheated his way through the preliminary eye tests by memorizing the correct answers in advance. His ruse came to an end when an officer asked Tommy what color a certain light was and he gave the wrong answer. Unbeknownst to Tommy, his older brother Anders, also color blind, would somehow manage to fake his own way though similar eye tests and be certified to fly Sabre jets for the Danish army.

"Tom was color blind," Hugh Ramsbotham recalled, "but he managed to get a copy of the book from which you had to read the colored numbers and desperately tried to learn the color codes by heart. The enthusiasm with which he was prepared to cheat his way into the RAF—there was almost an inevitability that he was going to do something like that again later in life. He was quite lucky to have gotten things wrong. At the same time, he could have been absolutely brilliant at something by getting things right. He could have been. But you never know which way these chaps are going to go, do you?"

Tommy, who had already lost his virginity to one of the "land girls" at New Barn Farm, was found to be "immature and undig-

nified" two years later, when F. R. Thompson, then the master of
Melvill House, discovered him in possession of what in England
had since the middle of the nineteenth century been called a
"French letter." When Thompson asked what it was he had found,
Tommy very politely replied, "Something for the weekend, sir. A
condom." When Thompson demanded to know with whom
Tommy intended to use this device, he wisely declined to answer
the question.

By then, Tommy and a few of the other older boys were doing
their best to have sex with the kitchen maids at the school. Hugh
Ramsbotham would later remember these girls as "traditionally
the butt of sexual banter and fantasy at the school. There had been
a case of two or three senior boys found in the maids' quarters just
before we got there. Tom may well have been involved in chatting
up the girls and even attempts to get into the maids' quarters. He
was clearly interested in sex and so I wouldn't be surprised that he
would get mixed up in something like that, real or not." Even if
Tommy never actually put the condom to use at Haileybury, possessing it was a clear breach of etiquette, and for this offense as
well as refusing to answer the master's question, he was caned.

At this point, Tommy was no longer the innocent boy who had
first entered Haileybury. The change in him can be seen most dramatically in a photograph taken in 1956. Now one of the oldest
boys in Melvill House, Tommy, clad in yet another tweed suit,
white shirt, and dark tie, slouches casually in his chair with an in-
souciant look of utter self-confidence on his face. As though disturbed by a passing breeze, strands of his unruly poet's thatch of
thick blond hair fly from his head in varying directions. By any
standard the best-looking boy in the photograph, he seems to
know it as well.

After he became a house prefect during the Easter term,
Tommy arranged a version of "Swing Low, Sweet Chariot," which
enabled Melvill to come in second in the house unison competition. In the house records, Tommy wrote with great approval of

the changes brought about in Melvill House by Richard Rhodes James: "If this trend can continue, there is no reason why Melvill should not become really prominent in Haileybury life. It is already outstanding for its enthusiasm and happiness, the most important; the remainder is easily possible."

With his time at Haileybury nearing an end, Tommy accepted his grandfather's generous offer to start him off in business by going to work for a highly placed executive at British Petroleum. When the executive sexually propositioned him, Tommy told him to "go fuck himself" and stalked from the office, never to return. Because Tommy never told his grandfather the reason he had left the firm, R. E. Weber was incensed. Calling his grandson a "very ungrateful bastard," the old man informed Tommy that from now on, he was on his own.

To repair the breach, Tommy wrote a letter of apology in which he thanked his grandfather for all he had done for him. In yet another storybook turn from the pages of English penny fiction, when R. E. Weber died suddenly on May 9, 1956, at the age of seventy-three, he was found at his desk clasping Tommy's letter in his hand.

In practical terms, Tommy's future as a captain of industry was now finished. After New Barn Farm was sold as part of R. E. Weber's estate, the proceeds were put in trust for Tommy's mother. In her brand new Jaguar, Pamela drove with her husband and two young daughters to Spain, where she built a magnificent house and took up painting. With his grandfather gone and his mother no longer living in England, there was now no one who could tell Tommy what to do. Because he had not yet passed his A-levels, he was, however, obliged to return to school.

During his last term at Haileybury, Tommy finally managed to accomplish the goals that his grandfather had always hoped he would achieve there. Becoming head of house at Melvill, Tommy decreed that no boys would be beaten for any offense so long he served in the post. He also won a coveted starting position on the school's rugby team, the exalted Haileybury XV. "In a boys' school," said Hugh Ramsbotham, "you don't get higher than that. There were certain games players who put themselves up like, 'Look at me, aren't I great?' But I don't remember any idolization of Tom, because he never did that."

Nonetheless, as Toby Parker, who teaches art while also serving as school archivist at Haileybury, noted more than half a century later, "If you were part of the fifteen, you were a god." On a team that won more than it lost, Tommy played fullback or sweeper. The last man between his opponents and the goalkeeper, a position for which he was ideally suited in size and disposition, Tommy was charged with the responsibility of making certain the other team did not score.

In his white-and-red striped Haileybury rugby jersey with the number of his position on the back, Tommy can be seen in a team photograph taken in 1956. Fifth from the left in the back row, with his hands shoved into the pockets of his knee-length rugby shorts, wearing striped white-and-red socks and studded leather rugby boots laced above the ankle, he stares into the camera with that same look of utter self-assurance on his face. By far the tallest member of the squad, he has legs like tree trunks and huge calf muscles. His hair is now so long that it has gone completely out of control.

That Tommy took the field each Saturday for Haileybury against Harrow, Tunbridge, Oundle, and Bracenose College, Oxford, has been commemorated on the school's weathered gray rugby boards, which date back to 1877. The boards hang beneath the vaulted arch beside the Atlee Room, which was named after Haileybury's most famous old boy. Along with D. A. Crichton, J. E. Phillips, M. W. Hardcastle, T. S. Churcher, R. G. D. Christie, and others, the name T. E. Weber can be found fourth from the bottom, beneath the year "1956."

Smiling broadly in an Eisenhower jacket, a beret with a regimental badge, leggings, and military boots, Tommy stands at attention in a photograph of the shooting team he captained that year. Melvill House, which had won the prestigious Capper Cup the previous term, lost it under his leadership because Tommy forgot the day of practice and so had to choose the team "blind." He did, however, win the St. Marks Cup for best shooting average, which, as he told the Melvill House recording secretary, he hoped "in some way offsets the above bloomer."

At a meeting of the House Society, Tommy rose to oppose the motion offered by Hugh Ramsbotham: "That in the opinion of this house modern trends in music are a disaster." Defining music as the art of exciting the emotions through harmony and melody, Tommy pointed out that since the temperament of the day was morose, it was the job of modern music to reflect this feeling. By providing an emotional outlet for the subconscious, modern music and modern composers were deserving of praise. When a vote was taken, the motion was defeated.

In an article he wrote for the student magazine titled "The Sports Car Enthusiast," Tommy explained his passion for speed: "To love driving is to want to drive well, to strive to handle a car to the best possible advantage. . . . The sports car driver wants performance and can get it not only from a special car, but from any car. The basic idea is to drive any vehicle as though its mechanism were fragile and to delight in mastering something because it is difficult, yet to attain a higher average speed than most people would expect from a machine of that size. . . . The true enthusiast seeks perfection and that quest is an entirely personal one, not requiring him to 'show-off.'"

Neatly, Tommy had defined his philosophy of life. Do your best, always go faster than anyone around you, but never take too much credit for your efforts. It was the code of the gentleman transmuted to conduct behind the wheel of an automobile. Driving too fast on every highway he could find without ever being certain exactly where he was headed, Tommy continued trying to get there before anyone else until the day he died.

Although he had already failed his trial A-level exams at Haileybury so badly that "it was a scandal," Tommy borrowed a set of essays written by Melvill House's leading scholar before he had left the school. By studying them, Tommy somehow managed to attain two A-levels in Medieval English and European History and two more in English Literature and Language, which enabled him to finally leave Haileybury.

Describing the path Tommy followed after he walked through the high wrought-iron gates and four Greek columns at the front entrance of Haileybury College for the final time on December 8, 1956, the school's bound ledger book simply states: "Gone into business." And so he had. Only not in a way that anyone at Haileybury would have understood or had ever done before him.

4
lilliesden and cambridge

As soon as she was old enough, Puss was sent to join her sisters Mary and Jenny as well as several of their female cousins at Lawnside, which Jenny would later describe as a "very recherché" independent school for girls on Avenue Road in Great Malvern, Worcestershire. Because Miss Winifred Barrows, the "ghastly, really terrible" headmistress, firmly believed the arts should play an important part in the lives of her pupils, the girls were, in Jenny's words, schooled in "Greek dancing and verse speaking" and made to visit the grave of renowned musician and composer Sir Edward Elgar, a local cultural hero of major proportions.

Mary, Jenny, and Puss, then thirteen years old, were all attending the school when the news of their mother's bankruptcy became a continuing story in the English press. "All I can remember," Jenny Ponte later said, "is that I was at boarding school and when the newspaper came out every day, they would cut out the centerfold because there was a photograph of my mother in it superimposed on a bicycle. If you knew my mother, you knew she could never ride a bicycle. Across the top, the headline said, 'Zip Goes The Million!'"

Although the school did all it could to protect the sisters, the scandal soon became common knowledge among the other girls. Puss herself would later tell a friend that it was for this reason she had been forced to leave the school. In truth, Puss engineered her own expulsion from Lawnside after an incident that could have come directly from the pages of a Victorian novel.

During a school holiday before the Coriat family left Twatley Manor, Puss was sitting with her sister Jenny in an automobile in the pouring rain with a girl who had already acquired a reputation for being the "local bicycle" (British slang for "local slut"). As the three of them watched a point-to-point, a steeplechase race in which riders on thoroughbred horses rode from one village church spire to another, the girl suddenly began unraveling what Jenny would later call "a fantastic story" about having taken a bath with a boy.

Pretending she was the girl, Puss wrote down the story and sent it in a letter to a friend at school. When the friend's mother read the letter, she demanded that Puss be dismissed from a school where the well-bred daughters of the English upper class were being carefully groomed to become proper ladies. "My parents were hauled off to Lawnside," Jenny recalled, "and they came back with faces like thunder. And Puss was sacked. She never told them the truth, and she wouldn't let me tell them, either. I tried, but she wouldn't let me."

Although she could have easily set the record straight, Puss preferred to be thought of as "incredibly naughty" by her family because it gave her the power to differentiate herself from her older sisters. Unlike Mary and Jenny, who remained at Lawnside even after the news of the family's bankruptcy became headline news, Puss was sent to Lilliesden, a school in Kent, that was, in Jenny's words, "a step down from Lawnside."

By then, Twatley Manor and everything in it had been sold at auction. Left with "practically nothing" from the sale, Priscilla and Harold Coriat moved with their young son to a rented house in South Gloucestershire, where the family lived on money the children received from their trust funds. Although Harold Coriat continued to dominate the household on a daily basis, his son now became the exclusive focus of his life.

By this point in time, Puss was already so good-looking that her beauty affected everyone with whom she came into contact. "Puss was sort of a honey pot at age fourteen," her sister Mary recalled. "And everyone said, 'Isn't it wonderful? She's so attractive.' From a very early age, she was a magnet." Although Puss now only spent time with her parents and siblings during school holidays, her beauty also caused a significant change in the family dynamic.

"The relationship between Puss and Camel wasn't very good," her sister Jenny recalled. "He was funny about Puss and sort of tolerated her. Then she turned into this fantastic beauty, and he was interested in her. There was always a sense of drama about her. She would come into a room, and the whole room would light up. She was like a little elf or a faun. She was also incredibly good at cartwheels and handstands. I remember her doing single-handed cartwheels in the garden at Lawnside when we were there. She was also fantastic with a Hula-hoop. She could do it round her neck, round her waist, and around her knees. Three going at the same time. Absolutely incredible."

At Lilliesden, about a hundred girls attended class each day in a Victorian farmhouse that was surrounded by terraced gardens. As Juliet Harmer, then a schoolgirl there, recalled, the girls all wore "a ghastly little tunic, thick lisle stockings, brown shoes, and serge knickers we had to play lacrosse in." Puss made an immediate impression at the school. "I remember her blowing into this all-girls boarding school with her sleeves rolled up and her cardigan around her shoulders, just sort of balanced there rather than actually on and people were going, 'Who's that?' She was very beautiful and exotic with long, dark hair and twinkly eyes, and I just thought she was heaven."

At Lilliesden, Puss quickly "palled up" with Diana Porteous and Lucy Mills, both of whom were also good-looking. "All her gang were pretty," Harmer said, "but Puss was incredibly sophisticated. She had picked up a lot of sophisticated habits from her older sisters, who were extremely clever and well connected, so she seemed a lot older than her age, more like fourteen going on seventeen. She was also very, very stylish. She could put clothes together and make them look fantastic. Whatever she wore looked cool and just right, and she blazed a trail."

The school was so old-fashioned that during the Saturday night dances, where the music came from a wind-up gramophone, the key question after one girl had asked another to dance was always, "Which one of us is going to be the man, and which one is going to be the woman?" With the nearest shop fifteen miles away and most of the girls "quite lonely, above anything else," the school was "an absolute hotbed of scandal, where people could be found lurking in the broom cupboard taking photographs of one another and creeping about, saying, 'Oh, we were only hugging, Miss.'"

Occasionally, girls would be asked to leave the school without anyone being told exactly what they had done to warrant such punishment. "When someone got expelled," Harmer later explained, "we assumed they had been doing things about which we actually knew nothing. We would just guess. You're highly sexed when you're fifteen, and it was like putting a lid on a pressure cooker. But as far as I was concerned, it was things like, 'Can I brush your hair? Will you brush my hair? Can I take a photograph of you and put it by my bed?' Quite innocent, actually. But it was an innocent time. No drinking. God, no."

Unlike Mary and Jenny, Puss, who "was not stupid by any means," did not care very much about school and left Lilliesden at sixteen before taking her A-levels. Because her mother had no idea what else to do with her, Priscilla sent Puss to Cambridge, where, in Jenny's words, she became "the only English girl at the Bell School of Languages. I think she was studying boys, actually."

By then, Jenny was at Millfield, a coeducational school in Somerset, where she studied with the playwright Robert Bolt as she prepared for her A-level and O-level exams. Mary was attending university at Lady Margaret Hall, Oxford, where she stayed for a year before being "kicked out for not doing enough work. It didn't matter then the way it does now. The reason I went to Oxford was to get away from home. My mother used to say, 'Mary's the clever one, Jenny's the funny one, and Puss is the pretty one.' And you weren't allowed to be different from that."

While walking down a street in Cambridge one day, Puss ran into her old schoolmate Juliet Harmer, who was at Homerton College studying to become a primary-school teacher. "It was absolutely brilliant to find Puss there," Harmer recalled, "because I had probably only read pony books by that point and Puss was talking about F. Scott Fitzgerald and Sylvia Plath and people I had actually never heard of. She came across to me as a font of wisdom and was saying things like, 'Isn't it wonderful to be able to read what you like and walk around with books under your arms for fun rather than *having* to read them?' She absolutely loved *Tender Is the Night*."

In Cambridge during the spring and summer of 1960, everyone Puss and Juliet Harmer knew was young, terribly good-looking, and "mad and romantic and living as though they were in a novel rather than in real life." After Puss borrowed a skirt from one of Juliet's very proper friends to wear to a party and then lost the garment, it became Juliet's responsibility to find out what had happened to it. "Puss had absolutely no idea. She'd given it to someone else, she'd lost it, it had fallen off on a punt, it was down the bottom of the river. I sort of made a choice at that time to be friends with people who didn't mind where a skirt had gone, rather than who did."

Becoming far closer in Cambridge than they had been at Lilliesden, Juliet, who looked like a young Julie Christie, and Puss, who was dark and exotic, soon found themselves swept up in a world that seemed to have come from a novel by Evelyn Waugh. "We went out with different men every night of the week," Harmer said. "You were trying people out and trying to find out who you were by going out with all sorts of different men."

Each date would begin with dinner, and then the boy "would have a pretty good go at getting you into bed afterwards." Because both Puss and Juliet had to be back at their colleges by eleven o'clock and often found themselves "climbing over walls" to get there, most boys "didn't really stand much of a chance." As Harmer explained, "There was a lot of snogging in cars but people didn't have affairs and relationships. I reckon very few people actually slept with one another in Cambridge. But I do remember getting pretty drunk, though."

At one point, Puss and Juliet both found themselves in love with the same boy. After Juliet had gone out with him, she came down with German measles and was confined to a sanatorium. By the time she emerged a week later, Puss was going out with the boy. "I was upset, but I thought, well, it couldn't have happened to a nicer person. I didn't mind, really."

Puss and Juliet soon joined forces with two other very good-looking girls to form "a little set. There were four of us, and we all had quite well-off boyfriends." One of them was Prince William of Gloucester. The third son of the Duke of Gloucester and a grandson of King George V and Queen Mary, he was then reading history at Magdalene College. When Puss and Juliet visited the prince at St. James' Palace, it was "quite exciting."

Along with her sister Jenny, Puss was then taken up by the "Ice Cream Set," a group of about ten very good-looking foreign boys, among them Parviz Radji, who would later serve as the shah of Iran's last ambassador to England. "They were called the Ice Cream Boys," Jenny said, "because they were all very good-looking and very slippery." The boy whom Juliet Harmer would later call the king of the Ice Cream Set was Alan Ponte, who, in Jenny's words, was "the most beautiful man I'd ever seen in my life. Absolutely gorgeous." Born in England and educated at Rugby before being admitted to Jesus College at Cambridge, he was the son of Captain Leo Ponte, a Moroccan Jew who, after France had capitulated to Germany, had escaped to London, where he became a captain in the Free French Army led by General Charles de Gaulle.

One afternoon, Alan Ponte, then in his words still a "gallant young undergraduate," met Puss for the first time on the street.

Ponte was "so struck by her that I immediately invited her to come punting with a group of friends on the river. She accepted sweetly and we spent some time chatting together on Jesus Green waiting for the others. She then ran away, overwhelmed by the prospect that she might have to deal with me alone, which was not intended at all."

To Alan Ponte, Puss looked like Jessica, the beautiful but ungrateful daughter of the Jewish moneylender Shylock who steals her father's money and then runs away to marry Lorenzo in Shakespeare's *Merchant of Venice*. "She was very beautiful but extremely coy. She had something rather Old Testament about her and she was entirely different."

At a "grand party" at the very exclusive Pitt Club at 7a Jesus Lane, Ponte then met Puss' older sister, Jenny. Still at Millfield School, she had come to Cambridge for the day to attend the gala and was wearing a long, black ball dress over a pair of rugger socks because "my feet were cold." Like her sister Mary, Jenny sported a beehive hairdo and affected the use of a very long cigarette holder. "We disliked each other on sight," Ponte would later say while also noting that he "much preferred Puss" because she was "more introverted" than her sisters and "had that wonderful ease with which people who don't know they're pretty but are pretty behave. She was lovely."

Although he was initially attracted to Puss, Alan Ponte eventually began keeping company with Jenny. Harmer recalled his saying "I'm going to marry one of those sisters, but I haven't decided which one yet." Further complicating the situation, Ponte asked Puss to dance with him one night at a party, only to discover he was with Mary instead.

By then, Puss had completed her year of study at the Bell College of Languages and had moved to London, where she was living with Jenny in the Rossetti Studios at 72 Flood Street in Chelsea. The studios had been built in 1894 on the property where the eccentric Pre-Raphaelite painter Dante Gabriel Rossetti had kept his extensive menagerie and where his pet elephant was said to have sprayed water from his trunk into the second-floor windows. Shaped like a curved, red brick medieval redoubt, the building stood in a silent cul-de-sac at the back of an arched brick tunnel that led in from the street.

Just a few moments' walk from the noisy tumult of the King's Road, the studios evoked an earlier, far more genteel era in London. In Jenny Ponte's words, the flat she shared with Puss "had a bath in the kitchen so you could sit in the bath and twiddle the stove with your toes. I remember Puss cooking spaghetti and getting in an awful temper because she couldn't work the stove and I was having a bath. But I laughed so much with her there."

Although she had never cared for school and had not paid much attention to her studies, Puss had educated herself by reading the poetry of Sylvia Plath, who eventually committed suicide, and F. Scott Fitzgerald's *Tender Is the Night*, the story of psychiatrist Dick Diver and his wife, Nicole, a former patient who suffers from mental breakdowns. The title of the novel comes from John Keats' "Ode to a Nightingale," which contains two lines that Juliet Harmer would quote many years later to describe her friend: "Darkling I listen; and, for many a time / I have been half in love with easeful Death."

Even as a young girl, Puss had modeled her life on what she thought and felt rather than what she had experienced. A great romantic who lived in her imagination, she was also the product of everything she had read. Nine years later, in a letter to her sons, Puss would write, "I have read too many books in my lifetime and it is because I am very frightened now that I am trying not to anymore. *please*: do pay attention: books are dangerous."

But not to an eighteen-year-old girl who had come to London knowing only that she wanted to be something more than a beautiful young heiress with whom men had already begun falling in love at first sight. Exactly what that was, Puss could not say for sure. Like a storybook princess in that great walled castle at 72 Flood Street, she was waiting for a gallant young knight to come riding out of the west to win her heart and claim her hand in marriage. Soon enough, he would be there. And, in the words of her sister Jenny, it was then that everything would go horribly wrong.

5

pont street

As Tommy walked to a business appointment one day not long after coming up to live in London in 1957, the sentry standing outside the gates of St. James' Palace, resplendent in his red military jacket, spotless white gloves, and towering black bearskin hat, saluted him. While Tommy's striped red-and-black Melvill House tie did look much like the one worn by former members of the Queen's Guards, it was the rest of his uniform—an impeccable pinstriped suit, a bowler hat, and the tightly furled black umbrella in his hand that marked him as an unmistakable member of the upper class who was clearly worthy of respect.

Before the Beatles, Mary Quant, and the fab shops on Carnaby Street brought flash and color to the streets of the city, London was still a drab, gray town where food rationing had only recently ended, coal was in short supply, and the social order remained much as it had been for the past half century. In a city where everyone was still living in black-and-white, Tommy set about creating for himself a life that could only have been shot in Technicolor.

He began the process by finding himself a flat in the very fashionable part of London, where he would live for the next fifteen years. "In those days," said John Green, who in time found himself in business with Tommy, "you could take leasehold apartments that were for rent and tart them up, and each time you turned one around, you made a thousand quid." Unable to sell one such flat on Pont Street, a road about three blocks from Harrods that ran along the back of Knightsbridge before ending near Belgrave Square, Green walked into an estate agent's office on German Street one day after lunch and offered to let him list it as a rental.

An hour and a half later, Green was back in his office when in walked "this tall, gorgeous-looking man, and he said, 'Are you John Green?' And I said yes. And he said, 'Well, I'm Tommy Weber. I'd like to buy your apartment in Pont Street.' I said, 'Don't be silly. Don't be stupid.' He said, 'No, I'm serious. I've just been into that estate agent. It's absolutely ideal. I'd like to buy it. The only trouble is you'll have to talk my trustees into putting up the money.' I said, 'If that's the case, if I can, I will.'"

Green, who was eager to make the deal, then contacted the executor who administered Tommy's share of his grandfather's estate. "Look," the executor told Green, "we've had a lot of trouble with this young man. He's got the money. And he likes you. Could you keep an eye on him for us?" Green, who was "dying to sell the bloody flat," said, "Well, to the extent that I'm able, of course I will." The terms of the sale were soon negotiated and Green was paid two thousand guineas (£2,200) for the flat. "I was happy," he would later say, "and Tommy was in the flat."

To his "horror" a few weeks later, Green learned that Tommy was running chemin de fer gambling parties in the flat—a practice that, as Green would later say, "was actually illegal. He was running private gaming parties in London." Nor did Tommy restrict his interest in games of chance to his new digs. A regular at a gambling club on the Bayswater Road, he also frequented a casino known as the White Elephant. "Tom was a gaming person," his friend Michael Taylor said. "And he gambled a lot. It wasn't legal then but you could go to the White Elephant at about seven in the evening, have dinner, and then gamble. I think he was a loser at gambling."

In fact, Tommy rapidly lost so much money gambling that he was forced to sell all the furniture he had inherited from his grandfather. When Tommy asked his mother for more money, she turned him down cold. Protesting her decision, he pointed out that unlike him, his mother and his stepsisters were all living quite comfortably on regular payments from R. E. Weber's trust fund. Pamela, who had been brought up to believe that women were not meant to go to work, informed her son that it was his duty as a man to find a way to earn his own keep.

The dispute over money was the final straw in what had become an increasingly contentious relationship between Tommy and his mother ever since he had returned from school to New Barn Farm to announce he had decided to become a race-car driver. "I remember him coming to take us out in a lovely old red sports car," his half-sister Lulu said. "The top was down, and my sister and I were sitting in the back screaming as he drove up the road at a hundred miles an hour. When he told Mum he wanted to learn to be a racing driver, she said, 'Not under my roof.'"

After he had been cut off from all further access to the family money, Tommy was forced to earn a living by relying on what were already his foremost assets—his good looks and great personal charm. In several photographs of him from this period, Tommy, his hair now cut suitably short and neatly brushed to the side, wears a pinstriped business suit, white shirt, and striped tie with a white handkerchief tucked into his jacket pocket. Impossibly handsome, he radiates the utter self-confidence of a young lord who has never known a hard day in his life. As he would later say, "They all thought I was going to be Howard Hughes the Second. The next multibillionaire. That was what was expected of me." It is precisely this image that he projects in the photographs.

Forced to rely on his own resources, Tommy became a good friend and business associate of Michael Taylor. Known as "Mikey" to his friends, Taylor bought and sold properties in London but was also a talented driver who after his first racing season had been asked to join Team Lotus, for which he drove at Le Mans with the legendary Scottish racecar driver Innes Ireland. In England, where only the upper class could afford this pastime, auto racing was then still the exclusive province of well-to-do gentlemen who pursued the sport for the thrill of competition rather than the money.

"Tommy was pretty wild in a car," Taylor said, "so he never really did all that well. But he was a great finder of deals. He'd find a property or two old widows who wanted to move. He could persuade people who didn't know they wanted to sell to do so, and he was very, very skillful at negotiating the prices of properties. He had great personal charm, and I made a lot of money with him in those days."

In a business that was completely speculative and not unlike gambling, Tommy soon became so good at the game that he would walk into a flat for sale, persuade the seller it was just what he had been looking for, and write a check on the spot to cover the deposit. Knowing he did not have enough money in his account to cover the deposit, Tommy would then stroll into the nearest pub, order a drink, and begin chatting up the other customers. Often, he managed to resell the flat for a profit before his check ever reached the bank.

Already buying and selling properties in a decidedly unorthodox manner, Tommy managed to earn enough money from the trade to afford an extensive social life. Known as "debs' delights," he and Michael Taylor were both regulars at what in England were then called deb dances—elegant dinner parties and formal balls at which debutantes were introduced to the best-looking, most eligible young men in London.

The nature of Tommy's nonstop social life is accurately reflected in a June 16, 1959 article from the *Daily Mail*. The item recounts the sad tale of how Sarah Drummond's dreams of becoming "Deb-of-the-Year" were shattered when she was thrown through the windshield of a Renault Dauphine after it collided with a three-ton army lorry as she was returning from "a gay weekend house party in Hampshire." In the article, "Six foot, blond, debs' delight Tommy Weber, [a] race driver who danced with her at the party," was quoted as saying, "We had arranged that I should drive Sarah back to London but at the last moment I decided to leave early. . . . I feel terrible, broken-hearted.'"

Years later, Tommy said of this period in his life, "I was the deb's delight for a couple of years, but it wasn't my line at all." Despite the way he had been identified in the newspaper, the only races in which Tommy had competed by then were on the streets of London, a city in which only those who had a good deal of money could even afford to own a car, much less drive it at high speed during an evening out on the town. In a bar one night as they were having a drink, Tommy and John Green made a twenty-pound wager to see who could get back to St. James' Palace first. "He beat me by twenty seconds," Green remembered. "But he had to go up the wrong side of the road to do it."

When Green bought himself a brand new Jaguar XK150S, then the ultimate status symbol for a young man-about-town in London, Tommy informed Green that although the sporty roadster was "a bloody good car," the factory-installed shock absorbers simply "did not do the car justice" and needed to be replaced. He then urged Green to go see a "mate" of his who was "a damn good fellow in a garage just off the Edgware Road." When Green arrived there at six-thirty that evening, Tommy saw to it that his friend fitted Green's new car with high-end Koni shock absorbers.

Tommy's obsessive need to make certain that fine automobiles received all the care they deserved did not also extend to the way he drove them. After Michael Taylor sold his wife's Alfa Romeo to Tommy, Taylor arranged bank financing so that Tommy could pay off the purchase price on time. On the second day Tommy had the Alfa, he wrecked the car and had to completely write it off. "*Reckless* is the word that describes him," Taylor said later. "And he was reckless from a young age. But full of fun. You always had a good time with him. He could always get the best table at a restaurant.

He knew how to deal with people. I sent him off to buy this huge house for seven thousand pounds, and he somehow raised the money through my bankers to buy it, and I never got the house, so we had a slight falling out over that. Slightly, he went behind my back and took it away. So we then didn't go on in business." The two men did, however, remain friends.

Tommy, who seems never to have spent a night alone at home during this period, was also a regular at a wildly fashionable restaurant called the Bistro. Located on Bourne Street, the establishment was run by Elisabeth Furse. The mother of English journalist Anthony Haden-Guest, Furse was born in East Prussia to Jewish parents. At a young age, she joined the German Communist Party. During World War II, she worked as a courier for British military intelligence, transporting secret messages and large sums of money in condoms hidden in her vagina. Because her favorite clients were "young men on the verge of making it," Tommy was always welcome in the Bistro, a dim room lit by candles and not so much a restaurant as "a club hideaway . . . a debating society . . . a womb to climb back into . . . a state of mind."

Tommy first met Puss through her sister Jenny. He and Jenny had become friends when Tommy fell ill with pleurisy as he was preparing to begin racing on a full-time basis in the fall of 1961. Jenny visited him regularly in her E-type Jaguar, bringing with her what he later described as "all sorts of luscious goodies, lots of cigarettes, and lots of wine." When Puss and Jenny decided to go see the newly released film version of *West Side Story*, Jenny asked Tommy to escort her while Puss went with Alan Ponte. When the movie ended, each sister left with the other man.

Years later, Tommy would remember that his first significant contact with Puss occurred while he was dining at the Bistro. Informed that there was a telephone call for him, he picked up the receiver and heard a woman say, "I'm Jenny's sister, and will you come to dinner tomorrow?" After he had accepted the invitation,

Tommy hung up the phone and told someone that he had just spoken to the woman with whom he would spend the rest of his life. As he would later say, "It was the voice that did it. Before I had even seen her. Her voice was very melodious and deep, very expressive and unique. It was a magic voice, and it completely bewitched me from the moment I heard it. It was a voice to fall in love with."

In England, where the way in which people spoke entirely defined their social standing, it was Tommy who had always had "the voice." Perfectly modulated and undeniably upper class, his voice and the way he used it had always enabled Tommy to persuade people that despite whatever unlikely proposition he was offering them at the moment, he really did have their best interests at heart. And yet it was Puss' voice that made him fall in love with her. "A lot of the people we knew at the time were sort of grand and talked in quite arrogant, Harrods-like voices," Juliet Harmer said. "But Sue had a very, very quiet voice. You had to strain to hear it."

Bearing flowers and "the obligatory bottle of wine," Tommy went round to have dinner with Puss the next night at the Rossetti Studios on Flood Street. "It was love at first sight, and we both knew it was right," Tommy said. "We were holding hands under the table while Jenny was with the poet Christopher Logue and I stayed there afterwards, and we consummated the relationship that evening. We were virtually inseparable from then on."

6
holy trinity church

Although everyone who saw them together knew that Puss and Tommy were very much in love, Camel Coriat strongly disapproved of the tall, blond racecar driver with whom his eighteen-year-old daughter was now keeping company. As always, Camel's objections were founded not so much on fatherly concern as how he, his wife, and their young son would survive once they could no longer count on a regular income from the trust funds of all four children.

By then, Camel had already begun what would become a long, rancorous legal battle to have the trusts equalized. As Christopher Coriat would later say of his father, "He felt very strongly that it was unfair that the older children had so much more. A lot of the difficulty within the family when I was growing up, especially with Mary, was around his campaign to try to equalize the trusts. There were court applications and all kinds of things. It became very relevant at the point when all three girls reached twenty-one and inherited their money. Then he and Priscilla would have been dependent on my trust alone to survive, and we couldn't have done so."

Jenny, acting very much like the middle sister, did all she could to ease what was a difficult situation for all concerned. "Mary and

I had inherited much more than Puss and my little brother," she explained, "and so my father was always trying to get us to equalize. He wanted money from us nonstop. I did equalize, but Mary never did. I think I inherited about a hundred and thirty thousand pounds, which would now be worth a million. And I gave Puss about ten or eleven thousand."

Due in no small part to the constant financial pressure exerted on them by Camel, all three sisters married during the same year. "He was always trying to get money out of me," Mary said. "When I was twenty-one, he tried to make me sign checks, and I felt I'd do anything just to get out. I did sign some, giving my money to him because he said it was for Mummy. I really hated it all so much that I tried very hard to forget it."

While Puss and Tommy's love affair did not cause their respective families to go to war with one another like the Montagues and Capulets, the situation was both delicate and complicated. As anyone who knew Priscilla might have expected, she was not the problem. "My mother was hopelessly in love with Tommy," Jenny recalled. "She wouldn't stop talking about him, and she had pictures of him all over the house. And I think she and Puss eventually fell out because of it."

To ensure his family's financial future and perpetuate the myth that he was thoroughly English, Camel wanted all three girls to marry very proper British gentlemen who had unlimited resources at their command. What no one knew was that in Tommy, who had already had a reputation as a rake, a playboy, and a womanizer, Camel saw someone much like himself. For all these reasons, Tommy recalled, "He did a lot of research into me and found out things about me that I had never done. Apparently, I was supposed to have burned down a hotel somewhere. It wasn't true, but somehow he knew about it."

Yet another motivation for his efforts was that Tommy's mother, Pamela, had worked as a secretary for Camel at Twatley Manor just after the war. "She wanted to learn how to look out for our estate in

Denmark," Tommy said, "so she went to him to learn about farming and how he looked after his own estates. Of course, he tried to get into her, but she didn't allow it." Confirming this, Tommy's half-sister Lulu recalled, "Funnily enough, my mother knew Puss' father. She had worked for him as a secretary in Wiltshire. She hated him. She couldn't stand him. She absolutely detested him. Weird, isn't it?"

Despite all the obstacles he was now facing, Tommy went to great lengths to win Camel's approval. Much like Edmund Rostand's Christian, who had asked Cyrano to plead his cause with the lovely Roxanne, Tommy enlisted a good friend to speak for him with Puss' father. "Tommy had to convince them that he was suitable for her to marry," John Green remembered. "Tommy said, 'Would you mind if they rang you up and would you tell them about me? I love this girl.' Whatever else you might say about Tommy, he was a very genuine guy. And I remember having this long conversation with a strange man called Camel Coriat, who didn't ring quite true to me."

After Green had interceded for him, Tommy appealed to Alan Ponte for help with Camel. Because Ponte's father, Leo, was then running the River Club, a well-known dinner and dancing establishment on the Embankment (Leo eventually sold the club to James Bond film producer Cubby Broccoli), Alan Ponte organized a table for dinner at the club one night for himself and Jenny, Puss and Tommy, and Priscilla and Camel.

As soon as Leo Ponte laid eyes on Camel, he informed his son that the Coriats were one of the best-known families in Morocco and that Camel's claim that his ancestors had lived in England for four hundred years was "rubbish." Making the entire situation that much worse, Leo at some point in the evening seems to have also informed his son that Camel's father was actually a sheep farmer who had lived one valley over from the Pontes in Morocco. In Jenny's words, "The irony was that Alan was in fact a Moroccan Jew, and so when I got engaged to him, my father went absolutely mad and said, 'Whatever you do, don't let the Pontes try and fool you about my background.' I didn't know what the hell he was talking about until my father-in-law came in and said, 'Camel Coriat, I know you. You're from one of the great families of Morocco.' And my father went absolutely mad and denied it."

Camel's objections to Tommy were rendered irrelevant when, as Tommy would later say, "Puss was found to be pregnant, and so she had to be married. In those days, there was no alternative. And that was how it happened." Before the marriage could take place, Puss had to persuade her trustees to honor the stipulation in her grandmother's will stating that Puss would receive her inheritance on her twenty-first birthday or her wedding day, whichever came first. As a ward of the court, Puss also had to apply for legal permission to marry. When Mr. Justice Pennycuick of the High Court ruled in her favor on July 24, 1962, the news of Puss and Tommy's engagement became a continuing story in the London tabloids.

That same day, the *Evening News* ran a story beneath the headline "Heiress Engaged": "Susan Coriat is to marry racing motorist and man about town Tommy Weber, 25, whom she met in London ten months ago. . . . She has been modeling for dress designer Kiki Byrne and he has been racing Mrs. Byrne's cars all over Europe." At the time, the two hippest shops on King's Road were Bazaar, run by Mary Quant, and Kiki, where Kiki Byrne sold her designs. After seeing Tommy drive a Ferrari in Nassau during Bahamas Speed Week, Byrne's husband had persuaded him to manage his racing team.

Below a photo of a smiling Puss and Tommy in the *Daily Mail* a day later, the subhead added: "they had to make sure he wasn't fortune hunting, says race-driver fiance." As they celebrated their good fortune in a pub in Chelsea, Tommy expressed his exasperation at how long the process had taken: "They had to make sure I wasn't fortune hunting. It would have been easier to elope to Gretna Green [a small Scottish town where runaway marriages were traditionally performed]." Identified as the son of a Danish army captain, Tommy was reported to be living with his mother on Eton Avenue in northwest London while running a garage and managing a racing team. He was also said to have won the Prix de Paris auto race earlier in the year, when in fact it was Michael Taylor who had done so.

Aside from the speed at which the wedding plans were now proceeding because Puss was pregnant, Tommy also failed to mention that if the two of them had eloped, his future wife would not have received her inheritance of eighty-seven thousand pounds (about a quarter of a million dollars) on the day they became husband and wife. While the article itself was classic English tabloid fodder, the reason it ran at length was the photo of Puss that accompanied it.

Perched on the hood of a car with her legs crossed and wearing a sleeveless dress with buttons down the front, Puss smiles at the camera with one knee draped over the other in a classic pose designed to show off her shapely gams. With her helmet of thick bouffant hair, penciled-in eyebrows, heavy black eyeliner, and copious lipstick, she looks like a mindless London dolly bird who has never let a single thought interfere with the ongoing party of her life. Too stylish for words but looking much older than her years, she seems like someone trying on an identity for size.

Assuring the reporter she would not waste her money, because she would have "to apply to the trustee every time I want some," Puss said, "The first thing I want to buy when I inherit the money is a sports car." In time, she bought herself a white Mercedes convertible with, as Jenny Ponte would later say, "left-handed drive so she could wave her engagement ring out the window. She ran out of petrol once in the middle of Sloane Square and just abandoned the car. And when she was stopped by police for leaving the car with the engine running and both doors open, she said, 'I'm pregnant and I went for a pee. When you're pregnant, you're allowed to go for a pee whenever you like.' And they accepted it."

Invitations announcing that Thomas Evelyn Weber and Susan Ann Caroline Coriat were to be married at the Church of the Holy

Trinity on Sloane Street in Chelsea at five-thirty in the afternoon on Thursday, September 6, 1962, were soon in the mail. Directly across the street from where Tiffany's and Cartier's are now located, Holy Trinity, a stolid red brick church that looks as though it has been fashioned from layers of gingerbread interspersed with vanilla frosting, was described by the poet and critic John Betjeman as "the cathedral of the Arts and Crafts movement." In every sense, it was the perfect place for Puss and Tommy to be wed.

A week before the wedding, the *Daily Sun* reported that the wedding promised to be "a swinging affair" because Puss had asked "the Negro cast of 'Black Nativity'" to perform during the ceremony. Although that plan was scrubbed, Tommy did decide at the very last moment that Mendelssohn's "Wedding March" would not do for the ceremony, and so he instructed the organist to play Bach's "Toccata and Fugue."

Four days before the ceremony, Jenny and Alan Ponte, who were scheduled to be married in three weeks' time at Caxton Hall with a reception to follow at Claridge's, suddenly learned that Ponte had to fly immediately to Brazil, where he had accepted what the *Daily Express* called a "big banking job." As Priscilla told a reporter for the newspaper, "We were at our wit's end. Susan and Jenny put their heads together and Susan came up with the answer. She asked Jenny to share her wedding reception and put the marriage forward to Thursday." As the article also noted, "All day long, Jenny rang her friends and said, 'We're getting married in the morning.'"

"We got married on the same day," Jenny Ponte said, "because Alan's family was Jewish and my father was going mad that his own Judaism had come to light. And so I said, 'Look, I'm absolutely fed up with all this. I'm going to get married the first day that Caxton Hall will accept us.' Which happened to be the day that Puss and Tommy were getting married. So we shared a wedding reception. Camel was there and was very pale-faced about me marrying Alan. He wasn't pleased."

Camel would have been even less pleased if he had known what transpired under his own roof on the night before the wedding. Violating the tradition that the groom should not see the bride before the ceremony, Tommy scaled the wall of the house that Camel and Priscilla had rented on Avenue Road in St. John's Wood for the wedding. Clambering hand-over-hand up the ivy like Errol Flynn in some swashbuckling epic of yore, Tommy vaulted into Puss' bedroom for a bit of fun with his beloved before their honeymoon began.

The two of them were "larking about in this rented house" when Tommy caught sight of "a picture that looked rather suspiciously hung." Behind it, he found a wall safe. "Apropos of my various adventures," he said, "I told her that I had been trained to open safes. Sure enough, I managed to open it in about five minutes." Although there was "nothing particularly of value inside," Puss was duly impressed by Tommy's never-ending array of skills. Suffering from what he would later call "stage fright," the two of them then had a lengthy, serious discussion about their situation. "I gave her the opportunity to call it off if she wanted to, but she didn't. It was obviously a shotgun marriage, but it went through."

As the fading light of late afternoon in London filtered into Holy Trinity Church through its great vaulted blue-and-green stained-glass window, Tommy, resplendent in a black morning coat, a formal vest, and a white tie with a red carnation in his lapel, waited for his bride. He stood in front of a massive altar, above which the images of the Virgin and Child, the Crucifixion, and John the Baptist had been carved in white marble. Tommy's good friend, Peter van Gerbig, an American millionaire who bought so many Bentley Continentals during his time in England that a collector's model now bears his name, stood beside him as his best man.

Puss' sister Mary, who attended the wedding with her husband, Charles Keen, and who was pregnant with their first child, later remembered Tommy as "looking glamorous in a rather louche way." The chief bridesmaid was Puss' good friend Juliet Harmer. Three-year-old Cathryn Harrison, the daughter of singer Noel Harrison and the granddaughter of actor Rex Harrison, also served as a bridesmaid. The young girl would later be seen taking a sip of champagne from a glass held by Puss in a photo in the *Daily Mail.*

As she walked down the aisle, the bride wore a very plain, high-necked, loosely cut dress designed by Kiki Byrne to hide the fact that Puss was now nearly three months pregnant. With a large white silk bow fastened to the back of her hair, which had now been cut short and swept back from her face, Puss held a beribboned bunch of white flowers in her left hand as her father walked her down the forty-foot-wide nave past the magnificent East Window designed by Edward Burne-Jones. To the swelling sound of Bach from the great organ ninety feet above the floor of the church, Camel escorted his daughter through a set of black and gold wrought-iron gates and then up four marble steps to an altar set with two huge brass candleholders holding thick candles before returning to his seat so the ceremony could begin.

At some point earlier in the day, Tommy had smoked "what I think was my first joint. It completely did me up, and we both got the giggles during the ceremony, and I made a complete mess-up of my part. There had been all this nonsense in the newspapers about me capturing an heiress, and in the oaths where one plies one's troth, I made a slip of the tongue and said, 'With all thy worldly goods, I do me endow.' I got it the wrong way round. It was true in a way, but a terrible slip, which I have never been allowed to forget. Many truths are said in jest, I'm afraid."

Jenny Ponte, who had been married earlier in the day but had not seen either Puss or Tommy at her wedding lunch because it was bad luck for the bride and groom to see one another before they met at the altar, would later say, "Puss looked very beautiful and very pregnant, and she was very funny. And Tommy behaved quite well. Except for saying 'With all thy worldly goods, I me endow.' But she loved it."

During the ceremony, Jenny sat near her mother. Although no one thought much about it at the time, Priscilla had watched two of her daughters marry on the same day in a manner that bore no resemblance whatsoever to her own magnificent wedding in a cordoned-off section of St. Paul's Cathedral before a huge throng of high-ranking British nobility, ambassadors, and foreign ministers. Whatever happiness she might have felt for Puss and Jenny was tempered by the sober realization of how different her own life had now become. "She did actually express feelings of regret," Jenny recalled. "Both of us being married under reduced circumstances and the press were impossible. She absolutely hated all that at that point."

After the ceremony, Puss, now Tommy's lawfully wedded wife, turned from the altar and walked back down the long center aisle with her groom by her side. In the fading gray light of what had become a rainy afternoon in London, the curving black latticework in the great leaded window over the front door took on an eerie life of its own, looking like a colony of bats taking sudden flight at sunset. As Puss and Tommy emerged onto Sloane Street, newspaper photographers who had been waiting for them in the rain began snapping pictures of the happy couple standing together beneath big black umbrellas held aloft by others.

Although it was an easy walk from the church, Puss and Tommy were driven to their reception in nearby Eaton Square, where great white mansions faced one another on either side of a central garden. Jenny, who at the time had eighteen hundred pounds in her bank account, "blew the whole lot on flowers, and there were flowers all the way down the street. In the *Evening Standard* that night, it said, 'I arranged all the flowers myself, said handsome Mr. Alan Ponte.' So I gave him hell for that."

In an oversized zebra-striped cloche hat that Audrey Hepburn could have worn in *Breakfast at Tiffany's* and a sleeveless black dress with a striped neckline, Jenny looked far more glamorous than her younger sister. The four newlyweds posed together for a

photograph, all of them holding glasses of champagne and lit cigarettes in their hands, that appeared in the *Daily Mail* the next day
below the headline "100,000 Pound Brides!"

After the reception, Puss and Tommy stepped into a white Rolls
Royce that drove them around the square again and again until
Tommy stopped the car. Leaping from the backseat, he bought all
the roses that a street vendor had in buckets on her barrow. As the
Rolls went around the square again, Puss and Tommy started toss-
ing roses out of the windows of the car. Even on what had already
been a remarkable day, everyone was astounded by this fabulously
romantic gesture.

Because Tommy did not own a car, he invited his good friend
Michael Taylor and Taylor's wife, Charlotte, along on his honeymoon. The four of them drove through France to Menton, where
they all stayed in Alan Ponte's house in a beautiful, unspoiled valley.
It was there Charlotte Taylor took the photograph of an obviously
pregnant Puss and a blissfully happy Tommy looking like figures
from Greek mythology as they sat in the sunshine on a veranda
with a white stone column and the mountains in the background.

"We spent most of our time down at the beach at the Eden Roc
in Antibes," Tommy said, "and we spent all our honeymoon money
on raspberries and champagne at a time when raspberries were not
in season. The head man at the Eden Roc said, 'Not since the Russian archdukes have we seen people spend money like this and only
take their champagne with raspberries.'" After running out of
funds in two weeks, Puss and Tommy went to Paris so he could enter a race and win some money.

To continue the endless party that their honeymoon had become, Puss and Tommy invited half a dozen friends from England
to join them at the Palais d'Orsay Hotel, where they shared the lift
with Orson Welles, who was then filming *The Prisoner* in the
nearby Gare d'Orsay. "I don't know who paid the bill," Juliet
Harmer said later, "but it was pretty bloody expensive. We had as
much champagne as we liked, and then we saw Tommy in his race.

I don't think he won, but at least he didn't get killed. That was what Puss thought might happen. They were definitely living on the edge."

In Tommy's words, "We were having a very lovely time, and both of us knew it wasn't going to last long, because we had no money, not a dollar, and the only way I was going to make any money was by motor racing, which I had only just started to do seriously. She had some capital, but it was all very well tied down by official trustees. Right from the start, it was a hand-to-mouth existence. Anyway, our son was on the way. We were married in September, and he was born on March twelfth."

By then Puss and Tommy were living in Pimlico so near Victoria Station and its multiple sets of railway tracks that they could hear the trains rattle by at night. With a view of a towering church spire down at the end of the street, their new home was so posh that one of the most fashionable magazines in England saw fit to describe it at great length. By any standard, Puss and Tommy were now not only the best-looking but also the most fortunate young couple in London.

7

cambridge street

S ix months after they were married, Tommy was driving home at two in the morning with a very pregnant Puss by his side when he went through a traffic light about a hundred yards from their home in Pimlico. A black cab cruising along at a far more reasonable speed clipped the rear of Tommy's car, causing it go spinning wildly out of control. In an era when no one wore seat belts, the resulting impact split open Puss' head and knocked her unconscious.

Gathering up all the cash for his hotel room in Monte Carlo, where he was headed the next day to pursue his dream of racing at the elite Formula One level, Tommy got Puss out of the car and carried her over a bridge and then around a corner into their house. After they had followed the conspicuous trail of Puss' blood along the street, the policemen who had been called to the scene of the accident were soon knocking at the front door of 23 Cambridge Street. Puss, who had suffered a severe concussion but had by then regained her senses, kept telling Tommy that on no account was he to let them into the house.

Somehow, Tommy managed to talk the police out of booking him for the way he had been driving, without ever mentioning how much he'd had to drink earlier in the evening at dinner with

Puss and Michael Taylor. Tommy then took his young wife to a clinic in central London, only to learn that he himself had broken his neck. The accident also caused Puss to go into labor, bringing on the premature birth of their son. Tommy witnessed the delivery as a patient in a nearby hospital.

Puss decided to name her son Jake because as, Jenny Ponte would later say, "She liked the letter *J* because of me and she liked *Jacob and the Amazing Technicolor Dreamcoat*, and she thought a short name was much stronger than a long one.'" The middle name Puss chose for her son was Taliesin, after the sixth-century Welsh poet whose work is celebrated in Alfred Lord Tennyson's *Idylls of the King*.

From the day that he was born, Jake never lacked for affection or attention from either of his parents. "It was a joy to have a child," Tommy said. "It was fantastic. Couldn't have been lovelier. The arrogance and the optimism of youth is absolutely astonishing. One just took everything in one's stride. There didn't seem to be anything wrong at all." As Jenny recalled, "They were both so proud of him. Puss was absolutely besotted by Jake. This tiny little yellow-haired boy with this beautiful black-haired mother. I can't tell you how attractive they were together."

The birth of their son only enhanced the widely held perception that Puss and Tommy were now, as Juliet Harmer would later say, "the most glamorous couple in London." Their standing was confirmed by a piece in the *Tatler*, a publication that ever since its inception at the beginning of the eighteenth century had concerned itself with the lifestyles of the rich and fashionable. As the magazine noted in an extensive piece accompanied by large photographs of their home, Sue and Tommy Weber lived on "one of those little streets in Pimlico" that was only just recovering from "a century of soot and clamor" as the nearby railway lines fell into disuse.

Because Tommy was a racing-car driver who drove "very fast cars which are fascinatingly constructed out of wood around a Ford Anglia engine" and a "property man" who dealt in "the nerve-racking luxury-flat market," his life was "tense," and so the Webers had "painted their house plain white all through," thereby "making it a light, relaxing place to come home to." Judging by their "superb, tailor-made furniture," notably the "long, mole brown interpretation of a Chesterfield" sofa in the living room and their "eight-foot-square four-poster" bed "hung with white chiffon," Tommy seemed "to be doing well" in these pursuits.

The interior of their five-story brick house was "unostentatious: austere, even—with a few strong touches like a giant marble and alabaster chess set on a little table; abstract paintings by Tommy's mother, Pamela Kerr;" and "a vast copper pot full of sweet peas." In the ground-floor nursery where Jake's nanny, a young Scottish girl named Maureen, whom everyone called "Mo," looked after him, the furniture was very spare but Victorian, consisting of a brass cot and a wooden high chair.

"They had an extraordinary flat," Juliet Harmer remembered. "It was completely minimalist. Very, very modern with white carpets, low coffee tables, and marble and glass. They had it designed by someone famous because they knew all those people. They had a magnificent chess set, but I don't think they actually played. It was all there for the style." Puss' brother, Christopher, then nine years old, would later remember "going to Cambridge Street and being wowed by it. Very modern and gorgeous. Fabulous ivory chess set. Everything was black-and-white and like nothing I had ever seen before. It was an amazing place. I also remember it being a little tense."

Much of the tension between Puss and Tommy was generated by his single-minded pursuit of a racing career. Although there was no mention of this in the story in the *Tatler*, the accident that brought about Jake's premature birth had also put an abrupt end to Tommy's hopes of earning a living as a Formula One driver during the coming season. The car crash had also introduced him to the salubrious effects of the painkilling drugs he had been prescribed for his injury.

"To keep the racing team in funds," Tommy said, "I had to keep driving. The pain was such that in order for me to get into the car before everything had healed up, I continued taking drugs." Although Puss was unaware of what he was doing, Tommy, who had smoked his first joint just six months earlier on his wedding day, had now begun regularly medicating himself so he could pursue the only career he had ever loved.

Even before they were married, Puss' greatest fear was that something terrible was bound to happen to Tommy if he kept on driving. "The motor racing was hard for her to take," Tommy said. "I would leave her behind sometimes, and she would somehow manage to turn up in some godforsaken place in the middle of Europe." Tommy was once scheduled to drive at Nürburgring, which was seventy miles south of Cologne and which world champion driver Jackie Stewart called the "greatest and most challenging race circuit in the world." Puss surprised Tommy by hitching a lift there in a plane "that got lost in the clouds over Germany." The plane was flown by Raymond Baxter, the former World War II Spitfire pilot and race-car driver who was then the BBC's motoring correspondent.

"I had gone out a week early to learn the course," Tommy said, "which is fourteen miles long and about a hundred and forty corners, all of them identical, and it took some learning. I would get her to drive the hire car, and I would have a blindfold on, and I would tell her what was coming up next. And that was how I would learn the course very quickly. She turned up to help me, but I should have realized then that she was a bit nervous about it all."

Confirming that Puss could never bear to watch Tommy drive, Jenny remembered sitting with her as Tommy raced at Castle Coombe in southeastern England: "Tommy was crammed into one of his mad little wooden cars, and as it passed the grandstand, he waved and Puss blew him a kiss. And his front wheel came off and rolled away, and Puss went, 'Oh my God, stop! My darling Tommy.' But he was okay. And when he reached the finishing line, he got out and did a very extravagant bow to her. But it was absolutely crazy. Puss hated it, and she was always terrified."

As he had so conclusively proved on the night before his son was born, Tommy was as dangerous on the road as on the track. "He was mad as a hatter," Jenny remembered. "He came to get me once in the south of France and drove me to the station in a Mini Cooper S, and he was going in the middle of two cars, one in the fast lane and one in the slow lane, and I've never been so terrified in all my life." Or, as Tommy would later say of himself, "In those days, one just drove like fuck, exactly."

On Boxing Day not long after Puss and Tommy were married, his half-sister Lulu went with Puss to watch Tommy drive at Brands Hatch near Swanley in Kent "with a picnic basket filled with leftovers from Christmas dinner and brandy and champagne. It was beastly cold, and she was terribly nervous about him. She finally put a stop to it because she just couldn't handle it anymore because of the children. I remember him stalling once, and he was twelve seconds behind, and he caught up and got into the front. He was totally fearless." Lulu was also at Brands Hatch on another occasion, when Tommy discovered that someone had put sugar into his gas tank before the race. "He was so angry that he wanted to kill the other drivers," she said, "but Mum said, 'You didn't see them do it, so you cannot even attempt to bash anyone up.'"

Michael Taylor, who won twenty-five races before being so badly injured in 1960 while driving a rear engine Formula One Lotus at Spa in Belgium that it effectively ended his career, later said of Tommy, "He was very fearless. Which is not very good for a driver. You can't live afraid all the time, but you've got to be sensible."

Less than two months after breaking his neck, Tommy was behind the wheel of his Marcos Ford, turning the fastest lap at Snetterton in Norfolk, where he came first in a race for grand touring cars. Despite his occasional victories, the Tommy Weber Racing Development team was never a profitable venture. Unfortunately for Puss, this made Tommy just that much more eager to get behind the wheel at every possible opportunity. After getting "all strapped up" and not telling "the medical officer about my accident," Tommy came second overall and first in the two-liter class in a race at Crystal Palace. "That was the last time Puss saw me racing," he said. "I could see it was getting her down, and so I came to an agreement with her that I would stop racing, which I did for a year. I gave it up for her."

Deprived of the adrenaline rush he could only find while driving a car at top speed for as long as it would hold together, Tommy became even more reckless in his business dealings, getting involved with property deals that were more or less outright scams. "He was selling land that didn't exist in Spain and France," Jake Weber said. "He and his mechanic, who used to tell Tommy he was going two seconds faster than he was to slow him down because he was so crazy in the car, had a scam going where the mechanic would pretend to be Tommy's chauffeur so people would think he had a lot more money than he did."

No longer working with Michael Taylor or John Green, both of whom he had alienated by doing deals behind their backs, Tommy began selling large plots of undeveloped land in Jamaica for Frank Duggan, another property man whom he had befriended. "If things were successful and Tommy was involved in them," Duggan said later, "his whole attitude would change and he would become a not very nice man and a bit of a know-it-all. He was going around London, saying, 'I did this. And I did that.' He had fuck-all to do with the original idea on the Jamaican venture. He was actually working for me and simply did what I asked him to do and earned quite a lot of money out of it."

Tommy's very expensive racing career and increasingly speculative property deals soon resulted in his owing so much money to so many people that he was, in Green's words, "beaten up quite badly" during this period. "Tommy had lots of racing-car debts that Puss paid off for him," Jenny said. "He treated her quite well, but his own affairs were in such a mess that he was always being done over by other bad boys. He got beaten up once outside their house on Cambridge Street, and Puss was desperately upset by it. I think he was involved in the underworld."

Left to her own devices by Tommy and determined to be more than a wife and a mother, Puss began pursuing an acting career. Then twenty years old, she was "discovered at a happening" by Sam Wanamaker, the well-known American actor and director who would later bring about the reconstruction of the historic Globe Theatre on London's South Bank. "She was sitting in a ball gown on a little wrought-iron staircase," Jenny recalled, "and they would send normal people through and film their reactions to this beautiful girl sitting in very strange circumstances."

In "Ambitious," an article that appeared on October 30, 1963 in the *Daily Express* accompanied by a photograph of Puss looking suitably artistic and very intense, the reporter noted that although Susan Coriat had come into a fortune on her wedding day, she was "not content to stay at home looking at her bank statements." Rather, she wanted to act professionally. As she told the reporter, "I have begun studying at a studio run by Charles Marowitz, who specializes in improvisation. I have my first part in public next Sunday in a play that has no script. It's an amateur part but good acting exercise."

Although Marowitz was a well-respected critic, playwright, and director who would later collaborate with Peter Brook at the Royal Shakespeare Company before founding the Open Space Theatre in London, Puss' first appearance for him on stage was also her last. "Tommy went to see the play," Jenny said, "and a man had to kiss Puss, and Tommy stood up and said, 'Stop fucking well doing that!' And he stormed out. So that was the end of Puss' acting career. She was very good at it, but she went running after him because he was more important to her than the play."

Denied a chance to become an actress by a husband who often sat in the lavatory at home "shouting instructions to everybody," Puss ran their house on Cambridge Street much as her mother had done at Twatley Manor. "Puss was always hopeless with money," Jenny recalled. "She asked her trustees once for a thousand pounds to buy machinery for Cambridge Street, and they gave her the money, and she spent it all on daisy plants for outside the house. So that when you got there, you almost couldn't get in the front door. There were so many daisies."

Two years after Jake was born, Puss became pregnant again. On November 25, 1965, she gave birth to her second son, Charley Beauregard Hercules Weber. The product of a difficult delivery during which he "nearly died" from a lack of oxygen, Charley was called "Mottle" as an infant because his skin was so discolored from being born as "virtually a blue baby." Puss soon put a halt to the practice so people would not think "Mottle" was his real name.

"She decided to get both of her boys christened in the garden in the middle of Belgrave Square," Jenny said. "And the priest went mad because she had called Charley by a pagan name. Hercules. And she said, 'I can be as pagan as I like over my babies,' and she stormed off. There was always a sense of drama about her. She was never boring."

Although Tommy adored his sons and Jake and Charley were still being looked after by Mo, their live-in nanny, thereby freeing Puss to spend her time as she liked, the strains of family life soon became evident to others. Whenever Puss and Tommy went to visit Priscilla, Camel, and Christopher at Forest Cottage in Chute, Andover, they would arrive in style with a modest amount of belongings, only to leave with ten times more.

"My mother said it was like the magic soup pot that would keep on making soup," Jenny said. "They would try to drive off while trying to cram all their goods in, and Tommy would be kicking the car, saying, 'Get in, you fucking kids!' They always had financial problems. Puss never had enough money to feed the kids. She'd have me come round for tea and ask if she could borrow fifty or a hundred quid off me. In those days, I had quite a lot of money and I always used to give it to her."

The family's financial situation became so dire that as Jake and Charley were playing in the kitchen one day, bailiffs arrived to repossess the long black sofa on which Puss was sitting. Refusing to budge, she made the bailiffs carry the sofa out into the road with her still on it. Continuing to appeal to her trustees whenever she needed money, Puss also began modeling for Maggie Keswick and Janet Lyle, two socialites who ran Anna Cat, a very hip boutique known as "the Biba of Brompton Road."

Although her knowledge of the subject was hardly encyclopedic, Puss also worked for a short while as a pop music critic on BBC radio, a position she seems to have been given primarily because of her good looks and upper-class bearing. In Juliet Harmer's words, "There were so few people in London then and so much less competition that you could literally walk into the BBC as a beautiful, trendy young girl and in ten minutes, someone would take you out to lunch and say, 'Do you want to present a program Thursday evening?' It was just that easy." Tommy later recalled first meeting Marianne Faithfull "through Puss while she was at the BBC. She knew nothing about rock 'n' roll, but they had given her a critical position. Puss had written something about Peter, Paul, and Mary, and Marianne was having her first broadcast of a song, and they were both sort of the same class."

A year after Charley was born, Tommy broke his promise to Puss and began racing what he would later call the "lethal Lotus BRM" at Snetterton, Goodwood, Brands Hatch, Mallory Park, Oulton Park, Crystal Palace, and Castle Coombe. By then, the financial pressure of family life as well as their own dramatic temperaments had transformed Puss and Tommy's passionate love affair into a far more traditional English upper-class marriage. "To start with," Tommy recalled, "it was very physical and very beautiful. We were extremely well matched. And she'd never had a man, so I was her first experience. We had Jake and Charley, and we were together for years until the itch came and I was behaving irresponsibly as usual, and we began growing apart."

In an attempt to revitalize what for Puss had become their un-
satisfactory sexual life together, she went with Tommy to see a
doctor, who informed him that his "foreplay was lacking." Although Tommy would later remember how happy they had been
together, most especially when "we used to go out on expeditions
where the four of us were very much a family," the good times
ended on the night that Puss and Tommy had a "very strange conversation on the street. I'd been drinking, and she was very upset
with my philandering. I didn't really understand that she knew.
But she came out with it and said, 'What would you do if I said
that I had been sleeping around?' And I'm afraid it was the only
time I hit her. I gave her a slap. Because I thought she was trying to
egg me on. It was a silly bad thing to do, and both of us had been
drinking a lot. It was the only time I ever raised my hand to her,
and it was awful."

By 1966, Puss and Tommy had come to a basic parting of the
ways. As Tommy said, "Puss had a life of her own, completely. She
had her own friends, and I used to meet them when we had dinner parties." In classic English upper-class fashion, Puss and
Tommy's marriage and the subsequent birth of their sons served
to give them both license to begin living separate lives. It was a situation that the social revolution about to sweep through England
would exacerbate in every possible way, blowing them so far apart
that they would soon have little in common but their children. "In
the end," Tommy said, "she became a dedicated super-hippie, mix-
ing with people I didn't know."

Alan Ponte, who returned with Jenny to England after living in
Brazil for two years shortly before this period began, later said of
the era, "By then, there was a change happening. One of the reasons we found it so odd was that people were wearing long hair
and jeans and caftans and the flower-power business had gotten to
London. And Puss was deeply into it."

Alan and Jenny Ponte would both later remember a party
where Puss, by then very much into peace and love, came wafting

up the garden path in a flowing caftan with a bow tied around her neck, only to be accosted by a large Great Dane that began barking loudly as it pushed up against her. In keeping with the ethos of the time, Puss did her best to calm the animal by saying, "Peace, peace." When that failed, she kicked the dog, told it to fuck off, and then cruised on up the path to the party.

8
the flying dragon

The speed at which Puss' life was now changing can be seen most dramatically in two contact sheets of black-and-white photographs that she had shot during this period for her modeling portfolio. Looking like a character out of *Blow Up*, Michelangelo Antonioni's iconic portrait of swinging London circa 1966 in the first set of prints, Puss plays directly to the camera in a pair of tight-fitting black trousers and a white sweater with embroidered sleeves. The outfit leaves her stomach bare as she raises her long, slim arms above her head.

Cut to shoulder length, her dead black hair falls perfectly over her left eye. Long before it became the style, a single, huge gold hoop dangles from her right ear. On her right wrist, she wears a watch with a thin black leather band. Between the second and third fingers of her left hand, she holds a lit cigarette. Her large, dark eyes are heavily made up. Her sensuously parted lips are coated with frosted lipstick. The intense, riveting expression on her face makes her look like a gypsy queen.

In the second set of prints, shot on a rooftop in broad daylight, her considerably longer, frizzed-out hair flies crazily in the wind. No longer looking into the camera, she wears a flowing, tentlike flowered dress into which three other people could have easily fit.

Barefoot with her arms outstretched, she looks like an exotic jungle bird about to take flight over the bare trees behind her into the cloud-strewn London sky. Utterly transformed, she now resembles one of the terrifyingly surreal female creatures from Federico Fellini's *La Dolce Vita* or *8½*.

The radical change in her appearance was due not just to the changing world of fashion in which she was trying to earn her living but to the fact that Puss by now was, in the words of Jimi Hendrix, "experienced." As Tommy later explained, "She was one of the first people into that whole LSD liberation thing. It was very early on, and not many people knew very much about it."

The introduction of LSD into the hip London scene in 1965 caused an authentic revolution in both style and sensibility. Unlike the working-class mods, rockers, and teddy boys, all of whom had been fueled by speed, the English upper class, as the noted antique dealer Christopher Gibbs would later say of his own experiences with the substance, "took to acid like a duck to water."

Like so many others in his rarefied social circle, Gibbs was first given LSD by Michael Hollingshead. An English trickster and con man of the first order, Hollingshead had turned on Timothy Leary, then a lecturer in psychology at Harvard University in December 1961. In September 1965, Leary sent Hollingshead to London with enough lysergic acid for five thousand trips, thirteen cartons of his *Psychedelic Review*, and a set of written instructions outlining a plan to rent the Royal Albert Hall for a "psychedelic jamboree" featuring the Beatles and the Rolling Stones. The "climax of the evening" would be the introduction of Leary himself as "the high priest" of a new religion he believed would change the world.

Operating out of the World Psychedelic Centre in his flat in Belgravia, Hollingshead began turning on many of the most influential members of the swinging London scene, Paul McCartney, Victoria Ormsby-Gore, and Christopher Gibbs among them. Hollingshead himself soon became addicted to methedrine. Smoking pot and hash constantly while also taking LSD three times a week, he was busted for possession of cannabis on Pont Street, where Tommy had lived after first coming to London. At a trial he attended while high on acid, Hollingshead was sentenced to twenty-one months in Wormwood Scrubs, effectively removing him from the scene.

Although Leary's master plan was never carried out, the door to Pandora's box had been opened. Perhaps because only they had the time and wherewithal to indulge in trips that lasted for hours and then took days to come back down from, LSD soon became the drug of choice for the hip young members of the upper class in London. As a group, they were usually referred to as "toffs," a British slang that referred to the "tuft," or gold ornamental tassel worn on the caps of Oxford and Cambridge undergraduates whose fathers sat in the House of Lords.

Right from the start in London, the LSD scene was always about music and fashion. "The center of it was Robert Fraser," said filmmaker Nik Douglas, who shared a flat with the art dealer for a year. "Christopher Gibbs and Robert were sort of hand-in-hand. Christopher had his coterie of fey friends in the art scene, and I think the common factor was that they had all been expelled from Eton or Harrow." Fraser, who was Paul McCartney's art dealer and confidant, soon turned Rolling Stones founder Brian Jones, his girlfriend Anita Pallenberg, and their good friend Keith Richards on to acid for the first time during the summer of 1966 in Brian and Anita's flat on Courtfield Road behind the Gloucester Park tube station.

In America, the counterculture then springing to life defined itself by its strident opposition to racial discrimination, the war in Vietnam, and decades of prosperity and overconsumption. In the words of Nigel Waymouth, the noted poster artist and cofounder of Granny Takes a Trip, then the hippest clothing store in London,

the acid revolution in England was "a reaction to the era of austerity and war. In the fifties in England, we didn't understand the
lyrics of the Beach Boys. We identified more with Mississippi
blues and terrible pain and squalor. Muddy Waters spoke to us."

As Michael Rainey, who then owned Hung On You, an equally
iconic London boutique near Granny Takes a Trip on the King's
Road, would later say, "We came out of a Victorian England that
in 1959 and 1960 was still bombed out. It was dirty. It was grubby.
The most far-out thing a man could buy in a shop was a pink shirt
to wear with a boring gray suit, and that was it. In England until
about 1961, when the first Beatles' record made everyone interested in music, in every single house of every sort of economic
and social level, parents would be saying to their children, 'Sit
down, take your elbows off the table, do your homework, take off
those disgusting American trousers, get your hair cut, stop listening to that disgusting American music.' Jeans were just coming in,
and everything was changing, and they couldn't stop it. They
tried, but of course, they couldn't."

Many of the early converts to the acid revolution in England
chose to express the newfound freedom they had first experienced
while tripping on acid through art, music, and fashion. "A lot of it
was aesthetics," Waymouth recalled. "Look at the photographs of
the kids in the Haight Ashbury, and then look at the photographs
of the kids on the King's Road. In England, it was very much more
of a party. America had bigger issues. Civil rights and the draft.
Yes, we demonstrated against the war, but we weren't being called
up to serve in Vietnam."

With Tommy "away a lot" pursuing the last vestiges of his racing
career as well as any other venture from which he might earn a dollar, Puss soon began hanging out with the artsy, Bohemian, aristo-
cratic King's Road set. Although it is impossible to say precisely
when Puss took acid for the first time, she did not do so with
Tommy. At a time when the gulf between those who had tripped

and those who had not yet done so was impossible to cross, Puss' acid experiences served only to further widen the yawning chasm between them while also freeing her to experiment sexually in ways she had never done before.

As Juliet Harmer, who by then was living in London while working as an actress in television shows like *The Avengers* and *Danger Man*, said, "Both Puss and Tommy were highly sexually charged, hugely beautiful people. I remember Tommy falling in love with some other girl who had moved in, just a girlfriend or a babysitter, and Sue came back and found her in bed with Tommy, and that was a real shock for Sue. But he said, 'You jump in, please.' And she did. That was what she said to me."

Tommy told a somewhat different version of the story: "She was the one who started it. She was the one was pulling [British slang for picking up women]. She said, 'Would you be upset if I told you I was sleeping with another girl?' And I said, 'No, not particularly.' 'Well, would you like to join us?' I said, 'Yeah. Sounds great.' So we did that with a few people. It was quite fun at the time, of course, but it was cliff hanging. It was no good. We were hanging on. By then, the essential relationship was gone because I had disappointed her in a number of ways. She thought I was the white knight she had been brought up to believe was her inheritance and her due. And I turned out not to be such a good guy after all."

Although upper-class women in England had been engaging in clandestine lesbian love affairs since long before Queen Victoria had declared that sex between women was physically impossible, Puss' willingness to experiment with other women was an honest expression of her own desires rather than a need to keep up with the flavor of the times. The fact that she was now regularly getting high on a variety of substances may have also been a factor in her decision.

As Juliet Harmer, who continued to be extremely close with Puss without ever sensing any sexual tension between them, would later say, "By the time Jake got to be about three or four, the atmosphere had become quite different at Cambridge Street. There were loads of people around, obviously all smoking dope, but more than that. There were other funny things going on. I was pretty scared of all that, so I really don't know what happened."

Perhaps because she did not feel completely comfortable with her newfound sexual freedom, Puss went to Tommy during this period. "She asked me," he recalled, "'What do you feel about me and my lesbianism?' And I said, 'If you want to do that, by all means, it's your business and I don't consider it the same as if you were going with a man. That would be entirely different.' She was a bit surprised by that, and relieved." In terms of Tommy's upbringing as well as the world in which he and Puss were then living, this was also the only proper response to such a question that a gentleman could make.

Now that he had finally abandoned his dream of driving a Formula One Grand Prix car, Tommy began an equally perilous career as a film producer. Vic Singh, a fashion photographer who lived on the King's Road, had by then already shot what was called "a music film" to accompany the song "I'm a Man" by the Spencer Davis Group, featuring a very young Steve Winwood on lead vocal. Edited by Keith Green, who lived nearby and worked at the BBC, the short film was shown with great success on the popular television program *Top of the Pops*.

Singh, who had photographed Pattie Boyd during her early modeling days and then become friendly with her and George Harrison, received a call from "out of the blue" from the Beatles' office, asking him to come film the group just three days before they were to complete recording "A Day in the Life," the final track on *Sgt. Pepper's Lonely Hearts Club Band*. When he met with Paul McCartney at his home in St. John's Wood the next day, Singh proposed putting 16-milimeter cameras all over the studio so the Beatles and all their invited guests could simply pick one up and shoot one another at will. As this was then "quite a far-out idea," McCartney gave Singh the go-ahead to film the session.

With no time to sign contracts, Singh and Keith Green showed up on the night of February 10, 1967, at Abbey Road's cavernous Studio One, which, as Beatle biographer Bob Spitz would later write, was large enough to "accommodate up to a thousand musicians where EMI's legendary symphonies had been recorded," only to be greeted by a carnival in progress. The Beatles, all of whom had already taken LSD and were deeply involved in the burgeoning London psychedelic scene, had invited a crew of their famous friends to join them.

The guests that night included Mick Jagger, Marianne Faithfull, Brian Jones, Donovan, Michael Nesmith, Pattie Boyd, Graham Nash, and Dutch fashion designers Seemon & Marijke. Stoned on grass, hash, and every other drug available in London during the winter of 1967, they were all dressed in flowing robes and waistcoats with long silk scarves and flared pants while the Beatles themselves were "tricked out in a wildly flamboyant, neon-rainbow wardrobe."

Seated on folding chairs in suits and ties, the violinists in the all-male London Symphony Orchestra, none of whom had ever before performed under such circumstances, were given red clown noses to wear while their section leader was fitted with a gorilla paw for his bow hand. Balloons were attached to the stringed instruments. Musicians in the brass and woodwind sections were made to don plastic spectacles, fake noses, and funny hats. As John Lennon handed out plastic stick-on nipples and fake cigars, people ran around the studio with blazing sparklers in their hands while blowing bubbles from little clay pipes. After doing five takes involving more than two hundred instruments, George Martin, who was at the board that night, called the session an "orchestral orgasm."

At the time, Tommy's familiarity with the London music scene was extremely limited: "I didn't know who the Beatles were. I didn't know which one was which. My very first job was *Sgt. Pepper*. Incredible story in itself, that. For the ending of the last song, 'A Day in the Life,' they filled the studio with the London Symphony Orchestra, who all had funny noses on, and there was a big party thrown and we made a very good film of it."

Although Tommy had never before done anything that even vaguely resembled this line of work, he would later say, "I was never one to be put off by something new. I just assumed I knew what to do and did it. I got about four times as many crew and cameras as anybody else would have done, as much film stock as possible, and just kept the cameras rolling so as not to get in the way of the performance, and preferably not be seen. It was really a cutting-edge exercise because we had lots of cameras lying around so anybody could use them, and then we cut the resulting footage together."

According to Singh, Tommy was not actually in the studio on the night when the footage, most of which was "out of focus or very shaky and could not be used," was shot. Nonetheless, Singh then spoke to George Harrison about making a film of the entire *Sgt. Pepper* album. Promised a fee of ten thousand pounds, Singh and Keith Green spent weeks working on a script with a writer supplied by the Beatles' office.

Unfortunately, the Beatles then decided to make their own film. Inspired by the trip that Ken Kesey and his band of Merry Pranksters had taken across America and fueled by their own supply of pure Owsley acid, John, Paul, George, and Ringo promptly set off in a gaily painted psychedelic bus with cameras whirring all around them. Screened for the first time on December 16, 1967, *Magical Mystery Tour* was eventually sold to the BBC for nine thousand pounds and was shown twice on television, to scathing reviews. The fifty-minute film ended up costing the group about forty thousand pounds (eighty-eight thousand dollars), which made it, as John Lennon told writer Ray Coleman, "the most expensive home movie ever."

"The next thing we heard," Singh would recall, "was that the Beatles had brought out *Magical Mystery Tour* and we were out of the running. I kept ringing them for the check, but it never arrived. Keith and I were desperate, and it was at this point we met Tommy. He kept popping up everywhere we went and promising us he would get the money from the Beatles and get us involved in other film projects, and he called us 'his boys.'"

Deeply in debt because of all the time they had put into the project, Singh and Green agreed to let Tommy handle their affairs. "Tommy came in and wanted to sue the Beatles through my company Peacock Productions," Singh said. "Keith and I voted against it but later on Keith decided to go with Tommy and Tommy's solicitor started the proceedings." Years after he had lost all contact with Tommy, Singh eventually received eight hundred pounds for his troubles from the Beatles' office.

Tommy's version of his time with the Beatles bears little resemblance to Singh's recollection of the events. As Tommy remembered it, the Beatles considered the footage shot while they were recording "A Day in the Life" their property and were only willing to pay for the cost of the shoot. Somewhat miffed, Singh and Green sent Tommy to the group's office to collect the money they were owed.

After Tommy accepted a check for the sum in question, the man in charge asked Tommy what he really wanted to do with the footage. "And I said, 'I'd like to make the whole film of *Sgt. Pepper*, of course. Complete it.' And he said, 'We don't see any reason to stop you. We'll sign a contract for you to make the film with the Beatles, and it will be the sound track.' I walked out of the office with ten thousand pounds for start-up financing."

According to Tommy, he then learned that "the Beatles were making their own film, *Magical Mystery Tour*, and they had run out of money and so they asked their people where it had gone. And they said, 'Oh, we gave it all to Tommy Weber to make the *Sgt. Pepper* film.' I was in full production by then, and John

Lennon and Paul McCartney both came on the phone and said, 'Give us our money back. Because we're broke.' I said, 'Why do you need it? You've got lots of money, and we were contracted to make this film.' And they said, 'Well, we don't want to make it anymore. You can make it, but we want to call it quits. And we want you to give us our money back.' Which I did. I gave it all back to them. Which, of course, left us without any funds for the project."

Although Tommy would later claim that Lennon told him "he would help in any way he could and might be in our film, the script had already been written and all the locations had been booked with crews, and the whole paraphernalia of filmmaking was in full swing. I suppose I must be one of the few people who ever gave the Beatles back some money. And that was the end of my very big chance in the movies." (The credibility of Tommy's story would seem to be belied by the fact that John Lennon himself was then still fairly oblivious to the state of the Beatles' finances and had enthusiastically endorsed the group's investment of £100,000 in the newly opened and ultimately unsuccessful Apple boutique.)

When the group announced plans to make yet another movie, the *Daily Sun* reported on November 21, 1967, that an application was to be filed in High Court for "an injunction against all four in connection with a cartoon film. Also named are NEMS Enterprises, Ltd. and Northern Songs, Ltd. The action by Mr. Thomas Weber of Peacock Productions, Ltd. has been started over *Yellow Submarine*."

"We went to court to get an injunction," Tommy recalled, "and the judge said, 'Your paperwork is absolutely correct, and if you go before a proper hearing, you'll win.' By that time, I was not interested in suing people, and I left it. I wish I had done so. Because it would have been priceless. I had the film rights to *Sgt. Pepper*. The synchronization rights and the world rights alone—it would have been a fabulous amount of money. It was the most successful album ever. But I rather goofed it. It was a bit of bad luck, and maybe I was a bit too honest. But it was their money. They needed it, and so I gave it back to them."

Although he had failed to produce a film about the Beatles, Tommy continued pursuing his new career. After Singh turned down the job, Tommy hired the photographer and future video artist David Larcher to shoot the all-star bill at the "Christmas On Earth Continued" concert on Friday, December 22, 1967, at the Kensington Olympia, a cavernous, hangarlike exhibition hall on Hammersmith Road that was used for horse shows and the circus. The show, which went on all night long and took its name from a twenty-nine minute film of an orgy shot in New York in 1963 by avant-garde film maker Barbara Rubin, featured the Jimi Hendrix Experience, the Who (who did not perform), Eric Burdon and the New Animals, the Move, Pink Floyd, Soft Machine, and the Graham Bond Organization. Although the event was sparsely attended, many of those who were there were high on acid.

Clad in full "Foxy Lady" gear in a brocaded orange-red sleeveless fur-trimmed Afghani vest over an iridescent purple shirt with huge flared sleeves and a sparkling silver medallion around his neck, an impossibly young Jimi Hendrix stepped onstage that night above a banner reading: "The Sound of Success—Marshall." With his bushy black hair jutting out from beneath a black wide-brimmed hat decorated with an orange-red plume and actual bird feathers, Hendrix dropped his cigarette but continued chewing gum as he told the audience, "Plug your ears. Watch out for your ears. Watch out for your ears, okay?" Without further ado, he then launched into a killer version of the title track from *Sgt. Pepper.*

That night, Larcher also shot Traffic, a last-minute substitute for the Who, featuring Steve Winwood playing lead guitar on "Dear Mr. Fantasy" with Dave Mason behind him sporting a walrus moustache that made him look much like John Lennon, circa "I Am the Walrus." Also appearing were Eric Burdon and the New Animals doing an endless version of Donovan's "Hey Gyp."

Despite the access Tommy had to bands at a time when few others were interested in filming them, he soon grew disenchanted with the business. "I had the first real video studio in London, but there was no use in making these films, because when they got into the theatres, the projectionists would turn the sound right down. I said, 'Forget it. I'm sick of it. I don't want anything more to do with films or rock 'n' roll, because the market is not up to it yet. We'll unload them all in twenty-five years' time.'"

Unfortunately, Tommy stored all the footage he had shot "in a house that belonged to a friend of mine. But his public company went bust, and the Grosvenor Estate moved in and took everything out of the house. All my archives were in the basement, and they've been lost to this day. Of course, now they would be worth millions. For a start, fifteen hours of Jimi Hendrix on his own. The Beatles, the Stones, Pink Floyd, Graham Bond, Traffic, the Animals. A huge portfolio."

After his film career ended as suddenly as it had begun, Tommy turned his hand to a new endeavor. Inspired in part by all the dope he had seen being smoked at the shows he had filmed, Tommy set off on his first overland journey to Afghanistan. Despite his long, blond hair and outrageous clothing, he returned to England with enough hashish to have made his trip worthwhile. In time, the long, perilous journey from London to Afghanistan and back again across multiple borders would become the prime source of his income.

Although Tommy no longer had any business dealings with the Beatles, he came home one night to Cambridge Street to find Puss entertaining George Harrison. "I gave him a couple of records I'd picked up in Afghanistan," Tommy said, "and he used one of them for the sound track of *Wonderwall*. I remember asking for a royalty. But I never got one." On another night at Cambridge Street when Harrison was visiting, Charley Weber's excited young nanny sent him into the room where his mother and George were smoking dope, so she could meet the very famous Beatle. "Their values were very much the same," Charley said of Harrison and his mother. "Both of them were introverted and quite spiritual. Tom and Puss were opposites. He was all about outside, and she was very deep. Which is not to say Tommy did not have depth. Mostly, I think he behaved like a child at heart. Which is good and bad."

By October 1967, Tommy and Puss had grown so far apart that she began planning a business venture of her own at 463 King's Road, just beyond the historic World's End Pub, which had once been "the last-stop watering hole on a medieval cart track leading west" from the village of Chelsea. During the seventeenth century, the cart track became the King's Road when King Charles II reserved it as his private route to Hampton Court Palace.

"Historically," Nigel Waymouth said, "that part of Chelsea had always had a great deal of notoriety attached to it. In medieval times and in the eighteenth century, it was sort of a den of thieves and had a louche reputation. It was the dead end of the King's Road, and we revived it by doing something that dragged people down there. Saturday was the big day. That was the parade on the King's Road. Every hairdresser in the world was there. Our first customers at Granny Takes a Trip were local debutantes and gays. Then John and Paul and Mick and Keith and Anita Pallenberg came in, and we started selling to the Saturday crowd. And the word spread."

At the epicenter of London's hip world, where everyone came to see and be seen on Saturdays, Puss first thought of opening a macrobiotic restaurant. Realizing that the kitchen on the premises was too small, she soon, in the words of designer Mike McInnerney, who worked with her on the project from its inception, "shifted her plans towards a teahouse serving light healthy meals."

Puss, who had already begun making LSD-influenced connections between events that others did not see as necessarily being related, was by then heavily involved with the *I Ching*. From the first hexagram, *Chi'en* or "The Creative," she chose "The Flying Dragon" as the name for her teahouse. When a nine occurs in the fifth line of the hexagram, the judgment reads, "Flying dragon in the heavens. It furthers one to see the great man." As Confucius said of this line, "Things that accord in tone vibrate together. Things that have affinity in their inmost natures seek one another. Water flows to what is wet, fire turns to what is dry. Clouds (the breath of heaven) follow the dragon, wind (the breath of earth) follows the tiger. Thus the sage rises, and all creatures follow him with their eyes. What is born of heaven feels related to what is above. What is born of earth feels related to what is below. Each follows its kind."

Mike McInnerney, who spent four very cold winter months perched on a scaffold painting the astonishing mural that covered the front of the tea shop, recalled, "As I got to know Puss, it came as no surprise that an ancient Chinese symbol system designed to identify order in what seemed like chance events would appeal to her. She was both physically and temperamentally beautiful and I saw her as a wonderfully gentle, kind, and very loving mother with a mystic's yearning for a kind of life that could be lived as poetry. But at times she also seemed sad and melancholic. I think her marriage to Tommy was not going well. I could tell she was lonely and missing Tommy and trying to understand why she was on her own with the children. Perhaps The Flying Dragon was a project that took her mind off her domestic problems."

The mural that McInnerney created for Puss was a twenty-by-thirty-foot representation of "the heavenly dragon descended to earth, the symbol of God's compassion. A tear in its eye waters the earthly dragon in the form of a plant (the street door entrance), the symbol of God's presence on earth. The dragon's fiery breath parts the water on the beach to reveal the glass window and the interior." Composed of several layers of hand-sanded primer with flamboyant coach paint mixed into it to produce a "radiant" color, the snaking body of the heavenly dragon was prepared with silver leaf by F. G. Fowle, a well-known fairground artist, before being painted. As McInnerney noted, "This was done to create a surface that would reflect the setting sun down the King's Road."

The interior of the Flying Dragon was no less extraordinary, with a rising white horse on one wall and a descending white horse on the other. After Puss had somehow obtained two huge Anchor Butter posters from the company's advertising agency, the image of the butter was cut from each one and the green grass that remained was pasted on the walls as a backdrop for the horses. "A moving cloud effect was created by two cloud machines placed in opposite corners of the room. Artificial grass was placed on the floor as a carpet with tables and cushions."

In Juliet Harmer's words, "Cambridge Street was getting out of control, and she wanted to find a quiet place, and she managed to get some money from her accountants to start this café up. I lent her a couple hundred quid as well. When I wrote the check, she said, 'Make it out to the Flying Dragon of the Heavens.' And I said, 'You must be joking. You can't do that. My bank manager will have a fit.' She said, 'We know what we're doing. It's going to be cool. Do you know where I can get hold of an Anchor Butter advertisement? We'll cut out the pat of butter, and we'll all lie on the floor in the grass and look up at the sky.' I said, 'You're completely mad. Why don't you come live in Gloucestershire with me? There's real sky and real grass there and you can lie in a real field.'"

During the period that the teahouse was undergoing recon-struction, Puss, who had already embarked on a vague spiritual search of her own, joined Mike McInnerney and his wife, Kati, at meetings held by "a growing group of people" who had become "Meher Baba lovers." An Indian spiritual master whose name meant "Compassionate Father," Meher Baba, also known as "the

Avatar," had in 1925 taken a vow of silence that he maintained until his death in 1969.

After Mike McInnerney repeatedly told his good friend Pete Townshend that many of his "own solutions to the great questions, including theories of reincarnations and UFO's" were contained in Meher Baba's writings, the leader of the Who "sought out Baba's book *The God Man*, and began a life guided by the teachings of its author." In part because of Townshend's interest in him, the iconic poster of Meher Baba's smiling, mustached face above the words "Don't worry, be happy" soon became a staple in hippie crash pads all over the world.

Occasional meetings of Meher Baba devotees were also held at the Flying Dragon. Mike McInnerney remembered: "For a while, Puss was interested in the idea of Meher Baba as a living master who could create a more complete sense of self by gluing together the patchwork of beliefs, rituals, and spiritual desires that she felt. But unlike her partner Barbara Allen, who became a lifelong devotee, Puss' interest in him did not last."

When the Flying Dragon opened for business in February 1968, it became a scene of major proportions, rivaling the nearby Baghdad House, where the crème de la crème of hip London society, Mick Jagger and Donovan among them, congregated in the basement. In Nigel Waymouth's words, everyone there "smoked joints and dropped Mandrax and acid while eating our kebabs. That was the first public place where people openly smoked joints in London. We did smoke joints at the Dragon, but we were a little more cautious because all those shops, my own included, would regularly get raided. The Dragon was a little phenomenon, and it was lovely. It was a sweet place, and Puss was there."

Christopher Gibbs, who lived around the corner from the Flying Dragon on Cheyne Walk, where both Jagger and Keith Richards owned houses, was another regular. "It was my local, as it were," Gibbs said. "I'd go and have breakfast there and see things projected on the ceiling while lying on cushions as all these very sweet, charming, beautiful people, Sue among them in some sort of Palestinian smock, went drifting by me."

For those who had not yet gotten high, walking into the Flying Dragon could be a major dose of culture shock. "I went to the Dragon one day to have lunch with Puss," Juliet Harmer said. "At that point, I hadn't had anything. I asked for Puss, and someone out of their mind said, 'Who?' I said, 'Is she here?' 'Who are you wanting to talk to?' The person was completely out of it. They all sat on cushions and smoked big spliffs, and I was a bit frightened of it all."

Sadly, the person whom Puss most wanted in her life rarely came to the Flying Dragon. "I only went in there twice," Tommy said, "because it was not part of my domain. She wanted to keep me out of it, although I'd had some experience in conversions and building and decorating. I think I helped her with the ceiling, that's all. It was a caravanserai tearoom, but nothing like you would have seen in Afghanistan, which were all dusty with broken teapots. This was just absolutely lovely. And very relaxed."

On March 12, 1968, just a month after she had opened the hippest tea shop in London, Puss spoke to a reporter from the *Daily Express* as she stirred a pot of potato soup at the Flying Dragon. "It's so peaceful here," she said. "There's only room for 15 people. We don't want more. We do soup but it is not a restaurant. Soon we will be having films and story-telling and books." And then, as the reporter duly noted, "she gave the potato soup another stir."

Completely clueless when it came to managing money, Puss did manage to make the Flying Dragon what Mike McInnerney would later call "a regular hangout for a particular hippie crowd. People would hang round and not buy much and I'm not sure that the teahouse made much money." The fact that Puss and her partner Barbara Allen were also "purchasing provisions for the teahouse from Harrods must have made a big dent in any potential profit they could have made from the place."

In December 1968, eleven months after it had opened, the Flying Dragon went out of business. By then, Puss had embarked on a full-time search for meaning in her life. Her quest soon became so extreme that virtually no one she knew in London could keep up with her, much less understand what it was she was really trying to find.

9
glastonbury and hugh street

Puss began a pilgrimage that would eventually take her halfway around the world in search of a new direction for her life by driving from her parents' cottage in Andover to Glastonbury, a small town in Somerset about 125 miles west of London. Leaving her car behind, she walked up the impossibly green hill known as the Glastonbury Tor to the roofless fourteenth-century stone tower that was the last vestige of the church of St. Michael, which had once stood there.

Beneath the ruined structure, a hollow tube of air and light and sound that seemed somehow mystically connected to both the heavens above and the center of the earth, King Arthur and Queen Guinevere were said to have been interred in the mythical Isle of Avalon. The site was also where Joseph of Arimathea was said to have come to bury the chalice containing the blood of Christ, the vessel known as the Holy Grail for which the Knights of the Round Table had searched in vain. In ancient times, Glastonbury had been part of a "triangle with the enormous stone circles of Stonehenge and Avebury—between them they formed a world energy-point." From the tor, ley lines, "hypothetical alignments of a number of places of geographical interest, such as ancient monuments and megaliths," ran across a ten-mile-wide circle in which the twelve "zodiac signs appear in their right order, formed by hills, outlined by roads and rivers."

A place of power where pilgrims had come for centuries to search for wisdom, inspiration, and mystery, Glastonbury was first brought to the attention of the hip London underground by John Michell, an English author and philosopher educated at Eton and Trinity College, Cambridge, in his 1967 book, *The Flying Saucer Vision*. As Michell later described the book, "It followed the idea, first put forth by C. G. Jung in his 1959 book on flying saucers, that the strange lights and other phenomenon of the post-war period were portents of a radical change in human consciousness coinciding with the dawn of the Aquarian Age. A theme in my book was the connection between 'unidentified flying objects' and ancient sites, as evidenced both in folklore and the contemporary experience."

Michell himself soon began escorting hip luminaries like Marianne Faithfull, Brian Jones, Anita Pallenberg, Keith Richards, and Gram Parsons on overnight excursions to the tor. Under the influence of LSD, those who accompanied him soon became convinced his theories were true. "The King's Road led straight to Glastonbury in those days," Barry Miles, who then owned the very fashionable Indica Gallery in London, recalled. "The people we knew led double lives, experimenting with acid, spending entire evenings discussing flying saucers, ley lines and the court of King Arthur. Other people waited patiently at Arthur's Tor for saucers to land."

Like so many others at the epicenter of the scene, Nigel Waymouth went to Glastonbury with John Michell, Brian Jones, and Jane and Michael Rainey to take acid and sit in the tor. As Rainey said, "John Michell was the first person who took us down to Glastonbury, and that was where my whole quest for the Holy Grail started. I got this vision of the Arthurian legend, and I thought, 'Wow, this is for real,' and I embarked on this Arthurian search and started chasing it around the country."

Sir Mark Palmer, who had run the English Boy modeling agency on the King's Road before dropping out to travel with his friends around England in horse-drawn carts, "often camped near the Tor," said Michell. "And while I was with them, we used to watch the nightly maneuvering of lights in the sky. Jung's prophecy of aerial portents being followed by a change in consciousness was evidently being fulfilled."

After a particularly rough marital patch with Tommy, Puss made her own journey to the Glastonbury Tor. In a long, rambling letter on her mother's stationery addressed to "My Darling Tommy," Puss wrote, "I have had a wonderful day, thank you, I love you so dearly. I am not very good at using words yet, where I was there weren't any and it was so easy without them."

Launching into an account of her day with very little punctuation, Puss noted that before leaving for "Chalice Hill," she had been given a

prayer to take with me, as you will see it is a very nice prayer and I said it and said it and lay up on the hill and the sun came out and I said it some more and I knew God was there and somebody asked what evidence have you that God exists and I looked up on the tor and there were two kites flying like griffins kissing in the air all blown towards each other and the cows were sleeping at the top of the hill around the church and a child running and jumping all the way down the hill and behind him a woman with a child carried in her arms and I said this is the evidence that I have and it may not be sufficient to prove but I have it as a most beautiful evidence and I lay in the sun & cried for joy because the evidence was so beautiful.

After losing track of how much time she had spent lying on the hill saying the prayer over and over again while thinking of Tommy, Jake, and Charley and loving them "most wonderfully because of the kites and the evidence," Puss suddenly realized the four of them had *all the time in the world in this one and all the other worlds together and I so look forward to the other ones because then we won't have bodies and the thing I seem to mind about being down here is that there are bodies other than mine for you to enjoy but it simply doesn't matter really because we won't have them anymore so mine will be as nice as anyone's and you will like me just as much.*

    Then I climbed down into the orchard which is just above Chalice Well garden and the first tree I reached I picked an apple & I sat down and took a big bite, quite unthinking & then I heard the tree say that was my only apple, and I had a look & indeed it was and I said I'm very sorry but it is a very nice apple, thank you. Then it said well I don't mind you having it but most people don't notice so you might just sit here under my branches while you eat it so I did and it was such a good apple. The tree said that one over there has got lots & I said yes I see that but your one tastes very beautiful to me and the tree was quite pleased and it said it's not really ripe yet you should have come in September and I said yes I know but I like it sour & the tree was quite happy & we were in agreement about its apple. When I finished I buried the core right close to its roots and said thank you and I said a prayer for it to have lots next year, I said I am not very good at this praying I only started today but it has worked well so far so I hope you get lots of apples next year and we parted very friendly.

In great detail, Puss then described the "very nice talk" she'd had "with a pig who was in the next field who had a very broad Somerset accent and so was difficult to understand" but nonetheless explained to her that the thing about pigs being dirty was all right so long as they had "a decent field to lie around in" but the things that humans shut them up in "got mucky & I did see that." Puss then saw "A RAINBOW," which caused her to laugh and laugh because it was so beautiful, especially after all the other wonderful things she had seen that day.

    Although she had been hoping to cross Salisbury Plain in the dark, it was still light when Puss reached it, but she thought, "well

I don't mind because it has been so lovely and just as I crossed the plain I looked up and there was a most incredible cloud painting over the plain, it was all there was in the whole sky, a huge cloud painting of a most beautiful flying saucer all lit with a rosy aura above the plain and I knew that God was showing off for me that day."

After asking for directions from a man who so delighted her that she "made him tell me again and he grew about 2 foot it seems to give people a tremendous sense of importance to be able to tell you the way and I was very pleased with his directions and we had a joke about there being no good turnings until Salisbury Plain," she began wishing for some honey, her favorite snack, which she usually ate while driving, thereby making the front seat of her car always sticky. Right around the very next corner, there was a place selling honey, and even though it had already closed for the day, they sold her some and also gave her a teaspoon with which to eat it "and I thanked God for the honey and said that is enough for one day it is enough for anyone what with the evidence & the apple tree the pig & the honey, it is quite enough."

Before she concluded her ten-page letter with the word "Peace," a drawing of what look to be mountains, and the letters "xxx," Puss wrote:

So thank you for the lovely day, and when I am cross remind me about the evidence, I know now that the only things that have me up are physical. Like not having enough safety pins for my clothes or my hair being horrid, these are the things that annoy me and one day they won't exist anymore and you & I and the boys will have eternity and all the stars to play around and we will be astonishingly happy for many dragon flying days of love.

Although Puss had always possessed a rich and fertile imagination and was almost certainly on acid at Glastonbury, her letter is not so much a whimsical account of a day filled with magical adventures as a chilling glimpse into a mind no longer able to order events in a rational manner. In the world of phenomena Puss was now experiencing, everything was of equal importance. And so she recounted her mystical encounters in the same tone as she expressed her childlike hope that there would be "chicken for supper but it turned out to be Knorr packet soup & frozen peas & I was cross."

While Puss was still able during this period to function in a perfectly normal manner, indicating that the state of mind she had depicted in her letter was not yet permanent, some of those who knew her had already concluded that she was not in touch with basic reality. "She wasn't a very stable girl," said Michael Rainey. "Both my wife Jane and I felt she wasn't on a beam. The beam was floating. A lot of people took a lot of acid and went hippie tripping but found something they were looking for on their trips that grounded them. Whereas with Puss, I felt there was no anchor and no grip. The best way of putting it was that she was sort of adrift." Christopher Gibbs would later tell Jake Weber, "The beauty of your mother was very compelling. I think of fineness with a touch of wildness, a big pinch of sweetness, and definitely a pinch of derangement in the soup, so to speak."

While Puss was driving back to London after having seen a fiery sign in the sky over the Salisbury Plain, Tommy was in the Speakeasy, then the hippest after-hours club in London. At the "Speak," where you could "speak easy, drink easy, and pull easy," only beautiful women and those with membership cards were permitted through the front door at 48 Margaret Street in the West End. That night, as Tommy said later, "There was this gorgeous little American girl dancing in the Speakeasy like a nutter. Most beautiful little thing, and I took her home because that was what one did in those days."

Tommy and the girl were together in the living room at Cambridge Street when "Puss walked in on me. She had come back from Glastonbury, where she'd had a very spiritual experience. She had seen a sign in the clouds, and she considered this as evidence, and she drove all the way back to tell me the good news and unfortunately discovered me in flagrante. She burst in on us and ordered the girl out of the house, and so I then drove her up to Hampstead. It was ghastly. Absolutely ghastly."

The American girl Tommy took home to Cambridge Street that night was Sally Field, a very successful twenty-two-year-old actress who had already starred in two hit television series in America and who would later win both an Oscar and an Emmy. "I would have done anything to not have done that," Tommy said later, "but it happened anyway. It was just my vanity. I just couldn't keep my hands off pretty girls."

Puss, who had come back to London to tell Tommy how much she really loved him and their sons, instead walked into her own home only to have all her worst fears about him confirmed. In light of all she had experienced during her magical day in Glastonbury, what for Tommy was a simple act of physical infidelity hit Puss like a thunderbolt from the gods.

"It was too much for Puss," he said, "and she was too badly hurt. And that was when she decided it was all over. And then I moved out. That was the end." When she talked to a *Daily Express* reporter in the Flying Dragon, Puss said of her teahouse, "It's my main interest now because my husband and I have parted. It's all quite amicable. It just didn't work out."

After he left Cambridge Street, Tommy promptly fell in love with a woman who was both physically and temperamentally far more like him than Puss. As he was driving past a doctor's office in Chelsea one day, Tommy saw an inordinately beautiful young woman "standing on the steps in tears. I knew her, of course. I'd met her at a friend's flat and seen her dancing at nightclubs and I'd always had an eye for her, thinking she was definitely the one for me."

Long, lean, and leggy, with a vulpine face, hawklike eyes, and razor-sharp cheekbones that gave her the on-screen presence of a young Lauren Bacall, Charlotte Rampling, then twenty-two years old, was just beginning her acting career. Discovered on the street in London at the age of seventeen, she had been cast in a popular British television commercial for Cadbury's chocolate and then appeared in a brief, uncredited role as a water skier in Richard Lester's 1965 film, *The Knack . . . and How to Get It.*

A year later, Rampling portrayed the best friend and flat-mate of the title character in *Georgy Girl*, playing what she later described as "a very outrageous, rebellious character. It seemed to correspond with who I was at that time, so it was very good typecasting." She had also appeared in an episode of the iconic British television series *The Avengers*.

Although her acting credits were hardly overwhelming and she never employed a press agent, Rampling, known as "Charley" to her friends, appeared with astonishing regularity in the English newspapers for a variety of reasons. Among them was her propensity for driving her Mini Cooper S so fast that she was arrested and taken to court after her second speeding offense in two months, thereby making her someone to whom Tommy could relate on many levels.

When the chairman of magistrates asked Rampling during the hearing who determined whether or not a car went fast, she replied, "The law," only to be told, "No! It's the motorist!" The newspaper account of her court appearance was accompanied by a photograph of Rampling sitting with tousled blonde hair in the front seat of her Mini in a short skirt, high boots, and huge sunglasses while cradling her black-and-white spaniel in her arms. Her extreme good looks, decidedly unconventional lifestyle, and willingness to discuss with reporters whatever was going on in her life at the moment soon made her the girl of the moment in London.

The youngest daughter of Godfrey Lionel Rampling, a British army colonel posted to NATO headquarters outside Paris, Charlotte Rampling had grown up speaking French. Although her father had won a gold medal in the 1936 Berlin Olympics, he never discussed it with his family because he had done so as a member of the 4x400 meter relay team rather than in an individual event. At the age of seventeen, Rampling dropped out of the University of Madrid and formed a cabaret act with her older sister Sarah. Their father, whom Rampling later described as "a crippling perfectionist," put an end to his younger daughter's singing career by sending her off to secretarial school in London.

When Charlotte Rampling met Tommy, she had just emerged from a period of great personal trial and trouble. Two months after giving birth prematurely to a child in Argentina, her beloved older sister Sarah had died of what Rampling told reporters was a sudden stroke. Seven hours after her sister's death, Rampling's mother suffered a severe stroke, which resulted in an extended stay in a series of hospitals and nursing homes. After breaking up with the thirty-seven-year-old actor to whom she was then engaged, Rampling left London to care for her parents. She then went off to make a film in Sardinia, only to learn that the stomach pains from which she had been suffering were caused by peritonitis. She underwent surgery in a hospital so understaffed that the film's English dialogue coach moved into an adjoining room to help care for her.

After her mother's death thirty-four years later, Rampling revealed that her sister had in fact committed suicide by shooting herself. "The death was what the French call the declencheur—the unclencher," she told the *Sunday Times* in 2004. "When something so obviously dramatic happens, you try not to be so futile, and I was leading a very futile life. Other things need to come in." As *Sunday Express* columnist Roderick Mann wrote in 1968, the actress formerly known as "the Chelsea Girl" who "wore her independence like a badge and looked bright and brittle and walked along the King's Road with a carefree swing" had now been "tempered by death and disaster" as well as "the onset of an emotion quite new to her."

The emotion was Charlotte Rampling's newfound love for Tommy. The two began an intense affair and were soon living together in what another *Sunday Express* reporter called "a high-ceilinged, barn-like room" with "white-washed walls covered with posters and photographs and posters" at 49 Hugh Street in Victoria. Although "not so much furnished as strewn with bric-a-brac" and "not the tidiest place in the world," the flat had, "as they say—atmosphere." It was also located just around the corner from 23 Cambridge Street, where Puss was still living with Jake, Charley, and their nanny, thereby making it impossible for Puss to ignore the fact that Tommy had set up housekeeping with another woman just a stone's throw from her front door.

As Rampling told a reporter from *The Observer* after she and Tommy had begun living together in March 1968, "I haven't been away on holiday this year because I am living with the man I love and looking after his children and that's my holiday. We've been together for six months. It took a bit of time to achieve a relationship with the children and for them to trust me. Now they know their mother and father don't get on and he is going to marry me one day and we will all live together for ever. We've spent whole days reading, or listening to records, or sitting on the front doorstep in the sun. We don't go out very much. If you really dig somebody and respect and like them as a friend, why bother? We have complete communication, telepathic closeness, we could do absolutely anything in the worst possible conditions, and probably enjoy it."

"At Hugh Street," Rampling said later, "we made steps to go up to a mezzanine where the boys slept. As a twenty-two-year-old girl, it was odd for me to be in this surrogate mother position with these kids, but I took it on board. Puss was then not really part of Tommy's life, but I never really met her, so I don't know if that was really true. Men say what they want to say, don't they? Men like Tom do."

In truth, Tommy's new relationship was the reason Puss decided to file for divorce. "Poor Puss took the brunt of it," he said later. "She was very unhappy about it. That was what finished it off. She just wouldn't stand for it. 'You're not going to have an open affair with her and stay married to me. Absolutely not.' Puss didn't like her at all. But I loved Charlotte. Absolutely."

Although the psychedelic summer of 1967 had come and gone, the 1960s were still in full, glorious swing in London. Tommy and Charlotte soon assumed their rightful place as one of the most beautiful couples on the scene. As she would later say, "At that time, it was all still very luminous and it was really about being young in the sixties and just being greedy and selfish and having fun. With Tommy, life was sort of an adventure. Every day was a party for him."

Shortly after Tommy and Charlotte began living together, Puss left London with Jake and Charley and their nanny for an extended stay at Port Eliot, the sprawling six-thousand-acre estate in Cornwall owned by her friend Lord Peregrine Eliot. A former partner in Seltaeb, the Beatles' merchandising company, Eliot eventually became the 10th Earl of St. Germans. Port Eliot House, which was thought to be "the longest continually inhabited dwelling" in the United Kingdom, had originally been built as a monastery in the twelfth century. It had belonged to the Eliot family for five hundred years and contained a priceless collection of portraits by Sir Joshua Reynolds.

After taking up residence in a cottage at the edge of the woods, Puss stabled her horse, Jerusalem Artichoke, as well as a pony named Bilbo Baggins on the grounds of an estate fronted by a Tudor gate that looked as though it had come from a child's storybook. She befriended an eccentric local poet who believed he was the modern incarnation of the goat god, Pan. Regularly, he brought her pheasant eggs, which she scrambled for the boys' breakfast. The poet also gave her an owl he had captured in the woods. Puss adored the bird, even though it kept defecating all over the house. While she was there, Puss also spent time with a handsome young lord she had first met in London.

Along with other members of the King's Road elite, Sir Mark Palmer joined Puss so they could all attend the Obby Oss Festival (from *'obby 'oss*, local dialect for "hobby horse") in the village of Padstow. The festival, which begins each year at midnight on the first of May, originated in an ancient Celtic fertility rite celebrating the return of the sun god Bel, who caused "the crops to grow and the hours of daylight to lengthen."

Dressed in "a great hoop of kind of tarred canvas and a mask," the man portraying the hobby horse is led through the streets of Padstow by a "teaser" who is bedecked in ribbons and bells and who dances around the hobby horse while prodding him with "a special padded stick." On its route, the hobby horse often stops to drag women "under its dark costume in quite a graphic attempt to portray a fertility rite. It used to be said that 'if you were caught beneath the veil that you would be pregnant within the year.'"

As the procession makes its way through the narrow, winding, very crowded streets of the tiny Cornish town, the revelers, dressed all in white with red kerchiefs around their necks and flowers stuck in their hats, sing a traditional song over and over again:

> Unite and unite and let us all unite
> For summer is acome unto day
> And whither we are going we will all unite
> In the merry morning of May.

Christopher Gibbs, who also attended the festival that year, recalled: "One of the things I remember most vividly about Sue was her performance there on May Day, because she decided to make a rather spectacular entrance. She was riding her horse Jerusalem, but Jerusalem was harnessed in some kind of a chariot very much festooned with flowers, as was she. The locals thought this was a lovely sight, but wondered, 'Who is this strange woman who has come among us? She's not Cornish, is she?' It was a very gracious, sort of otherworldly, very dreamlike performance. She was the toast of town that day and simply wonderful. But then everything she did was always very high flown and beautiful and a pleasure to behold."

What for those in Puss' rarefied social circle was an event of pure aesthetic delight seemed like something else again to her two sons. "Jake and I went down there with Puss for several weeks," Charley Weber recalled, "and we all stayed in this castle with no running water. She had her horse Jerusalem Artichoke with her, and Jake and I had this little pony named Bilbo Baggins. Every morning, we'd jump into this cart with our driver and get our Cornish ice cream on the corner. Our nanny hated where we were staying. She said it was a fucking dump."

Concerned that Puss had left London to stay for an extended period with people he did not know, Tommy drove to Port Eliot to have a look around. "He didn't want us living like that," Charley said, "so he grabbed us and said, 'I'm going to take the kids for a few days.' And then we were living with Tom and Charlotte at Hugh Street. Charlotte was okay. She would lecture me about how many pieces of toilet paper to use. Puss would never do stuff like that, but Charlotte was just trying to be a mum and didn't really know how."

A few months later, Tommy took his sons with him so that he could accompany Charlotte while she made two films in Europe. For Jake and Charley, it was the beginning of a pattern that would continue for the next three years. Shuttled constantly between a mother and father whose own lives were now completely separate, their primary form of education consisted of learning how to live like gypsies on the road.

10
london to sydney

Tommy, Jake, and Charley traveled with Charlotte Rampling to Italy, where she had been chosen by director Lucchino Visconti to play Elisabeth Tallman in *The Damned*, a film about the downfall of a family of wealthy German industrialists during Hitler's rise to power in the 1930s. With an international cast featuring Dirk Bogarde, Ingrid Thulin, and Helmut Berger, the movie was shot in Rome amid the kind of chaos for which the Italian film business was then famous. As each actor spoke the lines in his or her native language, construction workers building new sets hammered away in the background, creating a noise level that was constant and unrelenting.

Although working conditions were less than ideal, the stress of making the film did nothing to alter the state of utter bliss that Tommy and Charlotte were then enjoying. "We gypsied around in the car and camped out here and camped out there," she recalled. "We rented houses here, we rented houses there. With Tommy, life was an adventure. When I was working, he would have the boys on the set. He would be the father and the nanny, and everything fell into a natural rhythm. The French expression is *moment de grâce*. There are times when everything is just as it should be and it all fell into place and there were no problems. That was the enchantment of that relationship with him and those little boys."

During the filming, the critically acclaimed novelist and short-story writer James Salter flew to Rome to persuade Rampling to honor her commitment to play the female lead in *Three*, a film based on an Irwin Shaw short story for which Salter had written the screenplay and that he was also slated to direct. Unable to have dinner with him because she had to get back to Tommy, Rampling told Salter she would appear in the film, thereby enabling him to obtain the money to fund the project.

While shooting *Three* in various locations throughout the south of France during the summer of 1968, Salter, a forty-four-year-old West Point graduate who had flown more than a hundred combat missions as a U.S. Air Force fighter pilot during the Korean War, learned a good deal about his star. Little of it was particularly complimentary. As Salter later wrote in his memoir, *Burning the Days,* without ever naming her, his leading actress "chewed wads of gum, had dirty hair, and, according to the costume woman, wore clothes that smelled. Also . . . she was frequently late, never apologized, and was short-tempered and mean."

Viewing it all from what was apparently his side of the generational divide, Salter also noted that in the hotel room where Charlotte Rampling was then staying with Tommy and the boys, there were "soiled clothes piled in corners, bags of cookies, cornflakes, and containers of yoghurt. The boyfriend, a blond highwayman, was a vegetarian. He prescribed their food. 'Meat,' he murmured in a restaurant, looking at a menu, 'that'll kill you.'" In the mornings, Salter noted that the happy couple sometimes "danced manically in the street, like two people who have just become rich or had an enormous piece of luck. During the day, after every scene, she flew into his arms like a child while he kissed and consoled her."

While on location near Avignon, France, midway through shooting the story of three young college graduates on vacation in Europe during the 1950s, Salter would later write that his lead actress refused to continue working "unless her salary was doubled and her boyfriend took over as director." By this point in time, Tommy had expanded his film career by shooting footage of a doelike Rampling running through the English countryside in a chamois mini-tunic that did nothing to hide her long, lovely legs. He had also filmed her walking through the woods in a variety of different outfits, freak dancing while flipping her hair on a London street, and writhing orgasmically on the hood of a car. To the throbbing beat of Eric Burdon and the New Animals performing live onstage during the Christmas on Earth Continued concert, Tommy had then cut these images into a quasi-psychedelic montage as the band performed "Hey, Gyp" in *Watch Out for Your Ears*.

Although Tommy was not qualified to take over a movie halfway through production, much less one the screenwriter himself was directing, it was the 1960s, and in the film business, stranger things had happened. Fortunately, the producer refused to fire Salter and allowed him to complete the movie. When Salter learned of the "mutiny," he "found it hard to suppress my loathing, although in retrospect I wonder if it might not have been a good thing. The boyfriend might have gotten some unimagined quality from her and made of the well-behaved film something crude but poignant—that is to say compelling."

Although *Three* was a popular entry at the Cannes Film Festival the following year, the movie, which also starred Sam Waterson and Robie Porter, received decidedly mixed reviews in America and England. Salter then went on to write the screenplay for *Downhill Racer*, a far more successful film directed by Michael Ritchie and starring Robert Redford, Gene Hackman, and Camilla Sparv. Due in no small part to what he had experienced while making *Three*, Salter himself never directed again. In 1969, he did, however, lend his voice to Hunter S. Thompson's campaign for sheriff in Aspen, Colorado, doing the voiceover for a television commercial in support of Thompson's unsuccessful run for office on the "Freak Power" ticket.

By the end of September 1968, Tommy, Charlotte, Jake, and Charley were back in London living on Hugh Street. On November 24, 1968, Tommy's old friend Michael Taylor set off from London with Innes Ireland and Andrew Hedges in car 26, a Mercedes 280 SE that had been entered in the first London-Sydney Marathon. With the English pound having just been devalued and the British economy in a slump, British press lord Sir Max Aitken, who owned the *Daily Express*, and two of his top executives decided to create an event that the newspaper could sponsor and that would "raise the country's spirits" while also serving "as a showcase for British engineering" to "boost export sales in the countries through which it passed."

After leaving from Crystal Palace, the cars and their racing teams were put on the Dover ferry to France. From there, they drove to Le Bourget Airport in Paris and then through Italy, Yugoslavia, Bulgaria, and Turkey. Crossing the Bosporus by ferry, the drivers raced their cars on unpaved roads into Iran. They then took either the northern route across the Alburz Mountains along the southern shore of the Caspian Sea or "the shorter, but more treacherous route along the north edge of the Great Salt Desert" into Kabul, Afghanistan. After a 6½-hour rest stop, the drivers pressed on through the Khyber Pass across Pakistan and into Bombay. With no repair work allowed during the eight-day voyage by sea, the cars were shipped to Perth. Three days later, on December 18, 1968, the surviving cars arrived in Sydney. (Although Ireland, Hedges, and Taylor retired from the race in South Australia, they were the first to arrive in New Delhi, winning the Bombay Private Entrants Award.)

Racing under conditions that pushed man and machine to their utmost limits on the seven-thousand-mile course, the drivers braved snow, treacherously icy roads, washed-out creek beds, and head-on collisions with kangaroos as the cars sped through eleven countries in eleven driving days with only a single rest period, when they waited for the Khyber Pass to open at dawn.

Based on his lifelong desire to go faster than anyone else behind the wheel of every car he had ever seen, the race should have been the driving experience of Tommy's life.

Instead, the London-Sydney Marathon became his first real foray into a line of work that was equally dangerous but offered a far more dependable monetary return. "Why did I begin smuggling?" he would later say. "Well, it was there. Why not? The first time I did it was with the Mercedes Works car that had been crashed in Afghanistan. It was crazy, but that was how I started."

In large part, Tommy's decision to enter the lucrative business of bringing wholesale quantities of hashish overland from Afghanistan to London came about because of his long-standing friendship with Anthony Gustave Morris, who was known to one and all as "Taffy." A generic and somewhat derogatory name for all Welshmen derived from St. David (i.e., Daffyd), the patron saint of Wales, the name is also the subject of a nursery rhyme: "Taffy was a Welshman, Taffy was a thief; Taffy came to my house, and stole a piece of beef." As Tommy would later say of his friend, "Taffy was a Welshman. Taffy was a thief. Taffy was a very wild and extraordinary gypsy. One of the Romany who had been living in Afghanistan and Pakistan and knew it all well."

Tommy's half-sister Lulu, who in time would live with Taffy, first met him in 1965 while she was attending the Lilliesden School, where Puss had gone before her. "By then," Lulu said, "Taff and Tom were already great buddies. I was fourteen and still wearing my school uniform, and Taffy was Tommy's age [twenty-six], but he was totally giving me the eye and I was giving him the eye." A rugged-looking character who sported a moustache and long hair and always wore a Stetson hat, Taffy never stayed anywhere for very long. In Lulu's words, he "actually slept with one eye open." An inveterate thief of major proportions, Taffy stole, as Jake Weber later said, "everything from cheese to the crown jewels."

"The best one," Lulu recalled, "was when Taff took the jeans off some guy and tried them on because he thought they were such a good cut and wanted to go buy some. Then he walked out and left the guy without any clothes. Within five minutes of meeting you, Taffy would know exactly what was in your bank account and how many credit cards you had. Tommy felt an admiration for the way he got away with what he did. And he did it right in front of everyone's eyes. That was how Taffy got wagons and cars and everything else. He would take something and go off with it and never come back." In her words, Taffy soon became "one of the big shifters of dope from Afghanistan to England. Huge, huge shifter."

At the time of the London-Sydney Marathon, Taffy was living in a specially built Leyland exhibition van designed to transport horses that had, in Lulu's words, once belonged to a "famous spy" and was "filled with electrical equipment. It pulled out on both sides, and he would drive that east and stuff it with dope and come back." Taffy obtained the van in trade for the sleek Le Mans GT-40 racing car someone had brought around one day to show to Tommy.

"Tommy took it for a spin," she recalled, "and came back and said it was great, fantastic. Then it was Taff's turn, and he went off in it and never came back. And then he swapped the GT-40 for this amazing van." Behind it, Taffy towed "a Reading 1894 gypsy wagon, all cut crystal glass," which he claimed to have bought from the folk singer Donovan's father "for twenty five pounds. He probably stole it. He would sleep in the wagon and never stay anywhere more than a few nights."

The wagon itself figured prominently in Charlotte Rampling's relationship with Tommy. As she told the *Observer* in August 1968, "We have our weekends away, in a caravan that used to be in a circus. I didn't know what I was being taken to see, and then there was this beautiful caravan, still with photographs of the Gipsy who had lived in it. All kinds of strange vibrations hit me. When I was a child and we lived in France there were French Gipsies quite near us, and they were very happy. It could be that's part of it, associating him with that happy memory of being a child. But I don't think so."

In terms of the great London-Sydney Marathon caper, Taffy, who owned the wagon (which he later sold for a tidy profit to a museum in Australia), was most definitely the brains of the operation. After he learned that Michael Taylor had asked Tommy to fly out to Afghanistan to bring back car 35, a Mercedes 280 SE that had been driven by Robert Buchanan-Michaelson and that had left the race after passing through Teheran, Taffy put together a plan so elaborate that not even Tommy knew all the details before setting out for Afghanistan.

Leaving Jake and Charley with Puss on Cambridge Street, Tommy flew with Charlotte to Kabul. On the plane, he spent a good deal of time chatting up a girl he did not know, only to then learn she was one of Taffy's regular couriers. A genius at finding his way around the law in every country, Taffy had befriended a colonel in the Afghani customs service who in return for a cash payment and a night with the female courier would look the other way whenever Taffy took a load over the border. "This was Taffy's arrangement," Tommy later said. "I knew nothing about it."

Because the Mercedes 280 SE had blown a piston during the race, Tommy and Charlotte had to wait a week in Kabul for a replacement part to arrive by plane. Before the part got there, the Afghani colonel discovered to his great dismay that he had "caught the clap off this girl, and he had her picked up in Beirut, carrying, and she went down. I remember Taffy filling this huge syringe with penicillin and pumping it in this girl. But we carried on, nonetheless."

"What happened," Rampling said, "was that the car broke down in Afghanistan and I went with Tommy to fetch it. I had never been to Afghanistan, and it was really actually rather amazing. Because unbeknownst to me, all sorts of things were going on with the car. I thought they were trying to fix it. Because I was always told that it was the piston that had broken and the car had been so well made that nothing could happen to it except if the piston went. I didn't know what the piston was. Sort of the mythical piston. And we were waiting for this new piston."

In 1968, Afghanistan was still a wild and fairly lawless land where the last member of the Barakzai dynasty, Mohammed Zahir Shah, ruled as king. The only cash crops were opium poppies and towering cannabis plants, which after being pressed into thin blocks of black Afghani hash, was smoked openly in pipes and chillums throughout the country. Since governmental corruption and bribery were the order of the day, many high-placed locals were only too happy to sell their Western brothers as much hashish as they could transport out of the country.

With the help of Hyatullah Tokhi, who ran a hotel and rug shop in Kabul, and his brother Amanullah, who had worked as the maintenance supervisor at the American embassy, a hippie commune known as the Brotherhood of Eternal Love had already established a regular pipeline from Afghanistan to Southern California. On a regular basis, the brothers brought tons of hashish and regular shipments of hash oil to America concealed in their personal luggage, Afghani instruments and rugs, and then an entire Volkswagen packed with dope.

By the time Tommy and Charlotte arrived in Kabul, Taffy had already been, in Tommy's words, "all over the Mercedes before I came out and it was ready for me. I brought out a radio; that was the only thing that was needed." Driving the car south to "the lovely city of Kandahar," where Taffy loaded hashish into the second gas tank he had somehow managed to install in the Mercedes, Tommy and Charlotte headed back to Kabul, only to run into a problem not even Taffy could have foreseen. As Tommy later explained, "We had great difficulty getting out of the county. For one thing, the king of Afghanistan wanted this car. Because it was the car to have, and they didn't understand the rally rules."

As it would clearly not have been wise to offend the king, Tommy and Charlotte then tried to leave the country by driving to the city of Kunduz in northern Afghanistan, only to run into more unexpected difficulty. Taffy, who was now traveling with two girls he had picked up somewhere along the road, decided, in Tommy's words, "that he wanted to come back with me and Charlotte with the two girls in a car that only had two seats." After Tommy and Taffy discussed the matter somewhat heatedly, Taffy drew a gun on Tommy and fired a shot at him. "I hope he didn't try to aim at me," Tommy said. "I just burst out laughing at him, and that totally disarmed him, and I gave him a thousand dollars. And he got into a taxi back to Kabul and took his two girls with him."

Ensconced in a Mercedes loaded with hashish, Tommy set off with Charlotte for the long overland journey back home. Before reaching Iran, he carefully removed all the racing stickers and rally numbers from the car and made it without any further problems to the Bulgarian border. Arriving there in the middle of the night, they were met by a sergeant at the customs post "who was quite sure he knew what we were up to." When the sergeant told Tommy, "There's something wrong with this car," Tommy blithely replied, "No, no, it's just a rally car."

Refusing to accept Tommy's explanation, the sergeant looked under the Mercedes, only to see a sheet of titanium steel covering the entire underbody of the vehicle, "thereby making it virtually impossible to get to the front gas tank, which was the one filled with the hashish." Quite certain he was dealing with a smuggler, the sergeant put the car up on a ramp so he could begin undoing the metal sheet. "Of course, he couldn't get it completely off," Tommy said, "so he gave up the job halfway through."

In the morning, as Tommy was doing everything in his power "to make it take as long as possible, because that would have revealed the second tank," the sergeant and those under his command who had joined him were "just about to drop the huge metal guard under the car" when the commander of the post arrived. "We managed to talk to him in a mixture of Latin and French and English," Tommy said. "He was, I think, very enamored of Charlotte and said, 'Nonsense' to the sergeant. 'Have this man's car put back together again.'"

"I knew there were two gas tanks in this car," Charlotte Rampling said later. "But I was not aware of what was in it. I could have carried it off if I had known because when, you know, you take control of your destiny and say, 'Okay, I know. I'll go with it.' But I was just sort of the unknowing passenger. It was just another adventure, really. And we needed a stash. But I didn't know anything about it, and that's absolutely true. Which was also very sweet of Tommy. He absolutely protected me on that."

When Tommy and Charlotte finally reached the capital city of Sofia in western Bulgaria, the car broke down again. To his great delight, Tommy learned that "a new system had just been agreed to between the Royal Automobile Club and the Bulgarian Auto Club that any people whose cars had broken down in either country would have reciprocal arrangements. And so they said they would ship the car back to England via train. I thought, 'Oh, that's marvelous.' Because I figured my luck had lasted long enough."

With all his problems solved, Tommy was about to fly home to London with Charlotte when the local railway authorities informed Tommy they could not put the Mercedes on a train, because, as he would later recall, "in the small print of the reciprocal agreement, it said that if the car was still running, you were not eligible for the service." Although Tommy told them he had to get the car to the factory without running the engine anymore, his pleas fell on deaf ears.

Hiring a breakdown truck to follow him out of the city, Tommy drove the Mercedes to a remote location so he could blow up the engine. "And this bloody engine would not blow up," he said. "It red-lined at about seven and a half thousand revs, and it was well off the clock at about nine thousand revs, and this fantastic engine was still roaring away."

Pitted against one of the finest pieces of machinery that the engineering geniuses at the Mercedes factory in Stuttgart had ever built, Tommy did all he could, but still could not get "this wonderful engine to blow up. Eventually, after about five minutes and the most incredible racket and everything smoking and rattling, it went." After they had put the car on a train, Tommy and Charlotte boarded a plane to London with all their "bags and camel bags and robes and rugs that one collects in Afghanistan."

As Tommy was waiting to go through customs at Heathrow, he suddenly realized that his luggage also contained "two or three hand-pressed bits" of Malana Cream. Processed in the tiny town of Malana in the Kullu Valley in the Himalayas, Malana Cream was then considered the finest hashish in the world. As he later recalled, "When we arrived at airport in London, it was useful that Charlotte was there, because she was reasonably well known and that took some of the attention off me."

As the British customs officer was about to begin going through all the exotic goods the couple had acquired during their trip, Tommy looked him in the eye and, with the complete aplomb that his great friend Pete Prince later described as "sort of his version of the Jedi mind trick," Tommy said, "'Here you go. Where are we going to start with all this stuff?' And the man said, 'Oh, no. It's all right. *Go.*' So we were through, and the car got through as well."

Having made it back home in one piece with a gas tank filled with high-grade hashish, it would have made perfect sense if Tommy had never again wanted to lay eyes on the man who had pulled a gun and fired it in his direction in Afghanistan. "I didn't see Taffy again until I went especially to Paris to find him and give him his share, because I considered he deserved it," Tommy said. "I gave him about ten thousand dollars. Small-time stuff, these days. We became much closer then because he trusted me again. But he was the bane of my life, having crashed God only knows how many of my cars."

Because of Tommy's beneficent gesture, the two men formed a partnership. The way their operation worked was that Tommy would fly to Kabul to make the arrangements and then Taffy would bring the dope back into England in his specially equipped Leyland van. Compared with some who were involved in the trade back then, theirs was a relatively modest concern. Although Tommy began earning more from smuggling dope than he had ever made by racing cars or selling properties in London, he was, unlike Taffy, never into it just for the money.

Describing what truly drove Tommy to engage in such adventures, Charlotte later said, "For Tommy, it was absolutely the thrill of the adventure. To see what he could get away with. And that was the time. He certainly wasn't the only one doing that kind of stuff for the hell of it and the thrill of it. He liked dangerous situations, but he himself was not dangerous. I never did think he was."

Beyond doubt, Tommy had now proven to all concerned, Taffy foremost among them, that he had what the English called the "bottle" (Cockney rhyming slang for courage) to pull off any smuggling scheme imaginable with the best (or worst) of them. The fearless quality that had served him so well in Afghanistan soon became such utterly reckless abandon that even those who loved him could see that Tommy's life was now spinning rapidly out of control.

11

samye ling and lundy island

With Tommy and Charlotte looking after Jake and Charley at Hugh Street and the Flying Dragon out of business, Puss was now free to pursue her wildly divergent spiritual interests on a full-time basis. Along with a female friend, she made her way to the village of Esakdalemuir, not far from Lockerbie in southern Scotland, where Akong Rinpoche and Chogyam Trungpa Rinpoche, two Tibetan lamas forced to flee their native land after the Chinese takeover in March 1959, had founded the Samye Ling Monastery in 1967.

By far the more "charismatic and unusual" of the two, "Trungpa," as he was known to his followers, had been selected through a variety of tests and signs at a very young age as the next incarnation of the tenth Trungpa Tulku, a direct descendant of Karmapa, the black-hat lama of Tibet. After spending his childhood being trained in the monastery, Trungpa had walked with Akong Rinpoche and others for nine months through the Himalayas under extremely arduous conditions to escape the occupying Chinese forces.

After spending four years in India, Trungpa migrated to England. Awarded a Spaulding scholarship to study religion, philosophy, and fine arts at Oxford University, he quickly took to Western ways. As Nik Douglas, the author of *Karmapa: The Black Hat Lama*

141

of Tibet, would later say, "Trungpa liked his ladies, and he liked to get drunk and be outrageous. He did Zen-like paintings, read beat poetry, and was certainly was not the celibate, 'holier-than-thou' type lama that many people thought high Tibetan lamas should be."

After a calamitous automobile accident that left him partially paralyzed along one side of his body, Trungpa, who espoused the doctrine of "crazy wisdom," shed his traditional robes, married a sixteen-year-old English girl, and moved to America, where in 1974 he founded what is now Naropa University in Boulder, Colorado. In 1984, at the age of forty-five, he died of cardiac arrest brought on by a variety of alcohol-related causes.

By the time Puss journeyed to the Samye Ling Monastery, it had already become, in Nik Douglas' words, "a popular place for people on the London scene." Michael Rainey would later characterize it as the place "where all the upper-class rich girls would go and the Rinpoche [i.e. Trungpa] would get them to part with their money and their virginity."

On monastery stationery adorned with a Tibetan print depicting a barefoot, bearded sage seated on a throne before a bodhi tree and a mountain range with a crane by his side and a deer at his feet, Puss sent Jake and Charley, whom she addressed as "Taliesen" and "Hercules," greetings from her new home:

> THIS IS A PICTURE OF BABA
>
> PICNICKING UNDER THE TREES
>
> HE IS EATING POMEGRANITES [sic]
>
> THEY TASTE HONEY SWEET
>
> DO YOU SEE THE REINDEER
>
> KISSING BABA'S FEET?
>
> BABA BENDS THE RAINBOW
>
> BABA SHINES THE SUN
>
> BABA MAKES THE MOONGLOW
>
> BABA IS EVERYONE

IF WE HAD SOME BUBBLE CARS
WE'D PACK SOME MARS BARS & GUITARS
AND RACE THEM ROUND THE STARS
IF WE DROVE QUITE FAST, THEN SOON
WE'D REACH THE MAN THAT'S IN THE MOON
WE COULD HAVE A LOVELY LUNE
HE MIGHT INVITE US IN FOR TEA
LETS HOPE THE JAM IS RASPBERRY
I SUPPOSE WE'D BETTER WAIT & SEE

Showing no hint of the derangement she had exhibited in her Glastonbury letter, Puss wrote her "Darling boys" that she was

up in Scotland in a monastery which is a place where people learn to meditate which is thinking rather quietly. The monks are very nice yellow people and when they are not meditating they are playing with walkie talkie machines which are things that enable you to telephone from one tree to another, they are delighted with these toys and laugh a great deal while playing with them, they come from a country called TIBET *which is between India & China, but the Chinese are rather bossy people* [who] *shoved them out of their country (Tibet) which was very sad for them.*

She ended her letter by telling her sons that "because of all this meditating, one has to be very quiet here so it would not be fun for you, but I will come back to London to see you next Wednesday." Puss then apologized for having broken her promise to see them a week after leaving the city, indicating she had already been in Scotland for some time.

Puss wrote a far more frantic and somewhat desperate letter to "My Darling Tommy," reporting she had "received a terrible missive" from her solicitors. "I can't remember all the awful words but it says things about me living in such conditions, no bath, no nanny, too many gypsies, creating a reprehensible way of life, Tibetan Buddhism."

Telling Tommy that Akong Rinpoche had "knitted" her "into full lotus quicker than a trice" and was now going to teach her Tibetan "& never to be fearful," Puss noted, "He could teach the children these things too. It costs a lot of money to stay in the monastery & I have none so I am going to be the cook here. The children can stay in the house & have a wonderful time."

Expressing concern because her horse Jerusalem Artichoke was still in Cornwall with Bilbo Baggins the pony and because the *I Ching* said a white horse was meant to be ridden, Puss asked Tommy if the boys could go with her by train to fetch him. Hoping to spend the winter in India and Tibet, she wrote, "Please my darling let my sons share a part of my life. I don't want to fight any more with lawyers." Conceding that her way of life was "odd," she nonetheless wanted Jake and Charley to travel with her to Tibet. But if that was not possible, "which I think a great pity for them, as they would have such joy on the way, & really look forward to it very much; please let them join me for a while in Scotland."

Puss then expressed her deepest fear:

I think there is little time left for this planet as it is, so on every side it is said there will be a great wave of disaster, the communists will overrun the earth & a tide of blood will flow, then light & truth will be born again. It was so lovely to hear you talk of returning to Denmark. There is an organization called Universal Link which has its headquarters in Borup. They are in contact with Baba & the monastery, they have established a school where they say that when the wave is at its height & all are in utter confusion, then Baba will speak. There will also be a mass saucer evacuation. After this the earth will stop on its axis for one second & this will cause it to be purged by fire + its total geography re-arranged. People taken up in the mother ships will be returned to a clear world on another plane of consciousness there will be a thousand years of peace. I would like you to take the children there to Borup.

The Universal Link organization had been formed by a dooms-day group known as the Orthon Cult, whose members believed the world would end on Christmas morning, 1967. To ensure they would not perish in the nuclear holocaust that would then engulf the world, cult members built an elaborate fall-out shelter in a field in Borup, not far from Hald in Denmark. Wooden walls, partitions, and a roof were constructed eighteen feet underground and covered with twenty-five tons of lead to shield the inhabitants from the deadly radiation of the blast.

When the world did not end on Christmas Day, the cult split into different factions, but continued to generate the message that the end of the world was near, setting the new target date for spring of 1971. Although Puss never joined the group, she had seen a flying saucer while returning from Glastonbury and still believed this was the means by which those on earth would escape the planet.

Adopting a more balanced tone, she closed her letter:

Darling I have heard you are looking tired & am so sad to hear it. Please leave London soon, it is a pit of disease & filth. Come to Scotland with Charlotte or go back to your own country. Aryan parts of Tibet of Denmark & sweet Albion are all the very same. I want my biles [boys] *to take the right one. If the winds of my karma separate me from them in this existence I will try to accept it. I remember* [what] *the fortune teller said about them being taken away with dread but I know I will be with them sooner or later. Please lend your understanding.*

On January 8, 1969, Puss typed a very formal letter to her trustee with a handwritten mini–shopping list appended to the top: "Honey. Bio Strath [a Swiss herbal tea tonic]. Car Insurance. Get a *Goat.*" In the letter, she complained bitterly that her trustee had demanded a second opinion from a doctor other than the one she was consulting before he would consider her request for money so she could leave England to spend the winter in a warmer climate, preferably Morocco.

In a very clearly argued, entirely reasonable letter, Puss wrote that her own doctor's concern was with her

mental stability as well as my physical condition. I have been unable to cope with environmental pressures since early childhood and gradually with [his] help, I am learning how to organize my life in a better way, and above all how to fend for myself. I can only be very sadly grieved at your reluctance to permit me the chance to rest and convalesce away from England: I have now little hope of regaining my strength quickly in this climate.

To bolster her case, Puss wrote that her doctor had already pointed out to her that she had

misused large sums of money which you have permitted to me for financial ventures in the past, and that this fact has largely contributed to your disinclination to release the money which will allow me to leave the country. I would like to point out that the purpose of this journey is not one of speculation, or of finance at all, but of my own equanimity and my own physical strength in order that I may be equipped with the sanity and vigour to cope more successfully with my own life and economy.

She ended her letter by noting that if her trustee refused to believe "that it is strongly advisable for me in my present condition to go to a warm climate then you cannot have the consideration of my welfare at heart, but only the consideration of my funds."

Signing the letter "Mrs. Susan Weber," she added a handwritten poem:

What is fate that we should seek it
Wherefore question how & why
See the roses are in bloom, see the sun is in the sky
See the world is lit with Summer, let us live and love & die.

She also wrote that "obstinacy and arrogance are qualities ill suited to a would be disciple."

As though urging herself to become more enlightened, she added a series of observations and suggestions that accurately characterized her current state of mind.

Love. Obedience. Surrender. There isn't possibility of compromise about these 3 . . . I am disobedient & dishonest . . . There is a world of differ-ence between importance & necessity. Are bodily needs necessary, but not important? . . . Thank God God has a sense of humour . . . New Yrs. Resolution be cheerful.

And then, in a final note to herself: "Get a goat you stupid stoat."

The reason Puss was under a doctor's care was that she had tried to kill herself by swallowing an overdose of pills in Hyde Park, only to be found by a policeman who brought her to Charing Cross Hospital, where she was resuscitated. "Somehow," Jenny Ponte said, "they managed to pull her back. I went to see her there, and it was absolutely terrible. This beautiful, very fragile girl lying in bed in this terrible straightjacket, and I said, 'How could you have done it, my friend?' And she said, 'Because nothing can ever be as bleak as it is now.' She couldn't bear not living with Jake and Charley, and I think she missed Tommy terribly, too."

As her son Jake would later say, "She'd had a death wish forever. She was always talking about how the other place was better and how we were all going to be happy there." Tommy took both Jake, who was then five, and his three-year-old brother, Charley, to visit their mother as she recovered in the hospital. In Jake's words, "I remember walking into her hospital room and standing by the side of her bed and saying, 'Why? Why did you do that?' I was so angry with her, and she was sheepish. Like someone who had been caught doing something she shouldn't have done and knew it. Quite early on, it established our relationship. With me being the scold and her being the child."

After successfully persuading her trustee to give her the money to leave England for the winter, Puss departed for an extended stay in Afghanistan accompanied by the young lord with whom she had spent time at Port Eliot in Cornwall. Renting a house in the middle of Kabul, Puss stayed behind as he traveled through the northern part of the country looking for Afghan statues to take back to London for sale.

Adopting native garb, she bought herself a long maroon velvet Afghani wedding dress with heavy gilt embroidery. With her dark hair and exotic features, she looked much like a member of one of Afghanistan's wandering tribes. In a house surrounded by gardens, she cooked outdoors on a brazier and seemed very much at home in a culture where women played a decidedly secondary role. As Tommy had already learned when he had been there, it was not hard to purchase pharmaceutical cocaine in Kabul. Nor was it difficult to procure high-grade heroin. During her stay in Afghanistan, she also visited the Hindu Kush mountain range, which separates that country from Pakistan.

While Puss was gone, Tommy and Charlotte Rampling continued looking after Jake and Charley. Although in many ways Tommy seemed like a less-than-ideal father even then, he did include his sons in all aspects of his life, taking them with him and Charlotte when they went to see Jimi Hendrix perform at the Royal Albert Hall in February 1969. "We were at the back of the Albert Hall," Charley, then four years old, remembered, "and Tommy introduced me to Jimi Hendrix, who lifted me up, put me on his shoulders, and said, 'How ya doin', Charley?' Very cool guy. In the middle of the performance, Tom pushed me out onto the middle of the stage. As all the cameras went off, I said hello to Jimi and he said, 'How are you doing?' And then he did his fire thing."

Even then, Jake and Charley were already quite different from one another. Whenever Tommy took Charley to a screening room on Wardour Street to watch his footage of Jimi Hendrix on stage,

Charley would react so viscerally that Tommy came to believe the boy was destined to become a musician. Because he "always hated conflict," Charley from a very young age adopted the attitude that insofar as he was concerned, everything was always "cool." As Jake would later tell his younger brother, "You were always the extrovert, always smiling, the happy one." In Charlotte Rampling's words, "Jake always had this little observing face and was looking out for other people and seemed rather older than his age."

Having recovered her physical health and at least some measure of her mental equilibrium, Puss returned to England in the spring of 1969 and again began caring for her sons. Charley would later remember her taking him to the fun fair in Battersea Park so he could go on the rides. "One was this huge needle with a cylinder on the end, but I was too young and it was too weird and I freaked out at the top. Her reaction was very deep and primal. She yelled so loud that they stopped the needle way up in the sky, and I was left just sort of rocking there. It was as though she was protecting her cub."

Completely devoted to her sons, Puss still managed to upset them when they were together. "I remember the three of us going on holiday somewhere," Charley said. "We were on a train, and she jumped off to go into a shop while we were in the station, leaving Jake and me behind. It was just an impossible feeling. I kept thinking the train would leave without her. I would also have dreams about her falling out of the car while we were driving." If Puss saw a beautiful bird or a tree in a park while driving, she would, in Jake's words, "stop the car and go look at it and leave us in the backseat with the motor running. I remember her doing that once outside Green Park in London, leaving the keys and us kids in the car."

No longer looking after his sons on a daily basis, Tommy now had time on his hands. Thanks to Nik Douglas, who with his wife and baby daughter came to stay for a while with Tommy and Charlotte at Hugh Street, Tommy soon became involved in a scheme that made his drug-smuggling caper in Afghanistan seem like very small potatoes indeed.

A talented painter and jack-of-all-trades descended from the Duke of Buckingham, who in 1601 had refused to acknowledge King James I and so had been summarily stripped of all his extensive holdings, Douglas had been raised in the Middle East. Coming to London at the age of 15½ in 1960 to study nuclear physics, he had fallen into the music scene and begun working as a road manager for Graham Bond while also pioneering the overland import-export trade from Afghanistan, Turkey, and Lebanon. After spending several years in India, Sri Lanka, Nepal, Sikkim, Thailand, and Indonesia studying with Hindu yogis, Buddhist lamas, and Tantra experts, Douglas had been hired by the Rolling Stones to help the underground filmmaker Kenneth Anger direct a documentary produced by Mick Jagger and Robert Fraser about the Kumbha Mela festival in India.

While reading the newspaper one day in the house on Hugh Street, Douglas discovered that Lundy Island, located twelve miles off the coast of Devon in the Bristol Channel, between England and Wales, was for sale. Because his mother and father had met there and then chosen "Lundy" as his sister's middle name, Douglas was already familiar with the island's long and colorful history.

Granted to the Knights Templar in 1160 by King Henry II, Lundy Island, which then lay outside British territorial waters, had become a lawless haven for pirates and privateers. After changing hands several times, the island was bought in 1834 by William Hudson Heaven, who proclaimed it a free island, which soon became known as "the kingdom of Heaven." In 1924, the island was sold to Martin Harman, who declared himself its king and began issuing currency known as the Puffin, which was named after the bird that roosted there. Although the currency was eventually withdrawn, island residents did not pay English taxes and had to pass through customs whenever they journeyed to and from their homes. After Harman's son Albion died in 1968, the island, replete with a lighthouse, a castle, and a Victorian villa, was again put up for sale. As luck would have it, Douglas was also a good friend of Ronan O'Rahilly, the Irish businessman who in 1964 had founded Radio Caroline, England's first pirate radio station. Broadcasting from a ship anchored in international waters, Radio Caroline soon became a major cultural force in the United Kingdom by playing music no one had ever heard on the BBC. Convinced he could inveigle O'Rahilly into setting up another pirate radio station on Lundy Island, Douglas had no trouble selling Tommy, who was always up for everything, on the idea.

Accompanied by his wife, the former Eva Bjurenstam, who along with Nena Thurman had been one of Sweden's leading fashion models, and their baby daughter Tara, Douglas hopped into a car with Tommy and Charlotte to drive to Bristol so they could look at the island. As always, Tommy made the journey in record time. The terrific speed at which he drove that day was also due in part to the fact that with him from his most recent trip to Kabul, Tommy had brought back several "small screw-top jars of pure German pharmaceutical cocaine which could then be bought there in chemists' shops. He had been selling some as well and was flush with cash. He was very pleased with himself but I remember Charlotte being a bit perturbed by it all."

Although it could take as long as three hours to reach the island by boat, Douglas and Tommy learned they could rent a helicopter that would transport them there in thirty minutes. After doing so, they spent the entire day on Lundy Island, as Douglas said later, "scoping out the place. As there was some chat about putting a new Radio Caroline there, we were particularly interested in the lighthouse tower, the castle, and other high vantage points. I carried my small daughter around the whole island in a small basket."

Returning to the mainland, Nik Douglas and Tommy excitedly began discussing how to implement their plan. With Puss having only recently been at the Samye Ling Monastery in Scotland and Douglas having first met Chogyam Trungpa Rinpoche while the lama had been attending school in New Delhi, the key element of their scheme soon fell into place. As Douglas recalled, "Tommy and I had this flash idea that we could establish Lundy Island as sort of a Free Tibet and begin issuing Lundy Island passports for Tibetans who at that time were stateless and could only travel on United Nations passports. We also thought we could do corporate registrations, perhaps register ships, and develop our own currency, along with a pirate radio or TV station."

After Douglas persuaded Ronan O'Rahilly to come on board with the project, Douglas and Tommy set up a meeting with Trungpa, who received them lying in bed in a big house in Kensington, where he was recovering from his recent auto accident. While driving through Newcastle, Trungpa had blacked out, missed a corner, and driven his car through the front window of a joke shop, suffering injuries so severe that he would walk with a pronounced limp for the rest of his life. "He was quite badly hurt when Tommy and I met with him," Douglas remembered. "I did most of the explanation about Lundy and Trungpa was very excited and agreed it would be a great idea to establish a Free Tibet on the island, issue passports, and support it with revenues from a pirate radio or TV station."

From Tommy's point of view, this was a deal for which he had been tailor-made, In Douglas' words: "Tommy was never a real entrepreneur. He relied on others to come up with the ideas and lay out the script. He was however a great salesman and with a bit of coke in him to stoke him up, the right suit, and the right car, there was no stopping him. He was quite shameless, always very charming, and a real ladies' man as well as a man's man for those who admired a handsome, charismatic guy."

Douglas and Tommy then arranged a meeting with the solicitors who represented the seller only to be told that the island was no longer on the market but had become part of "a private arrangement." Investigating further, they learned that a British government official had somehow gotten wind of their plans. Understandably alarmed by the prospect of a coalition of radio pirates, hippies, and Tibetans-in-exile restoring Lundy Island to its lawless days of old, the official had contacted Jack Hayward, an ultrapatriotic British multimillionaire living in the Bahamas, and asked him to buy Lundy Island "and then donate it to the Landmark Trust so it could used as a bird sanctuary."

Although Douglas and Tommy had already persuaded Puss and Charlotte "to commit some funds to the project," it now looked as though they would have to fold their hand and get out of the game. When the two men learned Hayward was off in Scotland allegedly shooting birds, a story which, if true, the English tabloids would have loved, they decided to put the purchase money for the island in escrow and leak "the news" to the press.

Armed with the so-called information about Hayward, Douglas and Tommy went to Whitehall to confer with the head of the Landmark Trust. At the meeting, Sir John Lindsay Eric Smith, the scion of an old English banking family who was also the Conservative MP for London and Westminster, was accompanied by two operatives from MI6, Britain's Secret Intelligence Service for external affairs. Because Tommy was, in Douglas' words, "all coked up," the meeting soon became "very confrontational."

Intent on getting the deal done any way he could, Tommy "boasted that if the Landmark people wouldn't step aside, he would see to it" that the story about Hayward came out. Going completely over the top, Tommy "then went on to say he was sure that Spain would be delighted to have a military base on Lundy Island and in any event, he could put the Irish on Lundy and take it over within twenty four hours." Sir John Smith, who had most definitely never before dealt with anyone like Tommy, turned "red as a beet root" and became "mad, mad, mad. The two MI6 people muttered dark threats. The meeting was really scary and came to a bad ending."

As they drove away from Whitehall, Douglas and Tommy realized they were being followed. Going into full James Bond mode,

Tommy got rid of his pursuers by "driving the wrong way up a narrow street." For the next day or so, both men, in Douglas' words, "were under heavy surveillance. Charlotte was freaked. Then a big series of announcements were made that good Mr. Jack Hayward was indeed buying Lundy 'for the nation' and giving it over to the Landmark Trust." Hayward wound up paying £150,000 (about $360,000) for the island, which remains a bird sanctuary to this day, attracting thousands of visitors each year.

After what he would later call "the Lundy debacle," Douglas decided to return with his wife and baby daughter to India: "I wasn't that happy with what was going on with MI6. Tommy was totally uncool, and I feared if I stayed around much longer, I'd end up in jail. Or dead."

Fueled by cocaine, a substance that few people in London were then using on a regular basis but which soon became his drug of choice, Tommy had blown the Lundy Island deal by getting far too high on his own supply and raving at an august member of the British establishment. No matter how he had behaved at the meeting, it seems clear in retrospect that Douglas and Tommy's scheme stood little chance of success. Still, in an era when the line between fantasy and reality was so thin that the ingestion of any number of substances could suddenly cause what passed for everyday reality to entirely disappear, the chance of pulling off the impossible was always what mattered most.

Never one to be daunted by either failure or success, Tommy did not let the loss of Lundy Island keep him down for long. But then, as Charlotte Rampling later explained, "Tommy never closed on anything, so nothing was ever really attached to him in terms of work. He was always looking to do the undoable and constantly had these huge fantasy plans. Historically, that was what that very short spell in time was all about."

12

chester square

Before returning to India with his wife and child, Nik Douglas turned Tommy on to a house with but a few years left on its lease that had come on the market at a remarkably cheap price because of the sudden death of the owner. Taking advantage of a deal too good to pass up, Tommy bought the lease and moved with Charlotte, Jake, and Charley from Pimlico to the far more exclusive Belgravia section of London. Located on a quiet street around the corner from where Puss and Tommy had celebrated their wedding reception in Eaton Square, Tommy's new home at 53 Chester Square was a stately manor facing a private garden lined with benches just a stone's throw from St. Michael's Church.

"It was a huge mansion," Tommy said, "the most extraordinary place which had once belonged to the ambassador from one of those countries that had ceased to exist after the first World War. This millionaire ambassador had done the house up as the state-of-the-art of everything that had worked at the turn of the century, and nothing had been changed. Then the queen's doctor lived there. When he died, I bought the whole place lock, stock, and barrel off his widow for eight thousand quid [twenty thousand dollars]. Now, it would be worth about eighteen million pounds [thirty-six million dollars]."

For anyone else, 53 Chester Square would have been the perfect place to retreat from the hustle and bustle of city life in London. Tommy, however, soon transformed the house into a scene of epic proportions. "In Hugh Street," Charlotte Rampling recalled, "it had been just us and the kids. When we left there and went to Chester Square, Tommy became kind of manic because he was the lord of this huge mansion. He loved having all these parties where a lot of drugs were taken and there was a lot of drinking and always a lot of people hanging out."

On any given night, there was no telling who might stroll through the front door at 53 Chester Square to join the party. Jimi Hendrix stayed there. Steve Winwood, fellow members of Traffic, and record producer Jimmy Miller dropped by regularly. Keith Richards' good friend Stash Klossowski lived in the house for a while. Whenever he was in London after making yet another overland journey from Kabul, Tom's good friend and smuggling buddy Taffy was also around. Like a beneficent uncle, Taffy decided one day to take Jake and Charley for a ride in the sleek Ford GT-40 racing car he had purloined. As they crossed London Bridge doing a hundred miles an hour, Charley was delighted. Much like his father, he had always loved going fast. The same could not be said for Jake.

To look after Jake and Charley and help prepare the meals, Tommy recruited his twenty-year-old half-sister, Lulu. On the nights she did not cook, two beautiful twin sisters named Michelle and Nicole, who had appeared in a Roman Polanski film, handled the kitchen duties. On alternate nights, each of them was also sleeping with Taffy, who then began an affair with Lulu as well. Other visitors to 53 Chester Square included Helmut Berger, who had starred in *The Damned* with Charlotte Rampling; George Lazenby, the actor who had just replaced Sean Connery as the new James Bond; Roman Polanski; and Douglas Fairbanks, Jr., then nearly sixty years old.

Surrounded by the preeminent rock musicians of the day, Tommy soon decided to get into the music business by offering to manage Osibisa. An all-black aggregation founded by Ghanaian-born musician Teddy Osei, the band had just begun making a name for itself by playing pre-Afro beat, Santana-like jams at white psychedelic venues all over London. "We didn't have a manager. We didn't even have an agent," Osei recalled. "I was playing flute and saxophone and African drums and getting the gigs and running around trying to find record companies to listen to what we were doing. We met Tommy, we had a chat, and he wanted to do something with us."

After he had found a studio in London for the band, Tommy paid for all the session time so Osibisa could record what in different form eventually became their debut album. After the recording was done, Taffy came up with what seemed to Tommy like a brilliant notion. If they could find a bus large enough to sleep all seven members of the band on which they could also record, Tommy and Taffy could put the bus on a ship to Africa, where Osibisa would then play live shows in Ghana and Nigeria that Tommy could film and record. "That was a wicked idea, actually," Osei said. "Play shows as we moved along. Live on the bus. It was a great idea, and I welcomed it very much."

How Tommy could possibly afford to buy such a vehicle was a bit of a sticking point. Lest anyone think he was merely a run-of-the-mill, household-variety thief, Taffy then produced the bus. Exactly how and where he had acquired it, no one could say for sure. Knowing Taffy, it was better not to ask. To take Osibisa to Africa, Tommy needed a touring bus. Thanks to Taffy, he now had one. No more needed to be said. "He must have nicked it," Osei said. "Taffy looked crooked. He looked hard. You could see he had been traveling all over the world and that whatever he wanted, he would get it."

Just as Tommy was about to put his master plan for the band into action, the entire scheme fell to pieces, Osei said. "Everything was just freaky, and Tommy's family didn't like the idea that much. They thought he was spending too much of the money he inherited, so they cut him off. And that was where our relationship started to end."

Although it had been years since Tommy had depended on his family money, his income was subject to the vagaries of the overland drug trade from Kabul. If a shipment failed to arrive, Tommy had to scramble to set up another one so that he could continue paying for his wildly extravagant lifestyle. His increasing use of cocaine, a drug that encouraged wild flights of fancy, which rarely if ever came to fruition, was yet another factor in the downfall of his rock management career.

For Tommy, cocaine served only to intensify the abundant natural energy with which he had been born while making the comedown that followed just that much more severe. As Charlotte would later say, "Tommy's manic-depressive condition came on because of all the drugs he took. If you are of a highly lively nature and an unusual and original person, you swing over very quickly into those states. The condition would almost be inevitable."

Having never bothered to sign the band to a formal contract, Tommy let Osibisa, a band that went on to record sixteen albums and continue to perform to this day, slip right through his fingers. "Tommy loved us very much," Osei said later. "But he should have got a lawyer to organize everything, because most of the time, he was freaked out. He needed a secretary and a manager so his ideas could be carried out. But we loved him because the spirit he had for the band was bigger than anybody else's, and we were all very sad when his money was stopped."

As the scene at 53 Chester Square became progressively wilder, Tommy also had to deal with the reality of Puss' increasingly serious relationship with the young lord. Just as her mother had done after falling in love with Harold Coriat, Puss had turned a blind eye to the fact that the young lord himself had already been in legal trouble and had also acquired a reputation as a rake and a womanizer in the elite London circles through which he moved.

Slight and slim, with a face that stamped him as an undeniable member of the upper class, the young lord could not have been more different from Tommy in appearance and demeanor. As Christopher Gibbs later recalled: "I think Puss had a real thirst for and understanding of beauty, and this extended to her chaps as well. They were always kind of an aesthetic balance to her. Sort of Rose Red and Snow White. She didn't go for the beauty-and-the-beast side at all. But if you're always thinking about what things look like, that's a recipe for life which doesn't generally bring happiness."

While the young lord's good looks may have attracted Puss to him in the first place, it was his great charm that blinded her to faults that seemed painfully obvious to others. As Nik Douglas said, "I knew him when he first showed up in London with a seat in the House of Lords and no money. We became fairly close, but I was a bit suspicious of him because he was always looking for the next heiress to fleece. He was really pretty blatant about it."

Because the young lord had inherited only a prestigious title as well as a stately home that, in Nigel Waymouth's words, "was a white elephant, and like tearing up five-pound notes under the shower, he didn't have two beans to rub together." For a while, the young lord seems to have subsisted on what Waymouth called "the peerage dole," the five-pound fee that a peer received each day for taking his seat in the House of Lords while Parliament was in session.

Jenny Ponte recalled being told "a terrible story about him." On the opening day of Parliament, the usher of the Black Rod, a post dating back to the early fourteenth century, knocks on the doors of the House of Commons with a huge mace known as the Black Rod to summon the elected members to accompany him to the House of Lords, where the queen then opens the session by delivering her annual address. "The story goes that when he took his seat in the House of Lords, Black Rod dropped his rod. He was that surprised to see this unexpected presence. Dressed up like Robin Hood. Actually, it was Puss who told me that story."

Nik Douglas also described the young lord as "a bit of a Machiavellian character" who was always trying to make his way to the center of the "pure psychedelic scene" of the hip art world in London. Despite his shortcomings, Puss soon became, in Jenny Ponte's word, "very serious about him. She nearly married him." As Tommy himself was then living in luxury with Charlotte Rampling, there was precious little he could do about Puss' new boyfriend. Making the situation more difficult, both couples found themselves interacting socially at Chester Square.

"We were having a big party at Chester Square, and everyone was there," Tommy said. "Champagne everywhere, and Puss was there in a long, white, shimmering dress looking absolutely gorgeous. There was a big staircase leading up to the drawing room on the first floor, and she was standing at the top of the stairs. And as I came around the bend, she looked at me and literally just knocked me down the stairs. I was overpowered spiritually and blanked out. I dare say I had been feeding my nose with all sorts of things. Because by then we were getting more and more outrageous."

Until someone brought it to his attention, Tommy also had no idea what kind of drugs Puss was now using. All his worst fears were confirmed the night Tommy drove to Picadilly Circus and parked his car outside the all-night chemist's shop where registered addicts in London queued up at midnight to pick up their "scrip," a government-issued prescription for legal "jacks" of heroin which many of them promptly sold in the toilet of the nearby tube stop. "I had been directed to park in a certain place and wait, and it was obvious she was scoring. I was completely innocent about it. I thought she was just going to get some pills. She had even told me that this was all she was doing there."

So that she could pursue her new relationship, Puss had Tommy file an undefended suit for divorce on May 28, 1969, on the grounds she had committed adultery with the young lord. "He was cited in the divorce as the co-respondent," Tommy recalled. "In order for us to take Jake and Charley out of the hands of court, we decided I would do the suing, which was extremely ungentlemanly. Her family were arm-in-arm with the courts. They were almost part of the family, if you can imagine that. Because she had been through that all her life, she didn't want her boys to suffer the same fate and be hamstrung throughout their lives, and so she allowed me to have custody rather than the official receiver and the official solicitor."

As Puss and Tommy sat together in the hallway of London's Divorce Court on July 9, 1969, he was "nervous as hell. She was used to courts and I wasn't. We weren't enemies by any means, and we were still talking and she put a little note in my hand just before we went into court. 'I love you and don't let them get you down. We're all on your side.' It was very sweet, and it cheered me up." Although the judge did appoint the official solicitor as Jake and Charley's legal guardian, Tommy was granted custody of the boys.

Because Puss and Tommy continued shuttling Jake and Charley back and forth, the two adults remained in fairly constant contact even after the divorce. Then the young lord wrote Tommy a letter asking him to leave them alone for six months so they could sort out their relationship without any visits from Tommy. In a very civilized manner, the young lord explained that Tommy's visits might upset Puss, whom, as he openly conceded, still loved Tommy very much. In the letter, the young lord also assured Tommy he would look after the boys for as long as need be.

On the morning of August 9, 1969, a month after Puss and Tommy's marriage was officially dissolved, Tommy and Charlotte were sitting down to breakfast with Steve Winwood at his cottage in a remote part of Berkshire, where Traffic had written much of

Dear Mr. Fantasy. Opening the newspapers, they learned that Charles Manson and his followers had murdered five people at a secluded mansion in Bel Air, California: the actress Sharon Tate, celebrity hairdresser Jay Sebring, and heiress Abigail Folger, among them. The next night, the Manson family killed two more people.

Six months later, a young black man named Meredith Hunter was stabbed to death by Hell's Angels hired by the Rolling Stones to serve as security guards at their massive free concert at Altamont Speedway in northern California. Taken in tandem, these two events helped put an end to the widely held perception that the hippie culture was about to change the world for the better. The news, however, did not dissuade Puss from setting off on a journey that had already become one of the hallmarks of that culture.

Accompanied by the young lord, who had to borrow money from a former lover to pay for his share of the trip, Puss set off for Morocco to seek out her father's family roots. Continuing on to Afghanistan and then India, she hoped like so many others on the same road to find a teacher who would help her attain a more enlightened state of being. In an era when the journey East was meant to bring about real personal and spiritual transformation, Puss would return from her travels in a manner that no one, her two young sons least of all, could have ever anticipated.

Susan Ann Caroline Coriat,
eight years old

Priscilla holding her newborn son, Christopher, with Camel, Mary, Puss,
and Jenny at Twatley Manor, 1954

Thomas Evelyn Weber, fourteen years old, (second from right, front row), Melvill House, Haileybury, 1952 (courtesy of Haileybury and I.S.C.)

Haileybury XV, 1956, Tommy, eighteen years old (back row, fourth from right) (courtesy of Haileybury and I.S.C.)

Tommy in London, circa 1962

Puss, left, with Jenny, center, dressed for an occasion

Puss, center, with Juliet Harmer, right, bridesmaids at a wedding, 1962 (courtesy of Juliet Harmer)

Puss and Tommy on their honeymoon in the south of France, September 1963 (courtesy of Charlotte Taylor)

Jake, Tommy, and Charley in the snow in Hyde Park in London

Tommy and Charlotte Rampling in the south of France during the filming of *Three*

Jake, five years old, with
Charlotte Rampling

Puss, her passport photo, taken just before she left for India

Tommy and Anita Pallenberg at Villa Nellcote, 1971 (Dominque Tarlé)

Jake and Mick Jagger at a café in Villefrance, 1971 (Dominque Tarlé)

Jake with Keith's guitars and Mick Jagger, recording *Exile On Main St.* in the cellar of Villa Nellcote, 1971 (Dominque Tarlé)

Marlon and Keith Richards, Jake and Charley at the zoo in the south of France, 1971 (Dominque Tarlé)

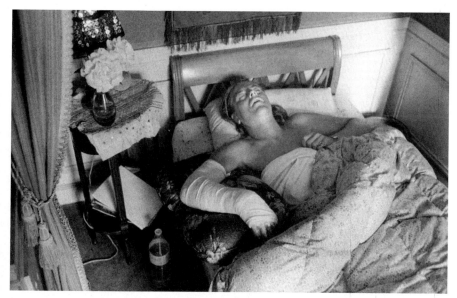

Tommy with his arm in a cast at Villa Nellcote (Dominque Tarlé)

Charley and Jake in Holland where Taffy was then holed up

Tommy, as he appeared in the BBC documentary about Jimi Hendrix
(Amy Whittern Hardy)

Charley, publicity photo,
We Are Juan, 2005

Jake kissing Patricia Arquette on *Medium* (CBS Paramount Network)

Pete Prince, Charley, and Jake in a pub in Rugby on the night of Tommy's funeral, September 22, 2006 (Amy Whittern Hardy)

Tommy, sixty-six years old, in Rugby, 2006 (Amy Whittern Hardy)

Puss' grave, Church of St. Lawrence, Ardeley, 2007 (D. Frantz)

13
almora

On January 1, 1970, in what Christopher Coriat would later call "suitably dramatic" fashion, "rather than facing the new decade," Camel Coriat was following his fifteen-year-old son across the fields as he hunted hares on foot with the Eton College beagles. Suffering a massive heart attack, Camel Coriat fell over dead at the age of sixty-six. Despite the distinctly reduced circumstances in which he had lived ever since his forced departure from Twatley Manor, Camel remained to the very end of his days a thoroughly "draconian" character who ruled his household like a divine-right king.

"My mother was not allowed to drive," Christopher said, "or express an opinion on anything and really was pretty belittled by him. He made all the decisions, and the household revolved around him. He ordained whatever was going on." Camel did, however, take incredibly good care of his son. "I was the center of his life, and he spent tons of what would now be called quality time with me, and we would go for walks with the dogs through the woods for hours and talk."

At the time of Camel's death, Christopher was already on his way to fulfilling his father's fondest hopes and dreams for him. After completing his studies at Eton, he would attend the Royal

Military Academy at Sandhurst as well as Cambridge University, serve as a British army officer, qualify as a single-and multi-engine pilot with an instrument rating, and then become a barrister specializing in offshore trusts and estate planning.

"I distinctly remember that on the day my father died," Christopher Coriat said, "we were driving to the meeting of the beagles in the car, and my mother dared to say something about the route we were taking or that we were going to be late. He was absolutely furious with her and stopped the car and said, 'What do you think you know?' He was unpleasantly tough on her, and it was extraordinary she remained so much in love with him."

Remarkably, Camel also managed to die with all his many secrets intact. A genius at confabulation, he had always told his son the reason the family never left England during Christopher's childhood was that during World War II, "Captain Coriat," as Camel liked to be called, had been "shot down over the North Sea and then spent twenty-four hours at sea and so really didn't like to fly." Even after his death, none of his children ever knew that he had served hard time under a variety of names in prisons in Australia, New Zealand, and England, a country Camel loved so dearly that he created an elaborate fantasy life so he could be part of it.

During the course of his lifetime, Camel Coriat, the renegade Moroccan-born son of a family of great Sephardic rabbis, had been a con man, a convict, a fox hunter, a bankrupt, and a member of the Royal Air Force who saw combat during wartime. Behind him when he died, Camel left a wife who grievously mourned his passing. For the rest of her life, Priscilla remained "unrelentingly faithful, not just physically but mentally as well" to the memory of her late husband.

To comfort Priscilla, Alan and Jenny Ponte drove to London, collected Puss, and then went with her to Forest Cottage in Chute, Andover. Thinking it would help ease the pain of her mother's loss, Puss, as her sister Jenny would later say, "put LSD powder in my mother's wine at dinner. We went and sat on my mother's bed because she became very ill in the night and was screaming the place down. She was away with the fairies. She was absolutely stoned out of her mind. Puss thought it would cheer my mother up and make her happy, but it completely freaked her out. I had the first row I'd ever had with Puss that night. But my mother did forgive her."

In a birthday letter Priscilla had sent Tommy two years earlier in which she had written that he "had been always a most generous caring & considerate son-in-law" while also noting how much she "had loved Charlotte from the moment we first saw her," Priscilla expressed her own concern for the welfare of her youngest daughter:

Naturally we long for Puss to find the same happiness & certainty that you both have and be able to re-create that atmosphere for Jake & Charley but no one knows better than I do (& I hope Charlotte too) that its the most astonishing bonus & miracle if human relationships in any context (man-woman-parent-child, etc.) work out. . . . But oh! God knows how easy it is to go back at my age & pronounce on such things— tho no one knows better than I do, that everyone has to work things out for themselves however long it takes, & no one least of all I can help Puss to get her life together now—the worst bit of having your children is the sitting back & watching & waiting & not having some big wealthy gift to pass on or some hard worn bit of advice or philosophy.

Six months after Camel's death, Priscilla sold Forest Cottage and moved to Gloucestershire. In Christopher's words, "She became quite active politically in the little village where she lived. She remained madly in love with my father and true to his memory, but because she had a fifteen-year-old son, she had to get into the parental role and she was tremendous. She actually came into her own and was very brave and impressive, living on her own in her old age after having grown up with servants and all the advantages." In 1996, Priscilla died at the age of eighty-two. Her ashes, like those of her late husband, were scattered by the banks of the Sherston, the branch of the River Avon that ran through Twatley Manor, where they had both once lived in pastoral splendor.

Shortly after her father's death, Puss set off with the young lord for Morocco. She soon wrote her mother that the two of them were so happy there that they had decided to buy a house. Now that she had finally found herself the right relationship as well as the perfect place in which to live, where everything would be wonderful, Puss urged her mother to persuade the trustees to grant her the funds she needed to make the purchase. Puss then set off to visit Mogador, the city in which her father had been born.

The decidedly psychedelic nature of the ancient fortified city and its four-mile stretch of open, wind-swept beach had already made Essaouria, as Mogador had been renamed when Morocco became an independent nation in 1956, a favored stopping-off point on the hippie trail. Jimi Hendrix himself had passed though the city a year before Puss arrived. While Hendrix had not written "Castles Made of Sand" about Essaouira, so many of those who loved his music thought he had that they began going there as well. Although Puss seems to have taken no notice of this, Essaouira then also had a reputation as a dangerous place for women who were traveling alone.

One day, as Puss was walking by herself on the beach there, she was raped. "It was a crippling blow," Tommy said. "She didn't give me any details, but it wounded her very badly." At some point before the incident, Puss may have eaten opium containing datura, a powerful delirium-inducing substance that, as Nik Douglas later explained, was given to a number of Western women who were then traveling in Morocco, causing them to literally "go out of their bodies and sometimes be unable to get back." In any event, Puss quickly abandoned her plan to buy a house in Morocco.

In a handwritten note addressed to her "beloved pomfrets," her pet name for Jake and Charley, that she wrote from Rabat,

Puss noted that as soon as the young lord made some money, they would

find a house in Turkey which used to be byzantium which was one of Jesus' most beautiful empires until an old Turk called Ataturk came down over the mountains and called it his. Anyway it is still very beautiful and we will find a house by the sea right in the sun and perhaps where there are some ponies and goats and fruit trees and we will have fish for breakfast when you come to stay . . .

Please ask Daddy to send us money soon so we can get there soon and see you soon. Also I feel a bit peculiar and would rather get out of here I think I have got cholera because I didn't have an injection for it and I can't breathe. . . . Send Dad my love and Charlotte and write quickly before we go so [we] know where to find you. Stay out of Dad's way if he gets in a huff and look after each other, love and hugs and blessings.

Mummy XXX OOO

Puss then flew with the young lord to Bombay. As she finished reading *Thus Spake Zarathustra* by Friedrich Nietzsche, the plane landed in "an Indian sunrise." In a letter to "Dearest Tom" from a hotel on Juhu Tara Road in Bombay, she wrote, "There are palm trees and rooks, no crows and a balmy warm sea; so unbelievable to take my clothes off and feel that kind of wind that touches you all over at the same time." She then added:

Very blue without the pomfrets, a lump of lead in my throat and in my stomach. My life is so utterly meaningless without them now. I just miss them. So much I feel empty and really ache without them. It makes me so sad that all my best goes to other people. I wish just for a bit, for a change, we could have a break. I suppose you know I love you more than most, can't help it, just keeps hangin' on. I don't want to infringe on you and Charlotte or you and the man in the moon I just wish sometimes we could have some fun again.

Noting that Tom's mother had told her she should stay away from him, Puss added, "Lord knows we bolted halfway across the world enough times, it seems I've grown on you like poison ivy." She ended her letter with a confession and her own version of the lyrics to the Beatles' song "I Will": "You know I had a freaky childhood. (show me someone who didn't) I can't survive Europe or a Christian climate because of that, I was brought up like a boy but I'm not, I am most definitely a young woman and I don't care if I do have to go east to make it, here ladies are a thing of great joy.

"Dearest T. miss you so much I could tell you the things in my heart when I see you but it never really mattered

> I will always feel the same
> Love you forever and forever
> Love you with all my heart
> Love you when we were together
> Love you when we were apart
> And when at least I find you
> Your song will fill the air
> Sing it loud so I can hear you
> Make it easy to be near you
> for the things you do endear you to me
> you know I will, I will"

Although Puss had been on a spiritual quest ever since her visit to Glastonbury, her trip to India was prompted not so much by an overwhelming desire to find a teacher as her need to escape the grim reality of the endless English winter. That she was now being pursued far more regularly by her own inner demons seems apparent from her subsequent letters. While, as Puss noted in another letter, the young lord looked "in the mirror far too often," she had little trouble finding one of the many opium dens then located on the upper floors of old buildings in the bazaars of the teeming city.

In one letter to her sons, Puss wrote charming doggerel about her new friend, a street child named Gita who had black skin and black eyes, wore only pink knickers, and whom she was teaching to do cartwheels. "I met her when I had eaten a lot of opium. It brings you closer to Jesus. but only for a bit and your head hurts."

After she and the young lord returned from Goa, the former Portuguese enclave then just being discovered as yet another paradise by the sea where drugs were cheap and plentiful and the natives looked the other way as Western hippies frolicked naked on the beach, Puss wrote Tommy a fairly incoherent letter from "steamy honking teeming seething" Bombay. Expressing her sorrow that he was broke, she told him again she missed her sons so much that "getting letters from the boys is almost too much pain." She also wrote "where am I I don't know [sic] I sent the opium to the laundry by mistake."

After a long, hot journey across India's central plain by train and then up into the Himalayas on a series of "ancient buses that made a lot of noise as they went round and round these hairpin turns," Puss and the young lord arrived in Almora during the first week in March 1970. A small village that had once served as a hill station where British government officials went each summer with their families and servants to escape the heat, Almora sat above the clouds with inspiring views of Nanda Devi, the second highest mountain in India.

Then still relatively unspoiled, Almora looked, in Nik Douglas' words, much like "an old Nepali town, like Katmandu. Very narrow little streets with poky little shops the size of a toilet with people squatting in them selling things. Steps going up and down both sides of the road and a couple of poky little temples." A stopping-off point for yogis and saddhus on their way to Mount Kailash in Tibet, Almora was where Swami Vivekananda, the Hindu monk who introduced yoga and Vedanta philosophy to the West during a visit to the Chicago World's Fair in 1893, had established an ashram before his death in 1903.

In 1964, Timothy Leary and his brand-new bride, the former Nena von Schlebrugge, who later remarried and became the mother of the actress Uma Thurman, had come to Almora and stayed at the Ambassador Hotel, a dark inn that was the village's only guesthouse. On foot, the couple had then continued further up into the mountains to Holy Man Ridge, where they had visited Lama Govinda, the Tibetan Buddhist philosopher of Austrian descent who lived with his wife, Li Gotama, in a house built by W. Y. Evans-Wentz, the translator of the I Ching.

In Almora, Puss and the young lord were the guests of Nik and Eva Douglas and their young daughter Tara at Chilkapitha, or the Eagles' Nest, a house in which Swami Vivekananda had lived during the rainy season and where his watercolor painting of Kali, the fearful incarnation of the mother goddess, still hung in the attic. A ten-minute climb down a steep hillside two miles outside the village, the house sat on the edge of the mountain with spectacular 180-degree views of the Himalayan peaks.

After the drugged-out hell of Bombay, Almora seemed to Puss like the place she had come to India to find. As she wrote in an aerogramme to her sons on March 8, 1970: "The girls are moving in circles with baskets on their head picking live herbs and flowers and roots, the men are driving the cattle and the oxen and the children drive the goats and sing songs on the hillsides, it is very lovely. They are looking after the earth as it is meant to be you see and it is like a song and a dance." As part of her return address, Puss identified herself as "Ruby Tuesday" after the Rolling Stones' song of the same name.

By then, Nik Douglas had already introduced her and the young lord to his spiritual guide and mentor. Bindu Joshi lived in what Douglas later described as a "typical Brahmin house with a front living area where he received people and a big yard where he had all his furnaces and would be firing all these alchemical potions. Bindu was a master of rasayana, one of the eight branches of ayurvedic medicine having to do with longevity, and an ayurvedic doctor. People came to see him from the crack of dawn until evening."

Then in his sixties, Bindu was "skinny, almost birdlike in looks," with an aquiline nose, dark skin, and "very long hands and limbs." Clad in traditional Indian clothing, Bindu looked "like any traditional ayurvedic doctor and was celibate. That was why he was called Bindu. *Bindu* means "sperm." He maintained his sperm forever. He was absolutely real, and I lived and studied with him for five years."

Quickly becoming part of the scene, Puss wrote her sons:

We spend most of the time listening to Bindu, we sit on his balcony in the sunshine and we talk about the world and how it is round. Doctor Bindu knows all about this having met Nik when he was peering through a hole in the window at Buckingham Palace, that is what he calls the Ambassadors [sic] Hotel here, and also Nik is properly the Earl of Buckingham and Doctor Bindu has very beautiful eyes with two white lights in them and is very keen on Italian footwear and on woolly socks because his feet get cold in winter and he wants [the young lord's] boots which are Italian footwear but too big for him, and he likes fountain pens more than anything, and on his balcony a little boy sits. I suppose he is about twelve and he is his apprentice, that is he learns from Bindu, he sits pounding gold and silver, mercury and lead, a costly preparation for the heart and all its ailments, he pounds it all day long in a pestle, and Bindu talks and jokes and jumps about and asks if we do not think him an idiot.

"He wasn't trying to transform lead into gold," Douglas said. "He was trying to transform the body into gold. He did an experiment while I was there where he regrew a leper's nose. He regrew some teeth on someone who had lost them all. I used to be one of his servants pounding stuff. He used a lot of gold and mercury, and he also used gems—pearls and rubies and diamonds. He would burn them for a year and create powders. Say there was a woman who couldn't give birth. He would prepare a special medicine and give her the teeniest small amount of it, and she would get pregnant. He never took any money from anyone. People brought him presents. He was highly educated, extremely well read, and very erudite. He would quote Robert Burns and Shakespeare."

Douglas confirmed that even in Almora, Puss was never all that serious about her own spiritual practice: "Bindu would complain to me that I ought to tell her how to sit. She used to sit with her legs open, and I would be apologizing for her, saying, 'She doesn't mean anything bad.' I was trying to interpret the hippie flower power thing to Bindu so he would understand that a lot of it was benign or just hadn't matured yet."

Although Douglas never saw either Puss or the young lord use drugs, "Bindu was a very open-minded guy. He'd had Leary and Ram Dass there, and *charas* [hashish] was part of the whole culture. It was perfectly normal at Doctor Bindu's house, if a saddhu came by, for him to light up a big chillum. Bindu wasn't into smoking, but he would make the most psychedelic preparations I ever had. One of the five ways of liberation is the use of drugs, and Shiva is the king of that, the yogi supreme."

While the idea of a mother doing opium, Douglas recalled, "would not have gone down well with Bindu," Puss had apparently brought some with her from Bombay or New Delhi, where a ball of the thick, black, gooey substance could be purchased for as little as ten or twenty dollars. As Douglas would later say, "You could eat that all day and go off into your own space. You'd be stoned the whole time."

Some two-and-a-half weeks later, Puss and the young lord were still in Almora. Calling herself "RUBY'S GROOVY," Puss sent a letter to her sons five days after Jake's seventh birthday. Written in all capital letters as though she were in a state of fevered excitement, Puss thanked them for their beautiful letters that had arrived just as Bindu had promised they would and again mentioned her desire to buy a house because she was tired of being homeless. She also wanted to give Bindu some money so he could rebuild his laboratory, which had been destroyed by a typhoon. He could then go on serving people, which was what people had been put on earth to do. Wishing that her sons were in Almora so she could look after them, Puss added, "OH POMMERS COME SOON PLEASE. IT IS COMING UP TO FULL MOON AND I AM BEGINNING TO FEEL FLIPPY & I WANT TO SEE YOU SO MUCH IT HURTS." She signed the letter "Ruby."

Overjoyed by the news that Tommy and the boys had at last agreed to join her, Puss, who by now was "painting prolifically," sent Tommy a letter on March 30, 1970, detailing the drawing paper "from Green & Stone next to antique market," "colored biros with fine points," and "Sable brushes: very fine, nos 00–10" that she needed them to bring her, as well as "—oh and box of water colours please."

Tommy, who never intended to make the trip himself, then put seven-year-old Jake and five-year-old Charley on an Air India flight to New Delhi with "a whole box of lovely pastels, lots of drawing paper and books, and a flask of mercury for her guru, Doctor Bindu, who was somewhat of an alchemist. The courts would have gone completely spare if they had known what I was doing, but she had written me to say she really could not do anything without the boys. So I sent them off to India on their own with labels in their buttonholes."

Puss, who had always done her best to look after Jake and Charley in a responsible manner, had long been importuning Tommy to send her sons to her. Another factor in his decision to finally do so was that Tommy was now not only broke, but also traveling constantly to set up what he called new "veins" for the transport of hashish from Afghanistan to London.

Because it was unusual for two young boys to be traveling to India on their own, the flight attendants made a big fuss over them during the long plane ride. "Looking back," Charley Weber said, "it sounds pretty horrific, but to me it was fun. The stewardesses spoiled us with sweets. Puss met us as we got off the plane, and we stayed at the Delhi Grand Hotel, where they had these Harley Davidson taxis with tassels on them before we went off on a bus trip up into the Himalayas."

Once Puss returned to Almora with Jake and Charley, Nik Douglas was "charged" by Dr. Bindu to look after the boys, for whom the young lord had "no use, none at all." As Douglas would later say, "She craved attention, but was continually being put down by him. He was no hero in any of this. He was like a scab." Douglas, who soon found himself "looking after Jake and Charley," would later say, "They were very beautiful kids, and I only have good memories of them. They were never difficult kids."

Less than two weeks later, Puss and the boys were forced to leave Almora after an incident that Douglas later called "the beginning of the fall" in terms of the unspoiled, idyllic life in the village. "I think she took off all of her clothes in the bazaar, which was on a fourteenth-century street with little Hindu temples. Or, she may have taken off all her clothes and gone into a Hindu temple and only male Brahmins were supposed to be in there. And was then rescued by someone from Doctor Bindu because it would have gotten to him and he would have arranged for her to get out of there."

Although Jake was not there when it happened, he later confirmed that Puss had run into the marketplace and "that everyone was very angry with her for going in there, and the men there started pushing her around and opening up her clothes because she was where she shouldn't have been. She was violated in some way there, and I know she was really traumatized by it. And I remember her being kind of shell-shocked by what had happened."

Always "conservative" in his own behavior, Bindu, who also liked "to play drama," then informed Puss there was a smallpox epidemic heading toward Almora. Puss later wrote Tommy that Jake and Charley would have been "particularly susceptible" to it, "having been so recently inoculated." In order to protect them, Puss needed to leave the village immediately.

"In Bindu's words," Douglas said, "Puss was 'tortured' and acting like a 'nymphomaniac,' meaning she was flashing wherever she went which is just not kosher in Brahmin society. He was also concerned about the kids and felt they should be back in school and she shouldn't have been there with her boyfriend or them. She certainly wasn't studying with Bindu. She was just there for tea and some sort of support, a rock to hold on to. If she had been on her own, she would have been a true spiritual seeker but she was not strong or not self-discovered enough."

In a letter to Tommy and Charlotte Rampling in France on May 25, 1970, Nik and Eva Douglas wrote that after having "disowned responsibility" for what Puss had done in the marketplace, the young lord had been "asked + advised to leave Almora—small mountain town freaked by freakout. Very heavy vibes for a week. She split with the Poms [Jake and Charley] alone (against our advice) about 6 weeks ago, supposedly to return to Europe via Greece. . . . Poms OK but should be looked after in a proper way by responsible guardian please. . . . Sue untogether when she split. Almora shaken + disturbed by all the events but now calm."

Although Puss had wanted to marry the young lord, she had proved to be too much even for him. Upon his return to England, he sought out his former lover who had paid for his share of the trip to India. As she would later say, "He turned up on my doorstep telling me how much he loved me, and I said, 'Yeah, but there is Sue. You can't leave her out.' And he said, 'Well, I fucking well wish I had.' And I said, 'Why?' And he said, 'Because she didn't wear any knickers and used to do cartwheels in the street.'"

Leaving Almora, Puss and Jake and Charley began the epic journey back to London. Before the trip was over, mother and child would reverse roles, and Puss would find herself being cared for by her seven-year-old son with more love and real concern than any man had ever shown her before.

14
on the way home

After a long, hot train ride back to New Delhi, Puss, Jake, and Charley went directly to the American Express office on Connaught Place in the center of the densely crowded, sweltering city. Beginning a series of missed connections that would continue for the next month, Puss sent a letter to Tommy at Chester Square asking him to wire them his mother's address in Turkey so they could visit her, as the boys very much "wanted to be beside the sea & see Lulu." Although Puss knew Tommy was now living at his mother's house in London, she did not have the address and so could only hope he was still picking up his mail each day at the only place where she knew how to contact him. When she tried to call Tommy at Chester Square, the phone number was "unobtainable."

Unaware that Tommy and Charlotte were in France for an extended stay, Puss dutifully went with the boys each day to the American Express office to join the long line of fellow travelers hoping for news and money from home, only to be told there was no mail for them. In unbearable heat, they spent ten days waiting for a letter that never came.

Leaving India, Puss flew with her sons to Istanbul, where Charley, who loved "the sweet tea and the pistachios and the smell of the Bosporus and the boats" lost the crimson silk pillow that was as precious to him as the big velvet Humpty Dumpty Jake had brought with him from England. Boarding a ferry, Puss went with the boys to Buyukada Island, the largest of the nine Princes' Islands in the Sea of Marmara. On the island, there were no automobiles and the only transport was by horse-drawn cart.

Staying in a "lovely old hotel" as they waited to hear from Tommy, Puss wrote that although "the pomfrets" were "disappointed to find no beaches—it is rocky and dangerous for swimming," they were "having happy times." Describing her sons as "wonderfully good and kind," Puss reported they were all "writing a book together, we do everything together really. We have some difficult times but never between ourselves, traveling is sometimes not easy; Pomfrets are innocent but we are learning to protect ourselves by behaving as well as possible and thank God I am no longer careless as I used to be with money and passports."

Although they were "alright for money," they did have "to be very careful so I'm afraid we can't send telegrams . . . We have to be thoughtful and work out exactly what we have per day to spend on food & treats and we have managed quite well so far with cheap but clean hotels—much nicer than the grand ones anyway, and the pomfrets are learning about not wasting money, as am I."

On May Day, Puss and the boys rode on donkeys up into the hills, where they found an old church "with blue ceilings and yellow stars and frescoes of George and the dragon . . . and [St.] John holding his head on a plate which they particularly liked; I told them about John and [the island of] Samos, so we thought we'd go there." In the hope that Tommy would join them there, Puss wrote they would be taking an overnight boat to the Greek port city of Piraeus and then go by boat to Samos to find "a fisherman's cottage" on the island "where John and Mark wrote their gospels."

In her letter, Puss admitted, "We have involved ourselves in a slight incident here." After arriving on the island, she and the boys had clambered into a horse-drawn carriage for the four-hundred-yard trip from the dock to their hotel on the top of a hill. When the driver began whipping his obviously exhausted pony, Puss said, "Look, we're not in a hurry. Please, sir, will you stop beating this horse? I won't have it." Refusing to heed her plea, the driver, as Tommy would later say, just "increased punishing this poor old nag. So she took the whip off him and horse-whipped him down the hill. And then, of course, she was arrested, and the whole town sent flowers to her room, and she was the heroine, one of those wonderful English lady eccentrics, and she created a wonderful stir."

In the manner of Thomas Coryate, the fabled traveler to whom she was not related, as well as a host of other English adventurers who had journeyed where no one had ever gone before while still insisting that the traditional rules of British conduct applied, Puss did this more than once during her brief stay on the island. As she wrote Tommy on May 2, 1970, in a letter signed "Ruby" from Buyukada:

There are horse drawn carriages, the drivers use whips on the horses and I have been reported to the police for using the whips on the drivers & then breaking them; the drivers have gone to the police to ask them for 15 lira for their whips which I have refused to pay. Since they are only old sticks with rope tied on them. . . . I see no reason why they should use them on the horses. We also refused to go to the police station because I won't take the pomfrets there; the police came to our room, which is full of flowers which the waiters brought us when they heard about it. They [the police] looked rather confused and friendly. They have gone away to think about it.

Nowhere in her letter did Puss mention that she had befriended, in Charley's words, "a Turkish bloke who had a scooter and was much younger than her but good-looking and a really nice guy."

Now that her relationship with the young lord had ended, Puss again began asking Tommy to come rescue her.

Like the star-crossed lovers they had always been, Tommy was doing all he could to find Puss, but to no avail. Because she had lost her passport in Turkey and then had "papers drawn up there and then again in Greece," Tommy managed to pick up her trail in Athens from "a friend of mine who was a junior officer in Greek naval intelligence. I went to the island where they had been, but I missed them and then I had to go back to work. The next week, I went to Athens again and then to Patmos, but they were gone." For a month, Tommy followed his family around Turkey and Greece, "being just about a week late" wherever he went. As always, he was "carrying on business, importing and exporting to Afghanistan, and that was keeping me extremely busy, but between those flights, I was looking for Jake and Charley and Puss."

What Tommy did not know was that with each passing day, Puss' mental condition was deteriorating at an alarming rate. By the time she and the boys reached Samos on their way to the island of Patmos, Puss was, in Jake's words, "becoming a lot sicker and delusional and more and more unglued. She became very blue, very depressed, and very superstitious. She would only let us walk on the right side of her because the left side was evil. Compulsive behavior. She was becoming insane."

Neither boy ever saw his mother take drugs in their presence. Nor was she traveling with anything on which she could get high. Rather, Puss was now living in a permanently altered state of consciousness in which she could no longer distinguish what was real from what was not. In a travel agency on one of the islands, Charley saw a poster of a big art nouveau ship against a star field. When he asked his mother if it was really possible that ships could fly, she told him to his great amazement that they could. During this part of their journey, Puss also threatened to take her life by jumping off a roof. Furious at her and "bloody sick of it all," Jake told her to just go ahead and do it, causing her to immediately abandon the notion.

Without telling them where they were going, Puss woke Jake and Charley up in the middle of the night in their hotel room on one of the islands, bundled them up into their clothes, and began walking with them through the deserted streets of the surrounding town. When at last they came to the beach, Puss informed her sons she had brought them there to wait for the flying saucers that were coming to take them away. As Jake railed angrily at his mother for being so foolish as to think this would happen, Charley played happily with the shells and the waves. Shushing Jake, Puss told him to be patient. Soon, the flying saucers would be there.

As they sat there waiting, Jake told his mother, "You're embarrassing yourself and us." When Puss told him there was no embarrassment in waiting for a miracle, Jake became angrier. That his younger brother seemed completely oblivious to what was going on made the situation just that much worse for Jake. Constantly thrust together in situations where they were the only children, Jake and Charley, who in time would become one another's best friend and protector, each dealt with the situation in his own way.

Charley was the dreamer, lost in thought, an adept who was good at everything to which he put his hand. Jake was the organizer and the straw boss, who in his own mind always felt that he was responsible for taking care of them all. As Charley remembered, "Older brothers always see younger brothers as annoying and foolish. Jake himself would tell you that he was always difficult and irritating where I was concerned and always trying to pick fights with me." Arguing constantly, the boys fought over who had eaten what at dinner and who had been given more dessert. Although Jake and Charley loved each other deeply, they were like oil and water. And despite the fact that Jake was now acting like Puss' father, he still needed his mother to hold him at night so he could fall asleep.

As Puss sat for hours on the silent empty beach staring up at the endless canopy of brilliant stars above, she pointed out the various constellations to Jake, among them Castor and Pollux, the twin brothers who in Roman mythology had shared their immortality. When the flying saucers did not come to rescue them, proving that Jake had been right in saying there was no magic carpet or instant escape route to another place, Puss gathered up the boys and took them back to their hotel. They awoke the next day only to find that Puss was no better, a situation made more desperate because no one but Jake and Charley even knew she was in trouble.

Possessed by the notion that she was meant to find some form of personal salvation on the island where St. John the Divine had received the apocalyptic vision that caused him to write the Book of Revelation, Puss went with the boys to Patmos. From Skala, the main town on the island, she led Jake and Charley along the trail to the Holy Cave, where John had foreseen the end of the world and the coming of the Second Messiah. Falling down inside the cave, Puss struck her head against the rock on which John had slept and which was said to still bear the indentation of his head. Although she was "bleeding and a little shaky," the boys managed to get her back to their hotel.

Waking up in the middle of the night, Puss decided to go for a swim in just her T-shirt and panties to an nearby island. "As she came walking back to the hotel down the main street," Jake recalled, "all the men of the town began following along behind her, howling like a pack of dogs and laughing and coming on to her." What was seen as a shameful act of public exhibitionism caused such an uproar that the local police promptly put Puss, Jake, and Charley on a boat to Athens.

"Okay," Charley would later say, "she looked for flying saucers and she swam out to the island, but a lot of it was internal. We were living perfectly well in hotels, and she was a mom and she took care of us a lot more than Tommy would have. Swimming out to that island was a self-destructive act. As Jenny Ponte says, those whom the gods love, they first make mad. In Africa, they say if they miss you on the other side, they call you back. What was she doing swimming out to an island? What was she looking for? Something was calling her."

At the British Embassy in Athens, the consul arranged a flight back to England for Puss, Jake, and Charley for which the Foreign Office would later ask Jenny Ponte to pay. Still grieving for Camel, who had died just five months earlier, Priscilla, who had never been able to bear such situations, did not come to the airport to greet Puss and the boys when they arrived in London. In her stead, Priscilla sent her oldest daughter, Mary, who herself had just given birth to a son. "It was just so awful," Mary said, "because Jake was in charge of her. Puss wasn't really there at all, and I couldn't believe Jake and Charley had managed to get her back, because she was absolutely off her head."

With nowhere to live in London, Puss went to visit her old friend Juliet Harmer at her cottage in Gloucestershire. Because Puss "was not capable of looking after them," Jake and Charley had been "put to stay" with a "lovely, apple cheeked" farmer's wife in Marlborough in nearby Wiltshire. Puss and Juliet visited the boys and took them out for the day. When Juliet told Puss that she should be with her sons on a full-time basis, Puss' very telling reply was, "No, no, they're happy there. She'll look after them fine." Doing all she could to help her friend, Juliet took Puss to look for a cottage. After Puss found one "in which she wanted to live," she "rang up her trustee to ask if he could send her a check, but he was making it difficult and they all thought she was not in a fit state to live down here." In no better shape than she had been before, Puss returned to her sister Mary's house in Oxford.

Mary, who had been deputized by her mother to take charge of Puss, consulted a general practitioner, who told her the situation was "very serious" and persuaded a psychiatrist from Oxford to come see her in Berkshire. "He was a terribly nice man," Mary said, "and he came out that night and said, 'She'll have to be committed.' I said I would drive her to the hospital in Oxford the next day. That night, she stood on the stairs being catatonic, and I watched her and worried. Feeling like a brute, I then drove her to a hospital where she didn't want to go. She didn't want to leave Jake and Charley. And I didn't know what to do with her, either."

On July 3, 1970, Puss was admitted as an "informal patient" to the Warneford Hospital for Mental Disorders in Oxford. At some point, two registered medical practitioners and an approved social worker submitted written statements that Puss was suffering from a mental illness or a psychopathic disorder so severe as to warrant hospitalization, thereby causing her to be officially "certified" or "sectioned" under the relevant provisions of the Mental Health Act of 1959.

So long as there was no objection from the person officially designated as Puss' nearest relative, the responsible medical officer in charge of the case could hospitalize Puss against her wishes for various periods of time and authorize the use of antipsychotic medications and electroconvulsive therapy. Convinced this was now the only option available to them, those trying to care for Puss had no idea how grievous the consequences of what seemed like a necessary legal step would eventually prove to be.

15

warneford and bowden house

An imposing gothic castle set on 160 acres of land atop Headington Hill in Oxford, the Warneford Lunatic Asylum, as it was then known, first opened its doors in 1826. In the belief that fresh air and views of the surrounding countryside could help those who had lost their mental equilibrium, it had been built "to recreate the atmosphere of a gentleman's country house" and was intended "for the accommodation of lunatics selected from the higher classes of society."

Surrounded by "very strange people who were nodding and bouncing," Puss was never a willing patient at the Warneford. "I went to see her there a couple of times," Jenny Ponte remembered, "and it was a terrible place. A complete, old-fashioned Victorian prison, and she absolutely loathed it. I remember a nurse coming into her room one night and saying, 'We must eat up our fish fingers, Mrs. Weber.' And Puss turned around and, as saucily as you like, said 'You eat the fucking fish fingers.' So there was still a spark left in her even then."

Which was not to say that Puss was also in her right mind. In Jenny's words, "She was mad as a hatter. She had that schizophrenic thing of thinking that if you looked at her, she would shatter like glass. Amongst all the real loonies there, she walked around like a shadow in a world of her own, listening to these voices. That was when I lost touch with her, really. Because you couldn't communicate with her. I just tried to love her like I always had."

As Jenny's husband, Alan Ponte, would later note, "They say of the Warneford that it gets more first-class degrees than any other college in Oxford. Meaning that everybody who has a breakdown at Oxford goes there and then comes out and gets a first-class degree. But it was just a horrid Victorian Gothic lunatic asylum with padded walls and horrid Gothic doors with bolts on them. Puss didn't like it, and of course, Jenny was appalled by it."

Using a brush and black ink on sheets of paper glued together to form what looked more like a child's attempt at calligraphy than a letter, Puss wrote Jake and Charley from the Warneford on July 23, 1970:

beloved pomfrets,
sometimes i am so sad I just don't know what to do. I try to laugh and think of you.

I have read too many books in my lifetime and it is because I am very frightened now that I am trying not to anymore. please: do pay attention: books are dangerous.

There is no way out of here, unless it is by magickall [sic] flying saucer. my family are determined to teach me manners. I know I haven't got any. what can I do? I miss you. Everything that went before I feel acute nostalgia for. I love you, please send me pictures, pray for us but warning; prayers are awefully [sic] dangerous too;

love Ruby Mama
XOX

Sorrowfully [with a drawing of a heart]

At the Warneford, Puss also wrote "reams" about visions that seemed to have come straight out of the poetry of William Blake.

She also talked about "Monster," a friend whom only she could see, and how Monster would save her. Although it took some time for those treating her at the Warneford to determine the exact nature of her illness, due to all the drugs she had been taking, they eventually concluded Puss was suffering from LSD-influenced schizophrenia, the same condition that ended Syd Barrett's career as Pink Floyd's guiding genius.

The desperate situation in which Puss now found herself was further complicated when Tommy returned to London after yet another smuggling expedition only to learn to his great horror that the unimaginable had finally happened. While he had been gone, Puss had fallen into the clutches of her family, whom he had never trusted, and been sent off to languish in an institution where, as he saw it, she should never have been put at all.

"I just wanted to get her out of there as soon as possible," Tommy said later. "I thought she just needed care by her family. I had no idea they were going to put her into a proper loony bin. It was disgraceful. That was what finally threw her as well, when she learned she had been certified by her own sister and, I think, her mother. The day she discovered that was the day she died. There was no way of covering up the disappointment when she realized her family had turned her in and thrown in the towel. I think it broke her heart."

Going full bore into his white knight/Soho gangster mode, Tommy, who was now living in Markham Square off the King's Road in Chelsea, set off with Charlotte Rampling for what he perceived to be the headquarters of the evil Coriat family empire. As Mary would later say, "He turned up in my house with Charlotte Rampling. It was very, very hot, and I couldn't think what to do with them. I was a bit worried about Tommy because he was furious with me for sending Puss to the hospital, and he was strong and I was alone in the house with my children. So I said I would take them swimming at a friend's pool."

What had been a dark and foreboding melodrama soon transformed itself into an English comedy of manners. Because Charlotte had not brought a bathing suit with her, Mary offered to let her wear one of her bikinis. "She didn't like any of them, but she said she would wear my broderie anglaise [a form of white English embroidery] bra and knickers. So I thought, 'Okay. Fine.' And she continued to wear them all day long after having swum in them. When my husband got back from the office with his briefcase, there was this sort of vision in our kitchen in my very expensive broderie anglaise bra and knickers from Liberty's, and she said, 'I'm Charlotte.' And he said, 'Oh yes. I'm Charles.'"

In photographs taken in the south of France before Tommy's visit to Mary's home, Charlotte sits in a tiny white shelf bra and panties alongside a bare-chested Tommy in front of a thick green hedge. With cocaine having stripped all the flesh from the bones of his face so that it has become a geometric arrangement of razor-sharp planes and angles and his long blonde hair hanging down to his shoulders, Tommy looks like a fierce Viking warrior who would have been perfectly happy to do whatever he could to free Puss from distress.

The most telling image is of Jake. The spitting image of his father with his own blonde hair falling over his eyes in a Prince Valiant cut, he stares at the camera with a heartbreaking look of utter confusion on his face. The picture of a lost child, he seems completely dwarfed by Charlotte and Tommy, the two impossibly beautiful adults by whom he is surrounded.

After he had spent a fairly civilized day relaxing in the sun with Charlotte and Mary, Tommy began ringing up Mary's husband on a regular basis to say that "terrible things were going to happen" to him if Puss was not immediately released from the Warneford. "He was so threatening," Mary said, "that we actually moved to my mother-in-law's house in Oxford because we got so worried. God knows what Jake and Charley were going through. Jake was at primary school with my daughter in Chilton Foliat in Wiltshire. He was adorable and didn't ask very many questions." Along with his older brother, Charley also attended the school.

By appealing to Puss' trustee, Jenny finally managed to get Puss released from the Warneford on September 5, 1970. Twelve days later, she was readmitted, remaining there until October 13, 1970. Upon being discharged, Puss was put on a monthly dose of twenty-five milligrams of Modecate, a powerful antipsychotic medication. Twice a day, she was to take twenty-five milligrams of Artane, a drug that was used to treat Parkinson's disease and that helped control the side effects caused by her other medications. She was also instructed to take a nightly dose of one hundred grams of Mellaril, another antipsychotic drug used to ease the pain of alcohol and opiate withdrawal, and, if required at night, one or two tabs of Mogadon, a sleeping pill and an anticonvulsant.

Taken in combination, this powerful cocktail of drugs, two of which are no longer used to treat schizophrenia because of side effects that include "shaking, stiffness, and facial tics" were intended to make Puss "robotic and compliant." The drugs also caused Puss to gain a good deal of weight without bringing about any positive change in her mental state. She was scheduled to enter the Richmond Fellowship facility, "a sort of halfway house" in Oxford, until Tommy, in Mary's words, "rode in like a knight on a white charger and took her away from there. Mummy didn't want to have her, and I said I couldn't cope with having Jake and Charley and the whole thing being so frightening with Tommy. I wanted a rest, so Jenny said she would have her. And I think she [Puss] was just incredibly miserable. She couldn't see who she wanted to be anymore."

Leaving Mary's house, Puss moved in with Jenny and Alan Ponte where they were then living outside Ardeley, a tiny village in Hertfordshire. "To some extent," Alan Ponte said later, "she was certainly classically mad. She would say something and then answer it and turn it completely on its head. It was just sort of a jumble, and there were moments when she seemed entirely normal. One would fall into the trap of responding to her, and you'd suddenly find yourself falling down a well of noncommunication. So that was difficult. She was, after all, Jenny's baby sister, and Jake and Charley were young. And that was why Jenny really wanted to try and give it a go at home absolutely against all categorical warnings."

Tommy, who believed that Puss would be right as rain again if only she was given the right care, then interceded once more. In March 1971, he arranged for her to be admitted to Bowden House, "a private nursing home in Harrow, which was also the drying-out paddock for the rich and famous."

Overlooking the lush, green playing fields of the very exclusive Harrow School with a view of London off to the east, Bowden House was a big redbrick manor at the end of a cobbled, tree-lined driveway atop Sudbury Hill Road in Harrow. Surrounded by shrubs, hedges, and towering trees in which big, black crows roosted, the main building and adjoining cottage housed no more than twenty-five patients at a time. With large, high-ceilinged rooms from which ornate brass chandeliers hung, the facility was a far cry from the Dickensian nightmare of the Warneford.

At Bowden House, Puss was soon befriended by a fellow patient. As either luck or fate would have it, Anita Pallenberg was then also at the facility, undergoing detoxification treatment for heroin use so she could join her companion Keith Richards of the Rolling Stones and their young son, Marlon, when they moved to the south of France. Although the ravishing Italian-born actress had by then appeared in seven movies, among them *Barbarella* starring Jane Fonda, she was better known for having been the girlfriend of the Stones' founder, Brian Jones, before leaving him to live with Richards.

During the filming of *Performance*, which had not yet been released because of its sexual content, Pallenberg had begun a torrid on-set affair with her costar, Mick Jagger. The Rolling Stones' lead singer, who also happened to be Keith Richards' good friend and song-writing partner, was himself then keeping company with Pallenberg's close friend Marianne Faithfull.

A stunning blonde beauty with an outsized personality whom no one could control, Pallenberg had turned both Jones and Richards on to LSD for the first time. She had become such a powerful influence on the Rolling Stones that she was considered by many, herself included, as an unofficial member of the band. At Bowden House, Pallenberg, who like Puss was then twenty-seven years old, was also being given Mogadon as part of what was then known as the sleeping cure for heroin addiction.

This course of treatment proved spectacularly unsuccessful because "Spanish Tony" Sanchez, whom Marianne Faithfull would later call "the dealer by appointment to the Rolling Stones," kept visiting Pallenberg at Bowden House with flowers and a gram of cocaine. On a regular basis, Pallenberg was also leaving the facility to score heroin from Sanchez in London, thereby causing her doctor to inform Keith Richards at one point that Pallenberg now had more heroin in her system than when she had first been admitted to the facility for treatment.

Intensely attracted to one another, Puss and Pallenberg began partying together with illicit drugs supplied by Sanchez. Their favorite song was "Leader of the Pack" by the Shangri-Las, and the two women loved singing it together. While Puss and Pallenberg were at Bowden House, as Tommy later confirmed, the two women became lovers.

It was through Pallenberg that Puss, who for the past year had been calling herself "Ruby Tuesday" after the well-known Stones' song, finally met the man who along with Brian Jones had written its haunting melody and then come up with its title while leafing through a fashion magazine one day. After downing a few margaritas one night and then doing a snort of cocaine, Richards decided to visit Pallenberg at Bowden House. Leaping into his pink Bentley with his friend, Stones' photographer Michael Cooper,

Richards crashed his car into an iron fence while entering Harrow at high speed.

Grabbing all the drugs with which they had been traveling, Richards and Cooper made a run for it, only to stumble willy-nilly into the front garden of the house where Stones' pianist Nicky Hopkins was living. Leaving his wrecked car behind as though someone else had been driving it, Richards then phoned for a limo to take him the rest of the way. When he called Pallenberg at Bowden House to explain why he was late, she screamed hysterically that if he did not get there soon with some heroin, she would check out of the facility immediately.

After what can only be described as a very harrowing journey to Harrow, Richards arrived with enough dope to get Pallenberg through the night. In a setting so surreal that it could have come from a play by Eugene Ionesco or Jean Paul Sartre, Pallenberg then introduced Puss to the man who, in "Ruby Tuesday," had created the indelible image of a woman whom no one knew and who was dying all the time but who was still determined to catch her dreams before they slipped away. In many ways, the description fit Puss perfectly. Richards himself seems to have approved of Puss, thereby paving her entry into the Stones' inner circle.

At Bowden House, Puss was also visited by Tommy, who somehow managed to spend the night with her in bed. As Tommy said, "Puss was not nearly as ill as Anita. She was still very much in love with me, but she couldn't have been all there, because she thought I was God. God was speaking to her through me."

In part, Tommy's renewed interest in Puss was sparked by the end of his relationship with Charlotte Rampling. After having lived with Tommy for three years, a remarkable amount of time, considering his utterly chaotic lifestyle during this period, she had decided to leave him in January 1971. In her words, "He was getting high every day, and it became nasty drugs. He said he wasn't doing heroin, but I knew he was, because I found the needles. And I thought, 'Oh, the dealer's coming round,' and I got really spooked, and I said, 'This is not on.'"

Throughout their time together, Tommy had never liked her "going off and was controlling in a very clever way because he was so charming." Leaving him behind in London, she went to America to do a "really weird movie called *The Ski Bum*, which was all about drugs. Everyone was completely drugged in that film, on screen and off, but I used it as an escape. I just said, 'Okay, I'm out of here,' and literally just left everything and went with hardly a suitcase. Because I realized it was all going wrong." Shortly after returning to England when the film was done, she decided to get married because "Tommy really wanted me back, and I needed to be protected against that because I knew I would go back. I needed to have a blueprint for sort of a normal life if I was going to survive. Because I could be very like Tommy, too."

Long after they had gone their separate ways, she recalled, "I don't dream that much about people I've been with, [but] he is somebody who has always haunted me, but in a really good way. When I say *haunted*, I mean someone you carry along with you, because the times we spent together were quite unique. We were young in extraordinary times, and I was right in them with somebody who was completely one hundred per cent in them. So I was able to ride on that wave, which was in me, anyway, and I had the perfect companion for it." After they parted company, she never saw Tommy again.

With his smuggling connections in Afghanistan having dried up and Charlotte gone from his life for good, Tommy was once more on his own and up for anything. For him, a brand-new world of possibilities of every kind suddenly opened up when he visited Puss at Bowden House. To his great amazement, Tommy discovered that Anita Pallenberg, whom he had met some years earlier in the south of France and immediately set his sights upon as one "of the top girls in the world," was not only in residence but also involved with Puss.

As Charley later said, "Bowden House was a very strange scene. Jake and I went to see Puss there, and it was very depressing. Anita was very sick, and when we walked in one day, Anita thought Jake was her son Marlon, and I just remember thinking, 'This is the strangest.' You can imagine the two of them in there. It was like Angelina Jolie and Wynona Ryder in *Girl, Interrupted*. Puss and I were always intimate and very close any time we were together, but she was distant and in another space. And I remember being freaked out by the whole scene."

Meeting Jake and Charley only served to inspire Pallenberg, who loved hatching mad fantasy plans that she would then somehow make come true, to begin spinning a black spider's web of dreams for Puss and Tommy and the boys. If Tommy could bring a large amount of cocaine with him to France as a wedding present for Mick Jagger, who was scheduled to marry Bianca Perez Morena de Macias in St. Tropez on May 12, 1971, he and the boys could stay with Keith Richards and Pallenberg at their new home in Villefranche until Puss could come join them. As Jake and Charley played with Marlon Richards in the brilliant sunshine of the French Riviera, Tommy and Puss could put their marriage and their family back together while living in rock 'n' roll splendor with the Rolling Stones.

For Tommy, the invitation was far too tempting to resist. But before he could put Pallenberg's plan into action, the doctors treating Puss at Bowden House decided that since the drugs she had been given were not helping, she would now be subjected to electroconvulsive therapy (ECT), more commonly known as electroshock treatment.

At the time, ECT was administered to patients who were fully conscious. Most likely on an every-other-day basis, Puss was placed in restraints with a rubber guard in her mouth so she would not bite through her tongue. Electrodes were then placed on either side of her head, and a sine-wave current of anywhere from 225 to 450 volts of electricity was shot through her brain for as long as a second, causing her to suffer a seizure lasting for at least fifteen seconds. Known side effects of the treatment include memory loss, confusion, cardiac arrest, and brain hemorrhaging.

Although, in Jenny Ponte's words, "Puss was terrified of the electric shock treatment and absolutely loathed it," she had already been certified and so was given ECT without her consent. As Jake said, "Anita said she came back one morning after they had given Puss the treatment, and she [Anita Pallenberg] was so terrified that she left that morning. She was scared for herself because she thought she was next, and so she booked out of there." Boarding a plane to France, Pallenberg joined Richards and their son Marlon at Villa Nellcote, a sumptuous mansion overlooking the sea near Villefranche, during the first week in May.

At Bowden House, Puss was now completely alone. Because all her medical records from that facility have been lost, there is no way of knowing how many sessions of ECT she underwent or precisely how long she remained there after Pallenberg fled to the south of France. After Puss was discharged, she went to live with Jenny and Alan Ponte in Ardeley while continuing regular outpatient treatment with a psychiatrist in London.

"We visited her at Ardeley," Jake said, "and it was a shock to me. She was so overweight and depressed that she couldn't bear to even speak to us. She had always been warm to us, but now she was so remote. She was literally barking at the moon. Talking to the trees and seeing visions and having acid flashbacks. She was not there. All she wanted to do was die."

Choosing to believe that Puss would soon be well enough to join him and the boys in the south of France, Tommy set about implementing Pallenberg's plan. After he had obtained what may have been as much as a kilogram of cocaine, Tommy flew with Jake and Charley on his customary smuggler's route from London to Ireland. Changing planes, he then continued with the boys to Nice.

Thanks to the very impressive wedding present he had brought with him, Tommy was welcomed as an honored guest at Villa Nellcote. With his usual reckless abandon, he quickly plunged into the never-ending round of pleasure that passed for daily life in that house on the French Riviera.

At Villa Nellcote during the month of May, Richards, Pallenberg, and Tommy often talked of Puss and how fabulous it would be when she finally walked through the great front door of the house. What with all the hubbub and commotion brought about by Mick Jagger's front-page wedding to Bianca as well as the constant stream of very stoned and famous visitors through the house, the talk remained just that, and nothing more.

As Jake recalled, "Dad was so busy hanging out with the Stones that he didn't get on plane to go get her. Instead, he was just waiting for her." At Villa Nellcote, everyone knew Puss was coming. When she would actually get there eventually proved to be not just a matter of time, but another story altogether.

16
ardeley

Once again, Puss was living with Alan and Jenny Ponte at Ardeleybury, a sixteenth-century redbrick mansion with fifty-six rooms and three Norman towers surrounded by a deep, dry moat on a gated estate John Lennon had once wanted to buy because the house resembled "a fairy-tale castle." Puss, who still seemed "pretty mad" to Jenny but "also okay" in her own way, soon struck up a friendship with the very pretty Italian girl who worked as one of Jenny's au pairs. Still desperately missing Jake and Charley, Puss seemed to be adjusting well to the circumstances in which she now found herself.

Every Monday, Puss would go on her own to London to see a psychiatrist who had already warned Alan and Jenny Ponte that it was a mistake to let Puss to live with them. Sooner or later, he believed, she was bound to try to kill herself again. The consequences of her doing so in their home would be unimaginable for all concerned. Disregarding his advice, Alan and Jenny gave Puss a room of her own in their "Gothic castle" of a house and did their best to cope with her behavior.

Puss, who had always been obsessed with her appearance, now felt mortified by how much weight she had put on. In part because the drugs she had been given served to stimulate her appetite, she ate manically and often went down to the kitchen in the middle of the night to raid the refrigerator. Although it infuriated Alan, Jenny actually put padlocks on all the refrigerator doors to keep Puss from opening them at night, only to then remove them again. So far as the Pontes could tell, Puss had settled into a comfortable routine and seemed more stable in many ways than she had been at the Warneford or Bowden House.

Before flying to the south of France with Jake and Charley, Tommy had come to visit Puss at Ardeleybury and again ended up spending the night with her in bed. Although Alan Ponte was so angry about what he viewed as Tommy having taken unfair advantage of Puss that the two men nearly came to blows, Jenny was "thrilled to bits" by what had happened. She believed that if Puss did join Tommy in France, the two of them could put their marriage back together and again begin caring for their two young sons.

At some point, Puss left Ardeleybury to visit her old friend Juliet Harmer in Gloucestershire. During the visit, the two women ran into the well-known British sculptor Lynn Chadwick at the local pub. When Chadwick asked Puss what she did, Juliet was surprised to hear her friend reply, "I am a mother." In "the early days of feminism," this was not the response Juliet had expected Puss to make. Later, she would come to believe the statement was "a key" to her friend's "very complex personality."

Juliet also took Puss to the Chichester Festival Theatre in Sussex to see eighty-three-year-old Dame Edith Evans' final performance in *The Seagull*, by Chekhov. Near the house in Chichester where her parents lived, Harmer and Puss heard a nightingale sing. Puss later described the event in a letter to Jake and Charley: "may is the most beautiful month in England full of lilac and magnolia and blossoms and nightingale. Have you ever heard one?"

As he had sat in the garden of the Spaniard's Inn in Hampstead in May 1819, two years before his death at the age of twenty-six, John Keats had written "Ode to a Nightingale," a poem that Puss knew well in which the poet expresses his reaction to the bird's melodious song:

> Now more than ever seems it rich to die,
> To cease upon the midnight with no pain,
> While thou art pouring forth thy soul abroad
> In such an ecstasy!

In her letter to Jake and Charley, who were now in France and whom she addressed not as the "pomfrets" but as the "pommes frites," Puss expressed her great love for her sons with an almost Buddhist kind of detachment:

I am very happy to think of you in the sunshine with Anita and Marlon; very nice people. . . . Juliet and I spent nights by the fire talking and making discoveries which you make all the time because your heads are new and not filled with memories and hopes, but we make only when we stop talking and thinking in tiny spaces which we call the present which goes on for ever when we don't choose to divide it into past and future and label it, as daddy says that is quite a mistake, to put names on things, because as soon as things have names they are sorted into divisions instead of remaining simple. For instance i think 'I miss jake and charley' and this hurts because i have names for this feeling but really the thing i 'miss' is contained inside me because i love you and if i didn't have a name for either it would be part of the same feeling. difficult to explain . . .

My life is very empty without you but I am exploring emptiness. What is empty? an O is empty. it is also full of space you see. . . .

. . . send me some pictures please my pommes frites and news of you and photographs if possible yes please.

lots of love, Mummy XXXXX

Before Puss could go to France to join Tommy, Jake, and Charley, she needed her passport. When she asked her trustee for it, he informed Puss that because she had been certified and was still under the care of a doctor who had specifically ordered that she not be allowed to travel, he could not give it to her. For Puss, as for her mother and grandmother before her, it was the curse of the Maple family fortune all over again. Ever since she had been a child, a court-appointed solicitor had been in control of her destiny.

Although Puss had never tried to hurt anyone but herself, she had, over the past year, been medicated against her will, confined to two mental institutions, and subjected to electroshock treatment. That she could not leave the country until someone else deemed her fit to do so was a crushing blow. Already headed down a road from which there was no return, Puss took her trustee's refusal to let her have her passport as a sign that she was meant to never leave England again.

On Monday, June 7, 1971, Puss left Ardeleybury for her regular weekly visit to her doctor in London. Before going, Jenny hugged Puss and kissed her good-bye. "Do take care of yourself," she told her younger sister. Taking Jenny's face in her hands, Puss replied, "I'll try to." To Jenny, Puss' calm demeanor that day meant that the peaceful country atmosphere was making her feel better. In truth, Puss had already made her decision, coming up with what everyone would later grudgingly admit was a clever and very well devised plan.

In London, Puss persuaded a psychiatrist who may not have been her regular doctor that Alan and Jenny Ponte were about to take her with them on a three-week holiday to France. Because her regular weekly prescription for Mogadon would not be enough to tide her over until she returned, Puss asked the doctor to give her a month's worth of sleeping tablets. Believing her story, he did as she had asked.

After getting the prescription filled by a chemist, Puss checked into a seedy hotel for commercial travelers at 30 Sussex Gardens near the Paddington tube stop in central London. Either to make it harder for anyone to pump her stomach or because she knew that food would help her keep down what may have been as many as sixty sleeping tablets, Puss brought a pack of hot dogs and a half bottle of whiskey with her to the room.

As she ate the hot dogs, drank the whiskey, and swallowed the pills, Puss wrote a note that said, "To Jake and Charley, my darlings, I still love you." Lying on the bed in a long green velvet dress in a London hotel where she would never have stayed by choice, twenty-seven-year-old Susan Ann Caroline Coriat ended her life in a world where, as Keats wrote,

> men sit and hear each other groan;
> Where palsy shakes a few, sad, last grey hairs,
> Where youth grows pale, and spectre-thin, and dies;
> Where but to think is to be full of sorrow
> And leaden-eyed despairs;
> Where beauty cannot keep her lustrous eyes,
> Or new Love pine at them beyond to-morrow.

When Puss did not return to Ardeleybury that night, Jenny became frantic. Alan told her it was not as though they could ring the London Metropolitan Police and ask them to go looking for Puss. The next day, Jenny, who was then running a company that made clothing for boys, was in the factory with the ladies who did the sewing when the manager came over to say, "Jenny, you're wanted on the phone." When she picked up the receiver, the trustee who handled both Puss' and Jenny's affairs said, "Jennifer, I hate to tell you. But Susan is dead." Dropping the phone, Jenny burst into tears.

Because someone had to identify the body before an inquest could be held, Alan Ponte went to London to perform the task. In a long green velvet dress with a cross on it that made it resemble a medieval mantle and a white cloth on her head, Puss looked beautiful to him, even in death. In "floods of tears," the young policeman who had discovered the body told Alan that Puss was "the most beautiful thing he had ever seen in his life."

Six days later, on June 14, 1971, the coroner for Inner West London conducted the official inquest. He determined that the cause of the death of the former wife of "Thomas Weber, a Company Director," was "tricholorethanol poisoning, self administered while suffering from schizo-affective disorder—killed herself."

Because Jenny wanted to bury her younger sister under a Gothic arch in the graveyard of the thirteenth-century Church of St. Lawrence in Ardeley, she and Alan had to get special permission from the parish priest to do so. On what Jenny recalled as "the most beautiful summer's day" anyone had ever seen in June, Puss' sister Mary and her husband, Charles; Priscilla Coriat and her son, Christopher, walked with Alan and Jenny up the drive from Ardeleybury to the ancient rough-stone church with a crenellated tower. Jenny and Mary had gathered wildflowers and fashioned them into great bouquets that they carried with him as they walked. The only other flowers at the service were "millions of lilies sent by the Rolling Stones." The parish priest, with whom "Puss had gotten on very well," conducted the service. After it was over, the note Puss had left behind for Jake and Charley was buried with her.

After the funeral, everyone went back to Ardeleybury, where Mary's husband, who had a beautiful voice, began to sing. As everyone sat around in shock wondering how this could have happened to someone so young and beautiful who still had two young children to live for, it seemed only right there was music because Puss had been the nightingale and now her song was done. Tommy, Jake, and Charley did not attend the funeral. As Jenny would later say of her sister's death, "It was absolutely the worst thing that had ever happened to me in my life. Bar none. Apart from my former husband and my children, I loved her the most of anyone I've ever known."

At some point, Puss had told Jenny that if she ever did kill herself, she would come back from the other side to see her if she could. For three weeks after Puss died, the front doorbell at Arde-leybury would suddenly begin ringing in the middle of the night, causing all the dogs to howl. Alan Ponte would go downstairs with a screwdriver to pry the bell out so the ringing would stop. The next night, the same thing would happen all over again. As Jenny said later, "I'm sure it was Puss, trying to get back in again to see me."

17
villa nellcote

For Tommy and the boys, the party at Villa Nellcote had started as soon as they walked through the front door, only to be greeted like conquering heroes by Keith Richards and Anita Pallenberg. The warmth of their welcome was directly related to the wedding gift that Pallenberg had asked Tommy to bring with him to the south of France when she and Puss were still at Bowden House. While a kilo of cocaine was a staggering amount of dope for anyone to smuggle personally across foreign borders even then, the way in which Tommy had done so won him immediate respect in that great white mansion by the sea.

After procuring the cocaine in England, Tommy flew to Ireland with Jake and Charley. Changing planes, they then boarded a Bulgarian airliner on which Tommy had booked them all the way to Sofia. Covering his tracks, Tommy got off the plane with the boys when it stopped in Paris and took an internal flight to Nice, where they all had to pass through French customs before Keith Richards' driver could pick them up at the airport.

In London, Tommy had divided the cocaine into two equal loads that he then taped to each of his sons. "It was more than a pound," Jake recalled. "Probably a kilo. He divided it into four packets and taped it front and back so our entire chest and back was covered with masking tape over plastic wrapped in a T-shirt so we wouldn't sweat from carrying it, which might have made the tape come off."

At the airport, Tommy was charming the daylights out of a female airline employee at the ticket counter when he suddenly caught a glimpse of the tape peeking out of Charley's shirt. Breaking off the conversation by saying he had to take his boys to the bathroom, Tommy collected their tickets and led Charley into a stall so he could readjust the tape beneath his son's shirt. As Charley, who was then six years old, said later, "All smugglers have tape issues, and Tommy was no exception. He had an obsession with tape."

Charley, who was still too young to know or care about what was going on, took what they were doing in stride. In Tommy's words, Jake "knew what was happening and that what we were doing was very dangerous. How he agreed to do it, I just don't know." In Jake's words, "There was no voting going on. It was just, 'Shirts off, and let me stick this on your back.'" Because Tommy looked exactly like someone trying to bring illegal substances into the Republic of France, the customs officer at the Nice airport immediately singled him out and began patting him down while searching his pockets.

Convinced his father was about to be taken away in handcuffs, Jake, then eight years old, made what he would later call a joke, saying, "Aren't you going to search us?" Caught off-guard by the remark, Tommy glared at Jake with an angry, frightened look on his face. Distracted by this unscripted moment of conflict between Tommy and Jake, the customs officer backed off and waved what he now saw as just another rich and eccentric upper-class English family bound for a late spring holiday on the French Riviera into the country.

When they all arrived at Nellcote, Tommy presented Richards and Pallenberg with what she had asked him to bring with him.

"The difference between Jake and me," Charley recalled, "was that when we got there with the drugs on us, Jake was a bit more of a momma's boy. He didn't want them to rip the tape off. Where I was like, 'Just take the fucking tape off.' Jake was more upset."

In the end, the coke Tommy brought with him to the south of France never did find its way to Mick Jagger as a wedding present. In Tommy's words, "Because it was much too much, Keith took it over, and it became his bag for the whole of summer. He said I'd be paid, but I never was." Tommy's impressive gift did, however, make him part of the inner circle at Villa Nellcote. "I know a lot of people would never talk to Tommy after they heard that story," Charley said later. "But I was just quite happy to be there."

While Jake and Charley played happily with young Marlon Richards in the sand pile strewn with toys by the winding stairs that led down to the private beach behind the house, Richards, Pallenberg, and Tommy began getting ready for the wedding of the year. Shortly before Mick Jagger was to wed his beautiful pregnant girlfriend, Bianca, in nearby St. Tropez on Wednesday, May 12, 1971, a chartered plane from London landed in Nice with seventy-five wedding guests. Among them were Paul and Linda McCartney, Ringo and Maureen Starr, Eric Clapton and Alice Ormsby-Gore, Ronnie Lane, Ronnie Wood, Jimmy Miller, Stephen Stills, Roger Vadim, and Lord Patrick Litchfield. As one of the Stones' people in London said at the time, "If the plane had gone down, there would be no music business."

Confirming that what Tommy had brought with him to the south of France never made into the hands of the groom, Mick Jagger phoned Spanish Tony Sanchez in London with the request that he bring three grams of coke with him to the wedding. The ceremony itself, conducted at the town hall in St. Tropez, was a media circus of major proportions, with a good deal of the world press pushing and shoving to get inside. Arriving late as always, Keith Richards, the best man, and Anita Pallenberg ended up sitting on the bride's side of the aisle. Along with Marlon Richards, Jake and Charley served as pageboys, an honor that must have pleased Tommy no end.

"The wedding was very funny," Charley would later say. "We were all there with big flowers. Jake gave Bianca a flower and kissed her. I gave her a flower and kissed her. Marlon was like, 'I'm not going to kiss her.' So I grabbed his flower, gave it to her, and kissed her again. Because she was pretty hot." After the wedding, the party at the Hotel Bibylos, featuring an all-star rock 'n' roll jam with everyone but Richards, who by then had already passed out in the balcony, went on all night long.

After the wedding, everyone but former Cream lead guitarist Eric Clapton and his girlfriend Alice Ormsby-Gore boarded the plane for the chartered flight back to London. Then in the early throes of what would become an ever-worsening addiction to heroin, Clapton was, as Tommy would later say, "clucking," a Cockney term for craving heroin while trying to withdraw. Not knowing where else to turn, Ormsby-Gore rang up Richards at Villa Nellcote to ask for help.

When Richards, who was himself clean at the time, told her there was nothing he could do, Tommy protested his decision: "Christ, you can't leave him like that." Richards' succinct response was, "Fuck him. He shouldn't have come out here if he didn't have his shit together." Although there were few people on the planet willing to confront Richards on any matter whatsoever, Tommy was not about to let the matter drop. Arguing that they had to do something for Clapton, Tommy continued the discussion until Richards finally said, "If you want to do it on your own, you can take the driver and go to Marseilles and sort him out. But you'll find that he'll be on your back."

As Tommy recalled, "Keith was just saying Clapton was a fool to come out there and not have made his own arrangements. He was a rich man. I didn't really understand it was that simple. I thought a bit of Red Cross work would be all right. So I went and scored for him in Marseilles and sent the driver in to take care of him. For which I was later paid back by the driver blowing the whistle on Keith in one of those outrageous centerfold spreads in the Sunday papers about the whole thing, the kids, and the wedding present. It was appalling."

In the world according to Keith Richards, Tommy had now distinguished himself for the second time in the short space of a few weeks. Like an Eagle Scout intent on earning as many merit badges as possible, Tommy cemented his standing in the house on Saturday, May 22, 1971, by escorting Richards and Pallenberg through Monte Carlo on the day before the Monaco Grand Prix in a manner that blew even their minds.

To his delight, Tommy discovered that Jackie Stewart, who won the race that year, was being followed around the course by a documentary film crew. "It was the same film crew I knew from *Three*, Jimmy Salter's film," Tommy said. "They recognized me, and I had a photographer's pass, and Keith and Anita had privileged passes, which meant we could go anywhere. Most of the marshals were English and had known me since my days of racing in England, so we were allowed to walk the whole circuit of Monte Carlo from the start to the finish line, up the hill on the right side of the road, round to the square by the Hotel de Paris and the casino, down past the Metropole, down past the station, and into the tunnel, where there was a restaurant overhanging the rocks you can't see from the road."

At a time when no one outside Mexico was drinking it, Tommy was also "carrying a bottle of tequila, which we consumed on our way round the circuit." Greeting many of the drivers like old friends as he and Richards, who had always loved fast cars, and Pallenberg, who just liked to have fun in the most outrageous manner possible, they "staggered around in a haze of tequila with these cars."

The day was yet another feather in Tommy's cap. Not only did he know all the right people on a first-name basis, but much like Richards and Pallenberg, Tommy could also consume massive amounts of alcohol, hashish, and cocaine and yet still stay on his feet. After Tommy introduced his hosts to the thrill of big-time gambling by taking them to the Monte Carlo casino where he had quite a run at craps, Pallenberg began calling him "Tommy the Tumbling Dice," after the song that would become the first single from the album the Stones were about to record at Nellcote. Tommy then found the classic wooden Riva speedboat, which she rechristened "The Mandrax" by scrambling around the letters of its former name. He also located a vintage Buick for Richards to buy.

As he had demonstrated beyond all doubt during his profitable run at craps at the casino in Monte Carlo, Tommy was now on a roll of major proportions. Unlike his many failed previous attempts at finding a role that suited his unique capabilities, everything he touched at Villa Nellcote seemed to turn to gold. By doing things for Richards and Pallenberg that no one else could, Tommy had plugged himself into the huge energy source that was the Rolling Stones, thereby making it possible for him to operate in a manner he had only dreamed about before. His newfound power was so obvious that Spanish Tony Sanchez, who had been with the Stones for ages, could only look on with envy as the man he wrongly called an "old Etonian" in his book assumed what had once been Sanchez's position as Richards' right-hand man.

Although Sanchez could not stand Tommy, this did not stop him or his girlfriend Madeleine from partying with Tommy on the night that Michele Breton, who had bathed naked with Pallenberg in *Performance*, came to dinner at Villa Nellcote. After dinner, everyone repaired to Sanchez's bedroom "to unwind by gulping down a few Mandrax tablets followed by hefty swigs of Courvoisier." In less than an hour, everyone had passed out cold on Sanchez's "vast Louis XIV bed."

Regaining consciousness at five in the morning, Sanchez heard "whispers and faint gigglings from two people on the other side of the bed." Thinking at first that it was Richards and Pallenberg, who then began to gently moan, Sanchez realized to his great shock and amazement as the bed began to shake that Tommy had "climbed stealthily" onto Pallenberg and the two were now "making love, gently at first and then violently" as Richards and Michele Breton dozed peacefully through it all. Falling asleep once more, Sanchez awoke to find Richards and Breton "stretching themselves and gradually coming to" while Tommy and Pallenberg were nowhere to be found.

As Tommy would later say, "The reason I was able to rationalize my appalling behavior was because I thought it was all sex, love, and rock 'n' roll. I had really fallen for that, and I thought Keith and Anita had, too. Keith sussed out that I was so stupid as to have fallen for all that, and he just couldn't quite understand it. But Anita kept saying, 'No, no, listen to this guy. He knows a lot more than you realize, and he's what we need down here.'"

Whether Richards also needed Tommy to be servicing the woman with whom he was then living was a different issue. Fortunately for all concerned, physical fidelity had never been a major issue for Richards, who during his own drug trial at the Old Bailey in 1969, had set the English establishment on their ear by proclaiming, "We are not old men and we're not worried about petty morals."

Hoping that Richards would toss Tommy out of the house when he heard the news, Sanchez made it his business to inform Richards the next morning that Tommy, in a very Victorian turn of phrase, had taken "a liberty" with Pallenberg the night before. Whether this contributed to Richards' highly combative mood as Sanchez, Pallenberg, Tommy, Jake, Charley, Tony, Breton, and French photographer Dominique Tarlé arrived at the harbor in Beaulieu in "a shower of warm summer rain" on a lovely June day to purchase a new speedboat, no one can say for sure.

After a minor accident, Richards launched into a profane shouting match with an Italian couple. Pulling a large German hunting knife from his leather satchel, he punched and/or was punched by the hulking giant of a French harbormaster who spoke no English. Going to his car, Richards returned to do further battle with what he later claimed was his son's toy pistol, causing the harbormaster to suddenly produce his own very real gun.

Having been through more than one street battle of his own in London, Tommy promptly disarmed Richards, taking away the real .38 revolver the beleaguered Rolling Stone had been brandishing. As Richards and Sanchez continued "having a lovely time having a brawl with all these uniforms," Tommy grabbed Jake and Charley, leaped with them into Richards' rented gray Dodge, and returned in record time to the villa so that he could "clean the place up before we had a big, big bust which was obviously going to happen."

Already familiar with the niceties of law enforcement on the French Riviera, Tommy knew that while Richards and Pallenberg had "protection from the prefect, they didn't have enough protection from the customs. And this was the harbor, so it was really serious and I had to warn everybody to clean up whatever was lying about because we were going to get a spin. And that was exactly what happened." Long before the local gendarmes visited Nellcote, Tommy had already dumped Richards' .38 in the harbor, thereby making it possible for Richards to claim that it was in fact his son's toy gun he had been using.

After the chief of police came to dinner at Nellcote and Richards gave him several autographed Stones albums as well as what may have been a fair amount of cash, the Stones' lawyers pleaded Sanchez guilty on a charge of assault. After Richards had paid Sanchez's twelve thousand dollar fine, Spanish Tony, now *persona non grata* with the French authorities, was forced to return to London until the heat subsided, leaving Tommy behind as the savior of Nellcote.

Proving beyond all doubt that he was now Mr. Indispensable insofar as daily life on the French Riviera was concerned, Tommy suggested to Richards and Pallenberg that the best way to deal with "*les cowboys*," the gang of young cigarette smugglers who hung out at Richards' favorite café in the port in Villefranche, was to hire them as assistant gardeners and cooks at the villa. By making them "feel important," as Tommy later explained, "we could get them to obey orders and keep them under control. They would also go down to score in Marseilles for us. That was what Keith and Anita saw as my value. I knew the coast like the back of my hand. I'd lived there on and off all my life, and I knew how extremely dangerous these Corsican French bandits were."

With everything going his way and one brilliant sun-filled day flowing into another, life for Tommy and the boys at Villa Nellcote soon became an endless round of pleasure. Jake and Charley, who had been shifted from one house to another ever since returning to England with Puss, were delighted to be living in one place with their father for more than a few days at a time. Nor was Nellcote a place where the ordinary rules of child rearing were ever in effect. Charley recalled, "Marlon was also a bit wild. He would eat ants, and Keith would say, 'He wants to eat fucking ants? No problem, man. Let him eat what he wants.' Marlon would put his hand into the butter in the middle of the big dinner table and eat it, and Keith loved it."

Jake and Charley would often go out on the Riva motorboat with Richards and Tommy to water ski or swim in the middle of the bay. At Nellcote, the boys were known as "the Rollies" because they rolled joints for the Rolling Stones, specifically Richards, who liked smoking hash just to pass the time of day. Nor were these simple twist-ups. They were authentic English hash-and-tobacco joints made of five separate cigarette papers glued together at right angles with a rolled strip of cardboard torn from a Rizla packet as a filter. As Charley later said, "We could roll a long one, a short one, a fat one, whatever anyone wanted. We used to roll the joints, but we were too young to drink or smoke. The norm was that we would dance around the room and get crazy to 'Brown Sugar,' and everyone else would get stoned."

All the while, Tommy was waiting for Puss to arrive. When she did, the never-ending party that was life at Nellcote would escalate to brand-new heights. On Tuesday, June 8, 1971, Tommy drove the Stones' Texas-born saxophone player, Bobby Keys, up to Alan and Jenny Ponte's house in the hills above Menton to show him "backup copies of the Gospel according to St. Thomas," which Tommy claimed he had obtained from "the guy who had financed the Dead Sea Scrolls" and was trying to sell as one of his many sideline scams.

When they returned to Nellcote, Richards greeted Tommy by saying, "Look, I've got some really bad news for you. Puss is dead." Richards then told Tommy he could stay at Nellcote for as long as he liked, adding, "We'll look after you and the kids." In Tommy's words, "There was no way I could face going back to the funeral with Jake and Charley. I was completely shattered. I felt totally convinced it was all my fault. And feel so to this day. I've been blaming myself ever since because I let her down completely and left her on her own to roam the world when she was really far too delicate to be left alone. She appeared to be strong, but she wasn't."

Taking Jake and Charley aside, Tommy said, "Boys, I've got some terrible news. Your mother has died." Making up a story as he went along, Tommy told them the death had been an accident caused by the fact that "she had taken the wrong pills by mistake." As Jake later recalled, "Everything just went white. I recall him saying those words, and then I heard a cacophony. Not a sound. Like a white noise. A cacophonous, symphonic thing like at the end of 'A Day in the Life.'" In Charley's words, "I remember us both breaking into pathetic sobs and the kind of hopeless emotion you go through when you hit the wall. And then for a couple of weeks, I don't really remember a hell of a lot."

Much like Charley, Jake would also later be unable to recall anything that went on after he learned the news. "I went immediately into uncontrollable hysteria, and it went on for days. In the haze of my grief, I remember clocking in on my dad from time to time and seeing him just blotto, like that Rodin statue with his head in his hands. I was just in a complete isolation chamber."

Charley tells a different version of the story. The night before he and Jake learned about their mother's death, the cook at Nellcote had given each of the boys a small bottle of Heineken to drink. Getting drunk for the first time in his life, Charley began dancing around to "Brown Sugar." In his words, "It was weird because I could see Tommy wasn't encouraging that sort of behavior. He was very somber. It was very strange because he was always partying and it was such an anomaly to see him straight-faced and sober. When he told us the day after, it all clicked into place. 'Oh, so that's why he was like that.' He had carried it around from the night before. We reacted by screaming, and he took us out into the garden overlooking the bay."

Two days later, Tommy received a letter Puss had written before her death, "saying how much she missed us and the nostalgia she had for the days when the blond boy she knew had driven around in a 1938 Packard. I treasured it for many years, but eventually it got lost. I wish I had it now. I've had many moves and lost everything."

18

on the riviera

With the Rolling Stones now jamming aimlessly each night in the basement of Keith Richards' house as they began recording the double album that would eventually come to be known as *Exile on Main St.*, the scene at Villa Nellcote changed dramatically. In large part, the atmospheric shift came about because of what happened the day Richards and Tommy decided to have some fun at the local go-kart track.

Tommy, who was getting as loaded as he could on whatever was going around to anesthetize his pain, was still having it off with Anita Pallenberg whenever they could find a time and place to do so. Finally taking note of their activities, Richards, in a line of dialogue only he could have delivered, casually told Tommy, "I don't know why you say you're a vegetarian. You seem to helping yourself to my meat." And there the matter rested until the two men decided to start racing their go-karts against one another in the blazing hot sun.

"It all started with the go-kart accident," Tommy said. "Keith drove straight at me and pulled his kart over my wheels, and the thing flipped. His kart turned over, and I had him with his head in my lap and the go-kart on top of him, his back scraping along the tarmac and opening up like steak while I was trying to slow both cars down. That was how fast it happened. It was murder. Definite, barefaced murder."

After they had extricated themselves from their tangled go-karts, Richards, who in the words of Stones' bassist Bill Wyman, had "torn all the skin from his back" and "looked bad and hurt worse," made a decision that would irrevocably alter both men's lives. "Now's the time, Tommy," Richards said, "for you to go to the doctor and get us some heroin. This is as good an excuse to start the smack again as any."

Without asking too many questions, the local doctor, who had already been sending someone around to Nellcote to regularly administer vitamin B-12 shots to all who wanted them, promptly wrote out a prescription to help ease Richards' pain. Hardly a novice with drugs, Tommy was relatively unschooled at shooting smack on a regular basis: "It was something I hadn't done before. And when Keith would give me a taste, it wasn't, 'No, thank you.' It was 'Yes, please.' I had never really used before then, and I was absolutely innocent in a way as well."

Downstairs at Villa Nellcote, there was now a constant stream of people trying to help the Stones record their new album so the band could tour America, thereby generating enough cash to sustain themselves. Retreating to the bedrooms on the second floor of the house, where no one but them dared to go, those in the inner circle, Tommy among them, began shooting heroin, snorting cocaine, popping Mandrax, and smoking opium on a regular basis. Because Villa Nellcote was Richards' house and these were his friends, no one could ask any of them to leave.

"I don't know if Keith had any real friends at that point," Stones' recording engineer Andy Johns would later say. "They all seemed pretty dodgy to me. Tommy Weber was a very typical, very dodgy weasel boy. He would sunbathe naked on the beach because it was hip, and I used to think, 'Please. I don't want to stare at your luggage.' I had a real job there, but at the same time, I was thinking, 'What are these bastards doing here? Apart from bringing drugs.'"

Although some of those who were then at Nellcote knew the real reason Richards had invited Tommy and the boys to stay at the house for as long as they liked, the story everyone had heard was how Tommy had used his sons to bring dope into France. Even if they had been aware of what had happened to Puss, it was not as though Tommy was a Rolling Stone. With all that was now at stake in terms of the new album, those who worked for the Stones cared only about the health and welfare of the band.

In his own way, Tommy was mourning the loss of his wife. This did not stop him from returning to the villa one day to report he had just had it off with Errol Flynn's daughter Rory on the derelict yacht in a nearby harbor that belonged to her brother Sean, a combat photographer who had gone missing and was presumed dead in Vietnam. As everyone sat on the back steps of the villa reading day-old English newspapers, Tommy's feat of derring-do became a source of amusing conversation for a while.

Like many of those who were hanging out at the villa for no apparent reason, Tommy was soon given a project of his own by the Rolling Stones. With the consent of both Richards and Mick Jagger, who were then seeing eye-to-eye on almost nothing, as well as Pallenberg's loyal support, Tommy was charged with the task of setting up Radio Rolling Stone, a concept that in every way was right up his alley.

Having failed to establish a pirate radio station on Lundy Island, Tommy now turned his attention to nearby Radio Monte Carlo, which had been "built on a slab on the side of a mountain as one of Hitler's projects for his thousand-year Reich." Radio Monte Carlo, which had first gone on the air in 1942, had a transmitter "so powerful that it could hit anywhere in the world." The general manager of the station was English and, as Tommy would later say, "I happened to know his son because he was a partaker, and so I started to put this deal together. It was going to be Radio Rolling Stone, and I was going to buy time from all the radio stations in Europe that were not broadcasting at night and so I would be getting them for just the price of the night watchman."

Long before anyone had thought of such a concept, the Stones, who had just founded their own record label, wanted Tommy to buy airtime from radio stations all over Europe for a prerecorded program that would be broadcast in AM and FM stereo from midnight until six A.M. To implement the plan, Tommy found a local recording studio run by "a CIA hit man who lived in splendor in the south of France who showed me all these appalling killer weapons" as well as someone "who was going to oversee the production and distribution of the air time."

Before any of this could happen, Tommy, who had not slept for two or three days, was driving a rented car at four in the morning on the Grand Corniche, "which is just like a track on the top of the mountains," with the son of Radio Monte Carlo's general manager in the backseat. Suddenly, Tommy became convinced that it was Puss who was now at the wheel. As it was then "about thirty days or so from the forty-nine-day grace period before her spirit would leave the earth," Tommy believed the two of them were again at "Targa Floria, Lake Garda, or Nürburgring," where he would sit blindfolded as Puss drove and he told her from memory which turn was coming up next on the course.

As he sped down "this treacherous road," Tommy suddenly saw a large "French truck going to market, and there was really room for only one vehicle, and certainly not for two." Guiding Puss as she drove, Tommy told her, "You've got to aim for his shoulder and hit him there. Otherwise, we'll both go over the top. This way, we'll connect and hopefully not push either of us over. We'll be entangled."

As he was "having a vision of her, and she was pulling me into the next *bardo*, she began screaming, '*Tommy! Tommy! Tommy!*'

And I suddenly realized I had fallen asleep and it was me driving and this truck was literally bearing down on me. And I had to hit this truck exactly where I was telling Puss to do it, and we entangled and everything was fine. There was an awful mess and everyone screamed, but everyone was all right."

Holding what would prove to be a broken wrist as well as the bag of cocaine he had been traveling with in the car, Tommy began making his way down the twisting mountain road until he reached "the first civilized building, which turned out to be a nunnery. And I went in there screaming, 'Morphine! Morphine!' And the old dears sat me down and very sweetly gave me morphine." In time, Stones' record producer Jimmy Miller and horn player Jim Price came to fetch Tommy. Knowing they could not take him to the hospital without arousing interest from the local authorities, they transported Tommy to the same local doctor who had already proved to be a reliable source of drugs, and he put a large plaster cast on Tommy's arm.

Never one to let any form of physical injury dampen his spirits, Tommy wrapped the cast in plastic and went water-skiing with Jake and Charley to impress, in Jake's words, "a girl with big tits who looked like Raquel Welch." No less accident prone on water than on land, Tommy and the boys were in the speedboat "when one of these huge liners came bearing down on us, and we all had to dive in the water to get out of its way."

Charley, a fearless child who was always thinking about "weird mechanics," would often leap from the Riva into the open sea just for fun while wondering whether he would "travel with the boat and land alongside it from inertia or land where I had jumped." He also loved going fast in Richards' E-type Jaguar and would later remember "a rift between Jake and Keith because Jake would try to get his attention by asking so many questions. 'Why this? What's that?' Finally, Keith told him to shut up. I missed the argument, but then came across Tommy trying to console Jake out by the driveway, and Tommy told me what had happened."

As Jake later explained, "Keith really loved Charley, and he couldn't stand me. Because as a child, my mantra was always 'It's not fair.' It wasn't fair, and I was right, but whenever I thought I was not being treated fairly, I would get aggressive. From very early on, I looked to see how I could work people, for our safety more than anything else. As a kid, Charley was always much more open and live-and-let-live than me."

Tommy, who by now had decided that the cast was crimping his style, promptly went back to see the doctor, who agreed to remove it with an electric plaster-of-paris cutter. "There was I sitting in his garden with no shoes on and dripping wet," Tommy said, "and he plugged this thing in, and I literally shot about six feet in the air, went up over a path, and landed on top of a hedge. Instinctively, I grabbed him in this survival grip of vengeance and he said, 'No, no, you bloody Rolling Stones! You're mad people!'"

Although the insanity of everyday life at Villa Nellcote had now reached another level, Tommy had still not worn out his welcome. How he finally did this can only be understood in the context of a house where everyone was always so stoned that reality itself was strictly in the eye of the beholder. Because the villa sat so high above the bay that those who lived there could look right down into the windows of the huge yachts anchored in the harbor below, Tommy had given Richards a pair of high-powered German optic binoculars.

While peering through them one night, Anita Pallenberg saw what to her looked like a pirate galleon. "You've got to see this," she told Tommy. "I've been trying to tell Keith, but he won't listen to me." Presuming the ship was "a joke, or one of those Hollywood makeup jobs," Tommy looked through the binoculars only to see what looked like the real-life incarnation of *The Flying Dutchman,* the ghostly vessel doomed to sail the seas forever without returning home. "Well, we've got to get on it," he said. Pallenberg replied, "That's exactly what I was thinking."

Driving to the harbor in the middle of the night, Tommy enlisted the cowboys to help him steal a fishing boat. Then they all set out for the bar of the harbor, where the galleon lay at anchor. The sea soon began to rise, the waves getting "more and more choppy, and halfway out there, we ran out of petrol. So, of course, it was, 'Okay, boys. All hands to the oars.' I was the galley master, and with Anita, we both got them to keep rowing."

When at last they came within hailing distance of the galleon, Tommy could see the ship was at least eighty feet long. One of the hatches was open, and an old-fashioned lantern clanked loudly as the ship rocked back and forth in the water. Trying to raise someone on board, Tommy began banging on the side of the ship with an oar. Although there was no response and the sea was now rougher than it had been before, Pallenberg insisted they clamber up onto the ship.

When Tommy demurred, "She began calling me '*un lache*' which is French slang for a coward. And I thought she was calling me a lush. She was always saying that my real drug was alcohol, which, of course, was true, and it took me years to realize she was calling me a chicken. The other incredible thing she said on the way out was, 'I don't know what we can do about your dick.' And I said, 'What do you mean? What's wrong with my dick?' No one had ever complained about it before. But she was really good at getting under your skin and unsettling you."

Despite Pallenberg's comments, Tommy for once in his life made the sensible decision and declared he was not about to jump out of the fishing boat so he could then shinny up the side of the galleon. Because the sea was too rough for either of them to accomplish a feat that would have daunted even Errol Flynn as Captain Blood, Pallenberg finally relented and allowed the cowboys to row them back to shore.

After they returned to Nellcote, Richards confronted Pallenberg and demanded to know where she and Tommy had been all night long. When she again began talking about the galleon, Richards just got angrier. When Pallenberg directed his attention to the bar of the harbor, the ship was gone. "Keith thought Anita had just gone off her head about the galleon," Tommy said. "But I am convinced to this day that I actually had my hand on the gunwales of this really enormous ship. And it was truly one of the most wonderful experiences of my life."

After a fairly explosive argument, Pallenberg declared, "That's it. I'm not standing another day of this. C'mon, Tommy." Grabbing her son Marlon, she got into the car with Tommy and the boys and directed him to head straight for the bank· in Nice, "where she emptied the Stones' accounts, and we went up to my place in the hills."

Not about to put up with such behavior, Richards, who by then would have had no trouble finding a replacement for the .38 revolver Tommy had tossed into the bay, went looking for Pallenberg and his son. As Richards and Pallenberg had spent a few days up at the house in the mountains a few weeks earlier, he had no trouble finding it. Rather than drive down into the valley for a physical confrontation that most likely would have ended in bloodshed, Richards decided instead to have dinner and then spend the night in a nearby hotel on the Rue Napoleon before continuing on to St. Tropez via the back roads. As Tommy would later say, "Had I met him up there, I would have been shitless."

After Tommy and Pallenberg had spent a couple of days at the house, he realized she was "really way out of my league and my class" and was just using him "as a goad to get Keith to pay attention to her." After she told Tommy he was "too boring" for her, he took Pallenberg back to Nellcote, from which he and the boys were then "sent out." Banished at long last from the court of the crimson king, Tommy, Jake, and Charley spent the next few weeks living in the house in the mountains. "It all settled itself," Tommy would later say, "and I would come down once a week with Jake and Charley and see how everybody was. And then they told me that things were getting extremely sticky, police in cars, and I could see the house was getting more and more decadent."

Continuing to work on the deal to put Radio Rolling Stone on the air, Tommy took the boys with him on regular trips to Monte Carlo to visit his friend, the son of Radio Monte Carlo's general manager. When the friend overdosed one day in his apartment, Tommy called an ambulance, gathered up Jake and Charley, and said, "Come on, we're off." Going down into the street, Tommy waited with the boys for the ambulance and then disappeared before anyone could connect him to the scene upstairs. Driving directly to the house in the mountains, Tommy cleaned the place up, buried all his dope, and headed straight for the Nice airport, where he flew with the boys to Paris and then Spain.

Three months later, shortly after Richards and Pallenberg and their young son had left Nellcote with not much more than they could carry, the local gendarmes raided the villa in force, arresting all the cowboys they could find on charges of bringing hashish and fifty grams of heroin to Nellcote on a regular basis throughout the summer. Nine months later, when the case finally came before the court, five defendants, Keith Richards, Anita Pallenberg, Bobby Keys, and Tommy among them, were not present for sentencing. Found guilty of the use, supply, and trafficking of cannabis, Richards and Pallenberg received one-year suspended sentences and a fine of five thousand francs (a thousand dollars). Saxophone player Keys was given a four-month suspended sentence and a fine of a thousand francs (two hundred dollars).

As Tommy would later say, "Eventually, they all got off and I was the guy lumbered with the blame for all of this. I've still got all these horrific charges outstanding against me in France. Which don't die. They don't have a statute of limitations. So I've never dared to go there again." (In truth, he returned there more than once over the years.) Although Tommy never spent a day in jail for bringing the cowboys to Nellcote and then getting as high on their supply as anyone in the villa, the bust at Keith Richards' house in the south of France was his first conviction. It would not be his last.

19
on the road

With no money, no real prospects, and two young sons who needed looking after on a daily basis, Tommy traveled with Jake and Charley to Marbella, a jet-set playground for the superrich on Spain's Costa del Sol. There he reconnected with a woman he had known from the King's Road in London and who had just opened the hippest local haircutting salon in town.

The woman, whom Jake remembered as "a Janis Joplin–type character with frizzy hair who was a little weathered but sexy and voluptuous," lived with a good-looking young Englishman who was the star of her staff in a beautiful house with a pool in Puerto Banus, a fashionable complex of shops and restaurants built around a new marina about six kilometers west of Marbella. Greeting Tommy like an old friend, she graciously invited him and the boys to live in her guest cottage at the end of the garden. Just as he had done with Keith Richards and Anita Pallenberg at Villa Nellcote, Tommy soon became the couple's new best friend.

For a while, life for Tommy and the boys was good in Puerto Banus. After he had taken Jake and Charley to a circus, Tommy came home with a monkey named Coco who had chewed through its own tail. Along with a wild fox that Tommy had begun feeding and a pair of caged canaries, one of whom was named Sing Sing,

Coco the monkey became part of the family menagerie. "Coco was so vicious," Jake said, "that he was like the anti-Christ. Eventually, Coco managed to open the cage where the canaries were kept. And then he ate both of them."

Long before Tommy realized what was going on, Jake could sense that the woman who owned the house was "directing her energy towards him. Then she was hitting on him, and he started sleeping with her." Although, in Charley's words, the woman had "a loose sort of relationship" with her boyfriend, he "was very upset and tried to take his own life" when he learned what was going on. "He slashed his wrists all the way up the arm trying to kill himself," Jake recalled. "It was bad, bad, bad. Really bad." Although Tommy saved the young man by taking him to the hospital, Tommy now "had this guy's blood on his hands." By now the woman had become so obsessed with Tommy that "she didn't care about her boyfriend, and it got really ugly."

Shortly after the failed suicide attempt, Tommy went on a "hard-core bender" of major proportions. Jake remembered this as "being the time when I was most frightened I would lose him. Dad would disappear for days, and Charley and I would be left alone in the house, and when he came back, he'd be hammered. Eventually, there was a big scene when we left the house, and he was driving around with a bottle of whiskey between his legs trying to find his old friend Mike Taylor in Marbella."

Moving with Jake and Charley into a development owned by a partner of his old friend John Green, Tommy sent his sons to an international school near Malaga. By doing so, Tommy unwittingly recreated the situation he himself had experienced after first coming to England as a boy. "There were maybe five English kids there, and the rest were German," Charley said. "The German kids were real Nazis, and it was like World War II all over again. A nightmare. Every day, they would chase us. It was literally like *Lord of the Flies*. Jake and I went there for maybe a term."

In Marbella, Tommy began doing shady deals with a London gangster who was "a partner in crime" of the woman who owned the hair salon. "Half out of his mind all the time," Tommy bought a greyhound from some local gypsies. Convinced he could race the dog, Tommy then planned to sell it for a good deal of money. He left the greyhound with the gangster, only to learn it had died in his care. After getting drunk in a bar one night, Tommy went "ballistic" and insulted the gangster in front of his friends. As Jake recalled, "The guy took Tommy out to the dump, made him take off his shoes, and beat him to within an inch of his life. He had to run away across the dump, and his feet were cut to shreds."

"Black and blue all over," as Charley described him later, "Tommy walked into the sea to cleanse his wounds and then walked back to the house. They pretty much did kill him, and it was terrifying for Jake and me. The guy then came by the house and poked his head in the door and said, 'Tom, you all right?' And Tom was terrified. I hated that he was that scared. Maybe the reason the guy didn't kill him was because Jake and I were there."

Jake remembered the scene occurring in a different place: "It was not in the house. It was in the car belonging to the woman who owned the salon—outside a hair salon and lounge where everyone drank. The guy who had beaten Tommy up came by and began screaming at Tommy that if he ever came near him again, he would fucking kill him. Charley and I were screaming, 'No, no!' And the guy said to us, 'You kids, your father is a fucking nutter!' All the while, Tommy was saying, 'Yes, man, yes.' He was terrified. And then with great bravado after the guy was gone, Tommy said, 'Did you see? I was looking for a knife so I could stab him in the face.'"

Leaving Marbella, Tommy took the boys to Portugal, where he tried to connect with an old racing partner who, as Charley later described him, was "some kind of royalty. Tom was very much in self-destruct mode and just drifting, trying to get something for free." By August 1972, Tommy and the boys were back in Marbella,

where he met Joanna Harcourt-Smith, a twenty-eight-year-old
heiress whom Timothy Leary later described as "a 21st century
fox" who had "boogied naked on the glass table-tops and run
hand-in-hand under the crazy moon" as the "snow queen of London's Chelsea district and madcap prankster of Europe's jet set."

Often mistaken, in Leary's words, for "Audrey Hepburn, Brigitte
Bardot, or Lauren Bacall's younger sister," Joanna Harcourt-Smith
was the daughter of a titled British naval officer whose father had
served as Lord Chamberlain to King George V and helped found
the Albert and Victoria Museum in London. Her mother was a
beautiful, domineering Jewish aristocrat from Poland who spoke
seven languages but never learned to drive a car or write a check.
Harcourt-Smith was also related to Stanislaw Ulam, the mathe-
matician who had helped Edward Teller invent the hydrogen
bomb.

At the age of seventeen, Joanna Harcourt-Smith had become
pregnant while having an affair with French singing star Charles
Aznavour only to abort his child. Three years later, she had married a Greek industrialist and given birth to a daughter. After their
marriage ended, she moved to America, where she married the director of a subcommittee in the House of Representatives and
gave birth to a son in February 1972. Six months later, while living
in "a beautiful house in Marbella," she took "a lot of LSD" and became part of the European hippie jet-set scene.

Small, dark, and intense, Harcourt-Smith, much like Tommy,
was always up for everything. An hour after "this beautiful creature sailed into my house," she and Tommy were in bed together,
with her husband "hanging on the sidelines. Tommy, who only
lived in other people's houses, said to me, 'Let's go to Switzerland
to see Keith and Anita,' and I said, 'Of course.'"

Scoring some morphine, Tommy and Harcourt-Smith went
with Jake and Charley to Villars-sur-Ollon in Switzerland, where
Keith Richards and Anita Pallenberg were then living not far from

former Harvard psychology lecturer and acid guru, Timothy Leary. After escaping from prison in America with the help of the radical political group the Weather Underground, Leary had sought refuge with Black Panther leader Eldridge Cleaver in Algeria only to be forced to escape again to Switzerland.

Granted temporary asylum by the Swiss government, Leary was being funded and controlled by Michel Hauchard, a tall, silver-haired man with whom Harcourt-Smith had begun a long-running affair when she was eighteen years old and he was forty. After spending several months in a French prison for embezzlement, Hauchard had moved to Switzerland, where he became involved in the international arms trade. Harcourt-Smith later described him as "sort of a gangster arms-dealer high-flying arriviste" whose tastes ran to "young girls, Cristal champagne, and the best Cuban cigars."

Switzerland, a country that had always been a haven for those who had money and nowhere else to go, was then also the temporary home of Richards and Pallenberg. Since the end of the Rolling Stones' triumphant tour of America in July 1972, they had been living in Villars-sur-Ollon with their son Marlon in what Charley Weber later called a "very sedate" manner: "It was not at all like Nellcote. Keith and Anita were very chilled, and they were trying not to use. Tommy said it was a great reunion, but I felt the whole thing was a little chilled."

During Tommy and Harcourt-Smith's visit, Richards spent most of his time downstairs playing electric guitar and piano while Pallenberg and Harcourt-Smith drank tequila, smoked dope, and snorted coke on the second floor of the house. As the night wore on and the drugs took hold, Pallenberg persuaded Harcourt-Smith that it was her destiny to meet and fall in love with Leary.

What Harcourt-Smith did not know was that Richards had already taken Tommy aside and said, "Look, I've got this guy Leary calling me up every day. It's driving me mad. Can you go and sort him out? I really don't want to meet him." As Pallenberg and Harcourt-Smith partied together late into the night, they came up with a mad plan to win Leary his freedom by offering to have the Rolling Stones do a quick tour of America to raise funds for Senator George McGovern, the Democratic Party candidate for president. After McGovern defeated Richard Nixon, he would pardon Leary. Although none of this was even remotely possible, it all made eminent sense to Pallenberg and Harcourt-Smith.

For Tommy, the idea of going with Harcourt-Smith to America to persuade McGovern's people that their candidate could not possibly win the forthcoming election without the Rolling Stones, with the quid pro quo that McGovern would then grant clemency to Leary, whom American authorities would soon brand "the most dangerous man in the world," was irresistible. Like Don Quixote tilting at yet another windmill, this was the kind of mission for which Tommy had been born. Although he had left Villa Nellcote in disgrace, Tommy also believed that if he and Harcourt-Smith could pull this caper off, he would again find himself in the good graces of Keith Richards, the man he revered above all others.

After Harcourt-Smith bought four first-class round-trip tickets to America, she and Tommy flew to Washington with Jake and Charley. "Washington was great," Charley said. "We stayed in Joanna's house, and we had a color TV in our room and Cocoa Puffs in the morning and McDonald's, all the stuff you want as a kid." After they had talked their way into McGovern headquarters, Tommy and Harcourt-Smith presented their idea to his aides, only to be told that they had come too late. McGovern was already so far behind in the polls that not even the Rolling Stones could help him.

Disappointed that they would not be able to put together a Stones tour for McGovern, Tommy drove with Harcourt-Smith and the boys to New York City. "There were a lot of drugs in the car," Charley recalled, "and Tom was doing his race driving thing and the police were chasing us. He chucked everything out the window, raced off, and outgunned the police between Washington and New York."

In New York, Harcourt-Smith visited her old friend Egon von Furstenberg and his wife, the noted dress designer Diane, who was "lounging around on a mink blanket." Harcourt-Smith also got a call from Michel Hauchard, whom she then met at the King Cole Bar in the St. Regis Hotel, where he showed her the large check he had just collected from a publisher for Leary's new book about his escape from prison. In no uncertain terms, Hauchard told his former lover the only way she would ever get to Leary was through him.

During their visit, Tommy and Harcourt-Smith left Jake and Charley asleep in the car. Woken up by a knock on the window, Charley was shocked to see a New York cop holding a gun and demanding to know what the two boys were doing there. As they began explaining their situation, Tommy returned from "either seeing Michel Hauchard or doing a drug deal upstairs" and charmed the policeman into letting them all go on their way again.

After Harcourt-Smith had seen Hauchard at the St. Regis, she and Tommy went directly to the airport. With the boys, they boarded the first plane to Geneva. Tommy and Harcourt-Smith then drove to Lausanne, where they went to Hauchard's house. "We rang the doorbell, and the Moroccan butler answered," she said. "Tommy got him stoned on hash, and I got into Michel's bureau and got his address book and wrote down the five different phone numbers he had for Timothy Leary." Tommy, Harcourt-Smith, and the boys then checked into the Palace Hotel in Lausanne.

As Tommy would later say, "The problem was that we were living in the top suite of the Palace Hotel in Lausanne, and we had run up a huge bill. My mother had come to Switzerland with my stepfather to check on their numbered Swiss account, and Charley had opened a bottle of Coke and sprayed my stepfather with it and there was Coke all over the walls, and they'd hit Joanna with a bill for thirty grand." Charley recalled, "Tom passed me a joint, his mum was horrified, and I shook things up with a bottle of Coke. Most embarrassing." The worst part of it was, as Tommy said, "Hauchard was a part owner of the hotel, and since Joanna wanted to have a dig at him in any way, she had done the most stupid thing and given him a check for thirty grand."

Knowing the check would bounce and fearing that Hauchard would have him killed if the hotel bill was not paid, Tommy returned to Hauchard's house and again got the butler stoned. Tommy had brought with him an array of drugs of every kind that he had collected while cleaning up Richards and Pallenberg's house in Switzerland before they had gone with their son to England. Tommy then proceeded to bury the drugs in Hauchard's garden. Knowing the police were "willing to do anything they could to get Hauchard out of Switzerland," Tommy phoned the arms dealer and informed him of what he had done. If Hauchard did not drop his claim for the money he was owed, Tommy promised to call the cops and tell them exactly where the dope was buried.

Hauchard responded to the threat by having both Tommy and Harcourt-Smith arrested. "I was actually in the cell Tim Leary had been in," Tommy said, "and I decided to drop some acid, and it was remarkable." When Tommy was taken from the cell to a courtroom inside the prison, he was greeted by he sight of "Joanna with her feet up on the judge's desk. The judge happened to be another of her boyfriends from her school days. And she had done a deal with him." Tommy and Harcourt-Smith were both soon back on the street again.

At some point in the proceedings, Tommy had called his half-sister Lulu in London and asked her to come join him in Switzerland. She flew there with eight hundred pounds, which she used to pay a portion of the hotel bill. When she heard Harcourt-Smith talking about Leary, Lulu said, "Oh, he's an old friend from the past." Lulu, who had attended school with Leary's daughter Susan on the Costa del Sol in Spain during the 1950s, then took Tommy and Harcourt-Smith to meet him. As Lulu would later say, "Tim and I were having it off together and having a good time, but Joanna was always walking in on us. I saw her talking to Leary on her own, and I knew there was some kind of scam going on."

Together, Leary and Joanna Harcourt-Smith devised a plan to get rid of Tommy by offering to send him to Amsterdam to buy a sailboat. With the boys, Tommy would then sail to the Caribbean and anchor the boat near Jamaica, where the Rolling Stones were recording *Goat's Head Soup*. From the boat, Joanna Harcourt-Smith later explained, "We would do an offshore radio station from which Tim would be able to broadcast and buy his freedom by rallying support."

To cover the deposit on the boat, Leary gave Tommy five thousand dollars. As Harcourt-Smith said, "Tim just paid him to go away." In Amsterdam, Tommy, Jake, and Charley stayed with Dutch Peter, a well-known dope smuggler who for a while was also Lulu's boyfriend. In Charley's words, "One day, Peter said, 'Do Charley and Jake want to do the canals trip and see the smuggling boat?' Sure, great. It took forever to go five miles in those canals, and Jake and I said we were shagged, so someone called a car and it drove up to meet us. Ten minutes after we had stepped off the boat, *boom!* Dutch Peter had double-crossed the wrong people, and they had put explosives on the boat and we literally walked off it just before it happened."

Before he had left Switzerland, Tommy, who by then was more than ready to be on his own again and thought the entire pirate radio plan was "hysterical," had told Harcourt-Smith and Leary that he would meet them "in Cairo for Christmas. Only they were stoned and he misheard me and they thought I said 'Kabul.'"

While Tommy was "waiting for them with Anita's girlfriend in Cairo," Leary and Harcourt-Smith were arrested after stepping off the plane in Kabul. Under armed guard, they were flown back to

America, where Leary was returned to prison. Acting as his common-law wife, Harcourt-Smith spent the next two years implementing a variety of schemes to set her "perfect love" free. Like so many of the women who passed through Tommy's life during this period, she never saw him again.

Although Charley loved Cairo and thought the city was "fantastic," he and Jake had by now come to know their father as few sons ever had. "It went from idolizing Tom to being very sad and very confused by what he was doing," Charley recalled. "The facade sort of crumbled. At that point, he was just off his head and embraced the darkness." As Jake would later say, "Dad went into a dark place of self-destruction and self-flagellation. He was partying and drinking to obliterate everything and got more and more strung out. A lot of his suffering was of his own doing. From guilt. And he was being cruel to us. He never hit us, but I remember him being very verbally abusive. He actually told me once it was my fault Puss had killed herself. Pretty bad stuff."

When Tommy learned that Osibisa, the band he had once wanted to manage, had finally made its way to Africa, he got on a plane with the boys and flew to Lagos, then the capital of Nigeria. "They took one look at Tommy," Jake said, "and decided he didn't have the right visa and threw us all into jail. We spent three days and nights in a Nigerian jail cell, and it was one of the most terrifying experiences of my life. It was so hot in there that we thought we were dying. Dad was so quiet, and I had never seen him like that before. We could have all died in there, and I think we were just in survival mode."

Finally, someone from Osibisa talked the authorities into releasing Tommy and the boys from prison. By then, Osibisa had a chartered plane waiting on the runway to fly the band to Accra, Ghana, where it was scheduled to play a show on New Year's Day 1973. Unfortunately, the band had left some of its gear at a Lagos hotel managed by Bobby Benson, a well-known African musician.

Because Osibisa had not paid the bill, Benson refused to release the musicians' equipment until they came up with the money.

Teddy Osei recalled, "We were all saying, 'Oh, Bobby, we all know you. If there is any problem, you let us go to Ghana and then we'll send you the money.' 'No, no, no.' The guy wouldn't budge. And the plane had come and it was waiting for us, and we couldn't go. Until Tommy went in there and hassled with the guy. Hassle, hassle, hassle. For hours!" Behind closed doors in Benson's office, Tommy began negotiating for the band's release.

"Eventually," Osei said, "Bobby Benson said okay. Tommy told him he was going to bring the band back to Lagos to do the show we were supposed to do there. But we had to go to Ghana first because we had a big contract there. I'm not sure if Tommy gave him some money. He must have done something like that. By the grace of God, we got everything and rushed to the Lagos airport and flew to Accra. We did the shows there, and it was perfect. But after that, we didn't see Tommy again. And of course, we didn't go back to Nigeria."

With the boys, Tommy then returned to Amsterdam, where they did not stay for long. Motivated by what Jake would later call his father's "nostalgic feelings for his homeland and a romantic notion of what life there could be like," Tommy flew with the boys to Copenhagen. On Christmas Day 1973, he arrived with Jake and Charley at Christiania, the legendary "free town" founded two years earlier by a large group of Danish hippies, squatters, and Provos who had taken over a neighborhood of abandoned military barracks and depots in the borough of Christianshavn, about a ten-minute walk from the Danish Parliament.

Refusing to obey any laws but their own, the citizens of Christiana had formed a self-governing community where all hard drugs, weapons, violence, and automobiles were banned but hashish and "Skunk weed were sold openly from permanent stands" on Pusher Street, the main artery. "I know we arrived there on Christmas Day,"

Jake said, "because some guy gave me a little puppy and we called him 'Happy Christmas,' which was later shortened to just 'Happy.'" Tommy, who had always adored animals, took to feeding the puppy with liver pâté. "We stayed there for a couple of months, and then we drove to Jutland in a rented Ford station wagon so Dad could find his father."

Before he did that, Tommy took Jake and Charley to Hald, the great house in which he had been born. The Danish International Student Committee was then running the estate as a hostel, and so Tommy and the boys "lived like students in a dorm" as Charley listened to the Doors doing "Riders on the Storm" over and over again. Nearly thirty years after his mother had taken him to England, Tommy was back home again. The great house in which he had been born was no longer his. The mother of his children was dead. He had no profession or real career and was no longer in contact with his older brother or his mother.

Sitting down at the piano where he had once been so joyously reunited with his mother after the war, Tommy, who could "play Chopin and fumble his way through cocktail music and some Thelonious Monk," began picking out notes on the keyboard. As he did, Charley caught a fleeting glimpse of "a ghostly figure" known as "the Old Gray Lady of Hald," who was said to have haunted the house ever since Tommy's father had entertained high-ranking Nazi officers there at dinner.

Embarked on a quest to reconnect with his past, Tommy left the estate with the boys and rented a little cottage in Jutland. Despite his obvious shortcomings as a parent, Tommy, who as a young boy had been forcibly separated from his own father and brother, was determined that Jake and Charley would not suffer a similar fate. Although he had no visible means of support and was hardly qualified to raise two young boys on his own, Tommy made it his goal to keep his sons with him. Because he had never liked or trusted Puss' family and now also blamed them for her death, Tommy was willing to do whatever he could to prevent Jake and Charley from falling into their clutches. The easiest way for him to accomplish this was to stay as far away from England as possible.

By stating that he now planned to live in Denmark with Jake and Charley in a house to which he had an actual lease, Tommy managed to persuade Puss' trustees to send him money so the boys could go to school. "At this point," Jake later said, "the family went 'Okay, we'll give them some money because this is as good as it's going to get.' Dad had never been back to England, and they knew they were never going to see us again. So they said, 'Stay in Denmark, and we'll give you money to set the kids up in school.'"

Living in "a little thatched cottage in the middle of Jutland near Aarhus," Jake and Charley began going to the local school while Tommy found work, in Jake's words, "as a lumberjack cutting down trees with a Barbizon chain saw in a giant wood. He straightened up. He would come home and have a few beers, but he had to get up the next morning to go to work. He grew a wild mane of blonde hair and a huge beard and really looked like a Viking god. He let the hedge around the cottage get so high that the neighbors couldn't see him when he sunbathed in the nude. On his day off, he would sit naked in the garden and smoke and drink strong Danish Elephant beer and play his guitar."

Although "the only money he was getting was from how many trees he cut down," Tommy opened a charge account at the local grocery store and sent Jake and Charley off to the local school. "We were in heaven," Jake recalled. "We were in a real school, which we'd never been in before, and we had this little cottage smaller than a living room. A teeny little thatched cottage with one bedroom, and we all slept in the same bed. All we had was a rocking chair, a bed, a guitar, and two bicycles. The inside of the house was decorated with pictures my brother and I had painted, wall-to-wall."

Sometimes, Tommy would go into town to pick up a girl, whom he would then bring back to the cottage for a while before sending her home so he could, in Jake's words, "go out and cut some more trees down. We had a dog and a cat. I was ten, and I was fluent in Danish. I was thinking in Danish, dreaming in Danish, everything." Through it all, Jake, a self-professed "momma's boy," was still missing his mother. "My brother always felt my dad was exciting and cool. But I was scared of him. My father had a temper, and he was a bully, and I was crying a lot. Because there was a lot missing."

As Charley would later recall, "When on alcohol, Tom became a demon. He was not a good drunk. He was teaching Jake how to make mayonnaise from eggs in the cottage in Denmark and he threw a plate at him in the garden which cut Jake on the shin. That event crossed the line for me. I thought, 'If he could do that, he could do anything.'"

After Tommy had established himself in Denmark, he took the boys on a day-long journey to the cottage where Poul Arkner was then living, in Jake's words, "in reduced circumstances" with his "mousy, deferential wife, who was very sweet. We knocked on the door, and he opened it and there was this freak with long hair standing there with two kids, and Dad said, 'I'm Tommy. I'm your son.'"

Sixty-nine years old but still vibrant and "very handsome, with a full head of white hair," Poul Arkner had not seen his son since the day Arkner had driven off with Tommy's older brother, Anders, after handing Tommy over to his mother in 1945. Living in South Africa, "Reggie," as Anders was now known, had long since cut off all contact with his father. He had also stopped speaking to his mother after she "bloody disinherited me in my presence" so that all her money would go to her daughters. Much like Jake and Charley, Tommy, who was barely on speaking terms with his mother, now had just one parent left with whom he could establish some sort of bond—his father.

"It was very awkward in the beginning," Jake said, "but they began to have a relationship, and we spent a lot of time there. We went back once a month for maybe four months, and the two of them reconciled. We would have big dinners, and they would get drunk together and argue." With each successive dinner, the tension between Tommy and "Fafa," as Jake and Charley called their Danish grandfather, increased. At what would prove to be their final dinner together, the two men began to argue after Poul Arkner called Charley a "bad-mannered, difficult brat" for refusing to eat the bean salad that Arkner's wife had prepared. Tommy then called his father a fascist. In Jake's words, "There was a lot of screaming and yelling, and Fafa threw us out in the middle of the night. Dad went into his office and took out his hunting knife and jammed it into Fafa's desk with a note. I don't know what the note said."

Tommy, Jake, and Charley then began walking to the nearest train station, a journey that took most of the night. "Tommy took turns walking with us on his shoulders, and we would take turns sleeping on his head. Walking in the freezing cold in the middle of the night in the middle of Denmark in the bitter cold winter. And that was the last time we ever saw Fafa."

All told, Tommy, Jake, and Charley spent about a year and a half in Denmark, the longest continuous stretch of time they had lived anywhere since leaving Villa Nellcote in August 1972. Their stay there began coming to an end when a man from the Hertz car rental agency showed up at the front door of their cottage one day to inquire about the Ford station wagon Tommy had never bothered to return. "This little nebbishy guy with a pocket protector from Hertz said he was looking for the car," Jake recalled, "and Dad invited him in, and he wound up living with us for a couple of months. Dad co-opted him and corrupted him and turned him into this little hippie guy. Eventually, he also got in trouble with the authorities and split."

Tommy, who by then had fallen afoul of the law by drinking and driving and also owed a considerable sum of money at the local grocery store, "got busted by the rental car people. The police came to arrest him, and he had a beard down to his waist. He was a mountain man and looked like Jeremiah Johnson." Unwilling to stand trial in Denmark, Tommy fled with boys back to Amsterdam. "We left everything," Jake said. "All the paintings Charley and I had done that were on the walls and my Humpty Dumpty that I'd patched up so there wasn't a square inch of it left that hadn't been patched up that I'd had since I was little kid that I couldn't sleep without."

Although he had been relatively straight during his time in Denmark, once Tommy found his old friend and smuggling partner, Taffy, in Amsterdam, he "got junked out with him" and fell in love with Taffy's seventeen-year-old girlfriend. In Jake's words, "Dad was doing some deals with Taffy and these gangsters, and there were shoot-outs and people with guns staying up all night."

In a city that was then a haven for drug smugglers of every nationality, Charley later remembered riding with Taffy in his truck one day, when Taffy stopped in the middle of the street and handed someone in a waiting car a bag filled with one or two kilos of heroin. "It was the size of a cat litter bag. The problem was—it *was* cat litter, and the guy shot it up without knowing that."

A day or two later, Tommy's half-sister Lulu, who had come to Amsterdam to be with Taffy, was driving his red Bedford TK Horsebox truck down the street with Jake and Charley beside her when two cars filled with the guys Taffy had ripped off tried to cut them off. Gunning the truck, Lulu took off with them in hot pursuit. "I drove back with the two kids and these people chasing us," she said later. "I was swerving down the road because they had guns pointing out the windows, and I would not let them get past to block me, and all the while, the kids were screaming."

After Lulu pulled up to where she and the boys were living, their pursuers pulled a guy out of the car who, in Charley's words, "had shot up the cat litter with a set of works and was green." In Jake's words, "He looked like a cat had shit upon him." As her pursuers screamed at her in Flemish, Lulu fiercely stood her ground and screamed back at them in English, "Take this up with Taffy! I don't know anything about it. Take it up with Taffy, then!"

Knowing that the guys he had ripped off would now be coming after him, Taffy, who, as Charley recalled, "was loaded with money, came back with a Camaro and shotguns and machine guns. And Tommy went, 'Okay. Let's go,' and we left Amsterdam." Taffy himself then returned to London, where someone reported seeing him trying to get a fix in Soho by selling entry for twenty quid to peep shows that had no idea what he was doing.

Just as he had done throughout his European sojourn, Tommy was able to leave Amsterdam on a moment's notice because, as Jake later explained, "Dad had all these blank airlines tickets from his old real estate deals. TWA. Lufthansa. British Airways. Whenever we were in trouble, he would fill one out and—*poof!*—we could get on a plane, and just like Puff the Magic Dragon, we were gone again. So we decided to risk it and go back to England. We were really nervous because we thought we would be arrested at the airport."

For reasons best known only to him, Tommy, who had been traveling on a variety of passports, including one issued to him in Denmark, decided after landing at Heathrow to present a document from some long since extinct international body known as the Commonwealth of Humanity. For reasons best known only to them, British immigration officials decided to let Tommy, Jake, and Charley back into the United Kingdom. After a four-year odyssey that had begun when he had left England with Mick Jagger's wedding present taped to the bodies of his two young sons, Tommy, now thirty-seven years old, was right back where he had started.

20
st. ann's villas

As out of control as he had so often been while traveling through Europe with Jake and Charley, Tommy was in his own way still mourning the loss of Puss and so could justify his behavior. After he returned with the boys to England, Tommy's continuing pursuit of the kind of oblivion he could only find through the constant use of drugs and alcohol became a goal in and of itself, defining him by any standard as someone who simply could not cope with life in any other way.

"We got back to England," Jake said, "and Dad went on a bender. He was back home with all his people, and Charley and I were sent off to sleep on couches with friends. It was the first time he had left us. We had been like millstones around his neck, and he couldn't deal with us anymore. He was done and worn out, and it was like, 'I'm home. Go stay with these people.' Who were taking pity on us."

Taken in by Tommy's former mechanic and his family, Jake and Charley found themselves sleeping on a couch in a council flat in World's End, not far from where the Flying Dragon had once stood. As Jake recalled, the entire flat was "smaller than a living room. We could hear them fucking at night. Dad was out and about doing deals and getting more and more strung out. And then he met Sally, who had a place of her own, and he moved in with her, and then they both got strung out on heroin."

The daughter of a Warwickshire farmer who had served as a tank commander in the British army and then become the chairman of the local dairy corporation, Sally had done some modeling after leaving school and then gone to London, where she had worked as a hostess at a nightclub. With fashionably frizzy hair, a fine-boned face, and large eyes, Sally was dark and good-looking but not nearly so exotic as Puss. Tommy was driving a friend's car when he first saw Sally walking down the King's Road with a girlfriend. The guy in the car with Tommy knew Sally's girlfriend, and so he introduced Sally and Tommy to one another. "I thought he was pretty tasty," she recalled. "And I'm sure he thought I was, too." The way Tommy liked to tell the story, he had been staring at Sally so intently before they met that he drove right into a lamppost.

Although they had never spoken to one another, Sally had first seen Tommy sitting with Jake and Charley at sunset on the beach in Marbella while on holiday there three years earlier. Thirty years old when she met him again in London, Sally was quite unlike any woman Tommy had ever been with before. Raised in a rock-solid middle-class environment outside Rugby, a small city in Warwickshire, she knew little about the world in which he had always lived.

The two became lovers, and Tommy moved with the boys into a flat that Sally's father had bought her at 11 St. Ann's Villas, a redbrick building on the corner of Holland Park Avenue and Queensdale Road. Although there were expensive houses nearby, the immediate neighborhood was fairly run-down and a steady stream of cars heading from North Kensington to the Holland Park roundabout rattled constantly past the flat.

Although Sally had never before done hard drugs, she was soon "smoking and eating" opium with Tommy. When Taffy appeared on the scene, they all began "chasing the dragon" by smoking heroin as well. Tommy and Sally then started injecting the drug while also smoking "a lot of cocaine." In Jake's words, "They were so strung out on heroin that all they were doing was literally staying in their room eating cheese and marzipan and shooting up and smoking cigarettes. That was it. They were like bears in hibernation, and Charley and I had to sit there and be quiet because Sally hated us and would come out screaming, 'You fucking kids! Shut up!'"

It was at St. Ann's Villas that Jake and Charley finally realized how their mother had died. After Tommy, who was "really strung out and engaged in some nefarious activity," had screamed at Jake and Charley, he left them alone in a car outside the flat. "We were both really shaken up and crying," Jake said. "And all of a sudden, I literally had one of those Isaac Newton moments, and I turned to my brother and said, 'Mom didn't have an accident. She killed herself.' And we both erupted into these huge, uncontrollable wails. I was eleven, and he was nine."

As Tommy and Sally got deeper into the desperate daily ritual of scoring and shooting, only to then have to score all over again— the ritual that is a junkie's life—the tension between her and the boys grew steadily worse. As she would later say, "We were strung out, and people put themselves first because they know they're going to feel sick in a few hours. Not little sick. Big sick. And you dread that. If you have some at night and you have to wake up without some to get yourself together, you get quite sick. If we had to choose between buying dope and a big supper for the kids, we would have chosen the dope. And I suppose I was worse than Tom. The kids were staying in the front sitting room, but it got to be a bit too much."

Because her father owned the flat, Sally and Tommy did not have to pay rent to live there, and so he could not afford to defy her. After having done all he could to keep the boys away from Puss' family, Tommy sent them to live with Jenny and Alan Ponte. "It was the ultimate betrayal," Jake said later. "Like, 'You're sending us to the enemy.' To his credit, he never gave us up until he was too smacked out to deal with us anymore. He always kept us with him, but it was like being handed over to the Gestapo. We went and lived in Alan and Jenny's castle with a moat in Ardeley, and I wasn't happy there, because there really wasn't a place for us."

In Ardeley, Jake and Charley visited their mother's grave for the first time. They attended the local school, where teachers discovered that Charley, who could speak Danish, Spanish, and French but had only ever been educated in Denmark, could not read English. At the house one day, Jenny was summoned by her gardener, who had discovered what he believed to be a dead body on the grounds of the estate. Rushing downstairs, she looked out the drawing room window only to see Tommy fast asleep on the veranda. With no money for the train, he had walked thirty miles from London to see the boys.

For almost a year, Jake and Charley lived in Ardeley with Alan and Jenny. In London, Tommy was barely eking out a living by selling prints on Portobello Road on Saturdays while also shoplifting to survive. Both boys hated being back there, because, in Jake's words, "They [Tommy and Sally] didn't have any food. Literally. They weren't eating. And if we asked for food, we would get chewed out because there wasn't any money."

Spinning a story that it was Sally who wanted them to go off to school, Tommy drove the boys to Summerhill, the boarding school in Leiston, Suffolk, founded by the well-known progressive Scottish educator A. S. Neill. Recalling their first day at the school, Jake said, "We got there, and Tommy said, 'This is Jake and Charley Weber, and I'm dropping them off.' And the woman said, 'We've been expecting you for three weeks now. The term has already started.'"

Unbeknownst to Tommy, Puss had always wanted her sons to go to Summerhill and so had already enrolled them there for that term. Because her trustees were willing to pay their fees, Jake and Charley spent the next four years at what Jake would later call "the granddaddy of alternative schools. Summerhill was like a life raft in the middle of a storm. You could do anything you wanted there so long as you didn't interfere with anyone else's ability to do anything they wanted."

Totally self-governing, Summerhill was run like a democracy, with each student having the same vote as the headmistress (A. S. Neill's wife, Ena) at weekly meetings where everyone decided on the rules for daily life at the school. As Charley later described it, "There were no uniforms, and you didn't have to go to class if you didn't want to, but it was a very pure and natural way of growing up with self-rule and respect for people that gave you values."

Clad in the only pair of jeans each of them owned that had been purchased at the Shepherd's Bush market for thirty pence, both boys flourished at the school. At Summerhill, Jake played football and appeared in various theatrical productions while Charley played electric guitar and learned to skateboard. "Jake did a little better on his exams there than I did," Charley said. "But I was good at art, technical drawing, engineering, crafts, and music. Although I was not a great student, I passed my maths, English, and biology. I had a band, and I was very happy while I was there, but also confused by all the mayhem at home—smack and the lack of legitimate child care."

Although Tommy visited his sons while they were at the school, Jake would later remember being "mortified every time he did so. He was really loaded and had hit bottom, and he would park in the field with his tent for three days at a time, and Charley and I would bring him food from the cafeteria."

During the long school holidays, the boys would return to St. Ann's Villas. In order to eat, they would knock on doors and offer to wash cars, clean other people's houses, and do odd jobs for money. Christmas was, in Jake's words, "always grim." Charley recalled, "It was terrifying during the holidays, and I was afraid of expressing myself other than with a skateboard or on a piano or a guitar, which I picked up after playing the drums." Because Tommy and Sally could not pay the bill, there was no electricity in the flat, thereby making it impossible for the boys to bathe, "because there was no hot water."

With the British government having criminalized the use and sale of heroin in England, there was now money to be made by dealing the drug on the street. Tommy and Taffy began doing business from the flat, a situation that did not go unnoticed by the local cops. As Charley said, "Tommy would set up these stings where he would do a drug deal and then get gangsters to come in with guns to steal the stuff. He would sell the drugs, get them back, and then sell them again."

One day, when Charley was about fourteen years old, he came back to St. Ann's Villas only to see Taffy standing across the road with a group of guys whom Charley did not know. Although Taffy gave him an odd look, Charley thought nothing of it until the front door of the flat flew open ten minutes later and "Bang, in came the Flying Squad shouting, 'Up against the walls, girls!' They put this gun up my nose, and I didn't know if it was really the cops or a sting Tommy had set up. When I realized it was just the police, I was actually relieved."

After both Tommy and Taffy had been busted, Taffy demanded to know why Charley had not warned his father about what was about to happen. "And I said, 'As far as I knew, they were all your mates.'" In fact, the people who had been standing with Taffy were cops. Found guilty of possessing cannabis and handling stolen goods in September 1975, Tommy was let go with a fine and a conditional discharge.

Somehow, Tommy managed to stay out of trouble with the law until 1979. After he had screwed up a sizable heroin deal by using most of it himself and then cutting the rest to sell on his own, an old friend saved Tommy's life by beating him up in front of some Russian mobsters who wanted to kill him for what he had done. In Jake's words, "He kept hitting Tommy until they were satisfied and would not kill him." On his own, Tommy then went after the guy who had refused to pay him money he was owed as part of the deal.

As Jake recalled, "Tommy took the guy and drove the wrong way up the on-ramp onto the M5 and said, 'Are you ready to go to the bank now?'" Someone who had witnessed the incident gave Tommy's license plate number to the police. By the time the guy had taken money out of his bank to pay Tommy, the police came to arrest him. Kicking the guy out of his car, Tommy took off on a high-speed chase through the streets of London.

After doing all he could to lose the cops only to realize that more police units kept joining the pursuit, Tommy led them all back to St. Ann's Villas, where he pulled up right outside the flat so that Sally could see what was happening and flush all their drugs down the toilet. Pulling Tommy out of his car, the enraged cops, in Jake's words, "beat him up on the street, handcuffed him, and then dragged him up the paddy wagon stairs. They were furious at him for making them chase him all over London, and they had a right to be, because at times he was driving on the sidewalk."

On July 3, 1979 as he sat waiting for his case to be heard, Tommy wrote a letter to Jake and Charley at Summerhill:

Well, I'm sitting in a police court waiting to be heard on a charge of Dangerous & Drunken driving and having a piece of hash—very bad & stupid. I just hope they are not too hard on me, tho' goodness knows I deserve it! But I just got a terrible beating by the crews of EIGHT police cars, who pounced on me as I got out of the car on Saturday night, outside the flat. Gosh, I must have really been out of my head. So I don't expect they will allow me to keep my driving licence, which is really a drag as I am in the car all the time. . . .

The court put the case off until September, thereby allowing Tommy to go with Sally and their newborn son, Buddy, whose middle name was also Evelyn, on holiday to the house owned by Tommy's mother in the south of France. While he was there, Tommy applied for a French driving license to replace the one eventually taken from him for what he had done. When the case was finally heard in court, Tommy was fined and disqualified from driving for five years, but again managed not to spend a day in jail.

After Jake had completed his studies at Summerhill in September 1975, his godfather, Peter van Gerbig, who had been the best man at Puss and Tommy's wedding but was now no longer on speaking terms with Tommy, arranged for Jake to come to America so that he could attend the Cate School near Santa Barbara. In what was in many ways an odd re-creation of what R. E. Weber had done by adopting Tommy and sending him off to Haileybury as a boy, Jake was literally plucked from the life he had been living and transported to a completely different world. "He saved me by taking me out of there," Jake said. "Charley was still at Summerhill, and the plan was for him to come out as well, but it proved too much for my godfather, who had a new family of his own. It was a lovely idea, but just wishful thinking." Three years passed before Jake saw his father or brother again.

"The whole thing about us separating when Jake went off to America," Charley recalled, "was that we would fight like brothers for hours, but we always had each other's backs. For me, it was harder losing Jake than losing Puss and Tom. He went away when I was fourteen, and I stayed another year at Summerhill, and then I split." Although the plan was for Charley to attend the Rhode Island School of Design in America, van Gerbig could by then no longer afford to bring him to America. Charley went instead to St. Christopher's School in London, where he studied computer programming and technical design before taking his A-levels and going on the dole "like everyone else I knew in England then." After a couple of months on the dole, Charley began working at a funky hotel in West Kensington while running an unlicensed parking facility on the side.

"It was hard at St. Ann's Villas when Jake and I were living there together," Charley said. "It was insanity cubed after he left. At that point, Tommy couldn't see straight. He'd sold my guitars. I had to give him my last five quid so he could get a fix. He was gone. I said,

'Tommy, if you want to do this to yourself, that's fine. But you can't do this to me. I'm out of here.' And I left." With her son, Buddy, Sally also left St. Ann's Villas and moved to Brinklow, a small village near Rugby where Tommy soon joined them

Charley, who now had no place to live in London, began hanging out in a flat on Hazlitt Road not far from the Kensington Olympia, where Tommy had shot Jimi Hendrix in concert. Charley, then eighteen years old, soon met and fell in love with a woman who was "twenty-nine and super beautiful." The two began living together in the flat on Hazlitt Road. At the age of nineteen, Charley rented an office in west London at the Nomis Complex, where bands like the Pretenders and Queen came to rehearse. He "shot about seventy-five music videos of different acts, most newly signed by Virgin, Polydor, and EMI. I also produced music videos for Emerson, Lake, and Palmer; Roger Taylor from Queen; and the Wonder Stuff." When Charley was twenty, his girlfriend gave birth to his son Beau. Whenever Tommy came down from Brinklow, he stayed with them.

One day, Sally, who had come to visit Tommy in the flat on Hazlitt Road, ran out into the street and cried, "Charley, Charley, Charley, you've got to wake Tommy up. He's going." Rushing inside, Charley found Tommy unconscious in the hall. Somehow, he managed to haul his father into the bathroom. "I'd seen that sort of thing before," Charley would later say, "and I'd heard you really had to slap someone about to wake them up. So I filled the bathtub with cold water while I was yelling and kind of hitting him. By then, he was totally blue. Finally, he woke up and said, 'Oh, hi, Charley, what's up?' And I said, 'You were dead, Tom. You'd gone. You all right?' And he said, 'Yeah. I'm fine.' By then, he was fixing constantly. Tommy could do more drugs than anyone."

By 1980, Tommy was, in Charley's words, "losing any semblance of sanity." During that year, Tommy was arrested and convicted for possession of heroin, failing to surrender to bail, possession of cocaine, drunk driving, possession of cannabis, and two separate counts of handling stolen goods. After his one-year prison sentence was suspended, he was again back out on the street.

Two years later, Tommy's luck finally ran out. After serving three months in jail in Brixton, he was transferred to Wormwood Scrubs. "The Scrubs," as it is known on the streets of London, is an imposing Victorian prison on DuCane Road in the Borough of Hammersmith and Fulham that to this day is the defining symbol of the penal system in England.

A veritable temple of punishment and confinement constructed with prison labor before the turn of the century, Wormwood Scrubs is a huge, sprawling redbrick edifice that accurately reflects the social values of the age in which it was built. Surrounded by a high stone wall with ornate turrets and iron-barred wooden gates, Wormwood Scrubs instills fear even in those who have never been inside it. As someone who drove by it each day to work said, "It is never summer at Wormwood Scrubs."

In the words of Tommy's old friend Keith Richards, who spent a single night there in 1969 after being convicted for possession of cannabis, "the Scrubs, that's hard time. The big house." As Richards told another interviewer, "I was only in there 24 hours, but it was the longest 24 hours I can remember. You get this goddamn shabby uniform, walk round in a circle and see the 60-foot-high granite wall. The cell was probably no worse than a lot of the Holiday Inns I've been in—the tough bit was the fact that you couldn't get out."

How Tommy finally found himself in Wormwood Scrubs as Prisoner Number 222181 under the name "Webber," one of the many versions of his last name he used to confuse the authorities, was a tale in and of itself. As always, it involved his old friend Taffy. Two years earlier, the cops had come looking for Taffy at St. Ann's Villas and found a small amount of opium in some kitchen jars as well as "some traces of smack" on the scales he used for his deals. As the householder, Tommy was also busted, but his sentence was suspended.

After Taffy had done a stint in jail for the bust, he popped up again, in Tommy's words, "strung out, sick & broke & begging for money of which I had none tho' he was unbearably importunistic." Telling Taffy he was no longer into pulling off petty crimes for money and unable to call Sally in Rugby for funds because "the phone had just gone on the blink," Tommy let Taffy talk him into going to the local post office to send her a telegram. Spying a wallet someone had left lying on the counter, Tommy pointed it out to Taffy and told him to do with it as he wished and leave him alone.

After stealing the wallet, Taffy came by the flat to pick up Tommy so they could go score. While Tommy was waiting in the car for Taffy to come back with the dope, the same policeman who had busted them at St. Ann's Villas appeared. Knowing Tommy was up to no good, he asked him to step out of the car, saw the wallet, and promptly arrested Tommy for theft. When Tommy appeared before the same magistrate who had suspended his previous sentence, Tommy was given 11½ months in prison plus the entire one-year suspended sentence that by then had just three months left on it.

Stuck inside a dark and foreboding prison that had freaked out even the unshakable Keith Richards, Tommy, who was now straight for the first time in years, became once more the highborn gentleman he had been bred to be. In a series of letters he wrote to Jake during his imprisonment, Tommy described his situation with the stylish aplomb of a nobleman who just happened to find himself in an institution soon to be supervised by David Ramsbotham, with whom Tommy had attended Haileybury.

On June 21, 1982, Tommy wrote to Jake:

Hi Jake, hope this rather obscure address doesn't shock you too much, but yes its the can & one can't move to there. Its not bad at all, it's just awful, tho' not in any inhuman way or anything, a bit tense and the company is a bit close and maybe not exactly what one would choose but then that is really about all one loses, choice, otherwise its just boring but then I've been in the system for about 6 months. . . . I'm actually here for sitting in Taffy, yes that fucking character of mine's-car-he ho. What a life.

Tommy closed his letter by telling Jake how badly he missed him and how much he appreciated having received a letter from him:

now the doors are closing & another identical day grounds into motion, a constant source of surprise. I shall soon be off to my slave labour for 5 pence per hour which is a hoot, the only way to earn stamps & smoke— well only legitimate way & its the bottom line & I love you & God Bless & have it good & don't worry (I hope this gets to you) all my love forever.
T.

With school having let out for the summer in America, Jake, who was then living in difficult circumstances with his godfather's family in San Francisco while "walking miles to this pizza place where I was working and doing gardening jobs for money," sent Tommy funds that were deposited in his personal cash account at the prison. Tommy wrote to thank him on June 27, 1982:

Your bounty astonishes me; I shall soon be so comfortable here that I won't want to move, if I ever can. . . . Scrabble is a dangerous blood sport in here, in case one happens to spell imaginatively or even just correctly . . . the most poignant card outside a cell I saw said, 'Sentence: Life + 30 days' I wonder if the 30 days is before or after ascensions, time on cross, rolling stone & resurrecting included? My 3 months in Brixton too should be 4 off here but in my case doesn't work like that. Catch you, 22 . . .

Describing the staff as "on the whole, pretty understanding," Tommy added that for him, Wormwood Scrubs was "no more or less than a bad 'good school' . . . very similar to St. Edward & Haileybury tho' more extreme in age & inactivity, boredom & bestiality." He also noted that he hadn't "cracked yet":

... it seems they have discovered my awful secret—no I'm not a latent queer not crazed klepto, sado/macho, wild psycho nor all-but-normal neuro, no, none of these but manic, a manic depressive, which is rather depressing if not too surprising. Don't worry it's not a plug-into-the-wall-and-chain job, just a daily dose of lithium salts to 'ease' me out. Ha! This 'short-sharp-shock' straightened me out far quicker & better, personally, but maybe they are planning on keeping me here, so the lithium will be helpful. . . . He, the shrink, assures me its not 'habit' forming which is disappointing without being any relief.

Finally diagnosed with a disease those closest to him had long suspected was one of the reasons that he was continually self-medicating with drugs and alcohol, Tommy closed his letter by noting that personally, he agreed with Timothy Leary that the "most suitable jail juice" was opium because it served to kill the libido.

Shortly after he wrote the letter, Tommy received a visit from Sally and their three-year-old son, Buddy, whom Tommy adored. In Buddy's words, "I remember walking down the big wall into this room that looked like a gymnasium that was the meeting room with one table for each guy. They had a little confectionery store so the families could eat while they waited, and I remember giving him a bit. He had a really big bushy beard there. For the obvious reasons. Because he was a bit of a pretty boy, so he roughed himself up to look a bit more masculine. So he didn't get approached in the showers. I remember tugging on it."

On June 27, 1982, Jake, then nineteen years old and about to enter Middlebury College in Vermont after having graduated from the Cate School, returned to England to see his father for the first time in three years. In a letter he wrote Jake the next day, Tommy noted, "*There is a very important secret.* Work is much more interesting than play and if you are lucky enough to be able to make your work your play and your play pay, well then you're in clover."

A month later, in his final letter from prison after Jake had visited him again, Tommy wrote that although their life together had

been quite a long struggle but it will have been well worth it—tho' I know its been a terrible torture for you, especially so far away and having to build a new life, friends & environment: but it will have been worth it, especially if we can all be free & united on a June day living & laughing under the same roof.

He expressed wonder at his own current "predicament":

It causes others more pain than I, which is the best reason I can think of for getting out & never returning, but we must bow to our destinies, they are more than only of our own making. It must be most frustrating to be thrust into the institutionalized security of the zoo; and I've often wondered on which side of the bars/fence one is; its very much more a question of point of view.

. . . the good news is good, for a change: for really its not anything as bad as one imagines or needs and though in general incalculably wasteful. . . . there are glimmers of hope & good will, tho the general principle is appalling and quite devoid of any of these graces. No hope, No bail, No dope, just jail! . . . And sometimes still this old dream looks to get the better of me 'Ain't it just like Life, Turn out to be a dream come true . . .'

After spending about eight months behind bars, Tommy emerged from prison only to discover that all the money from the sale of the flat at St. Ann's Villas he had hoped to use to "go around the world" with Buddy and Sally had gone instead to her father. As though he had learned nothing from his time in prison except that it was a place he never wanted to go again, Tommy, now forty-five years old, was soon drinking and using heroin again.

21
rugby

Tommy's life in Rugby, an "oppressive market town where farm boys come from twenty miles around to strut about and kick each other's asses on the weekend," really began the day he first wandered into the ruined old redbrick building at 92 Lower Hilmorton Street, which housed the Rugby Youth Project, a local charity for the young and unemployed. At "the YP," as everyone who hung out there on a daily basis called it, the funk was so thick you could cut it with a knife. The scene itself was distinctly working class. Nonetheless, it was at the YP that Tommy found what became his second home.

As Pete Prince, then a nineteen-year-old art student at the local college who played in a band called the Dark Side, from which he earned "no money at all," would later say, "Somewhere in that building, there was a weirdness magnet that used to just pull them in. Anybody weird who ever came to Rugby got drawn in. Italians who couldn't speak English. Tommy. All these weird people. We'd be sitting there, and they'd just come in off the streets."

Now forty-seven years old and looking a good deal like the actor Peter O'Toole, Tommy was older than most of those at the YP. His posh, upper-class accent marked him as not just an outsider but someone who the regulars believed had to be working for the police because, in Prince's words, "There was a scene going on, and they don't like anything going on in this town, because of Rugby School."

In Rugby, daily life was still dominated by the exclusive boarding school in the center of the city that had been founded in 1567 and that had given its name to the game first played on its lush green fields in 1823. Over the centuries, the separation between town and gown in Rugby had become so complete that the locals knew that their lives had nothing to do with those of the sons and daughters of the rich and powerful who attended the school. After completing their studies there (as Tommy's former brother-in-law Alan Ponte had done), most of them would go on to brilliant careers all over the world, leaving the locals behind to continue earning a living in a far more traditional, working-class manner. Many of those who could not find work of any kind ended up spending most of their time at the YP.

"Upstairs," Pete Prince would later say of the YP, "there was a print works that did printing on low budget for charities and other people who did not have a lot of money to spend. So we used to do all the band posters and handouts for all the gigs and all the tickets. All the bands would come into the YP to get their printing done. They'd start hanging out with us and practicing in the rooms downstairs, and we'd end up recording them in this really basic studio we had." While the YP was then the center of the burgeoning Rugby underground art and music scene, it could have all just as well been taking place on the dark side of the moon rather than ninety minutes by train from London. Rugby itself was just that self-contained.

Which was why no one believed for a moment the fantastic story that Tommy himself had once hung out with the Rolling Stones until the day someone brought in a book of photographs only to find Tommy right there on one of the pages, back at Villa Nellcote. Duly impressed, someone showed the book to Tommy.

Promptly throwing it across the room, he stalked out of the building and did not return to the YP for a couple of weeks.

"He never brandished his past," Prince recalled. "But little bits would seep out when we were all drunk. When he'd get booted, he would say, 'It's me, Tommy the Tumbling Dice!' But only when he was booted. He would never sit there and say, 'I used to hang out with the Rolling Stones.' Because in a strange sort of twisted way, Tommy was exactly like us."

Not everyone at the YP approved of Tommy. In the words of Pete Bain, a member of Spacemen 3, then the most popular psychedelic band in Rugby, "He threw pills at people like Smarties because he wanted you to binge with him. He'd come staggering in, talk shit at you for an hour with garbled words like a radio that had to be tuned to a certain frequency, and then stagger out again like a drunk. He'd had a public-school education, and the upper class are trained to be selfish and egocentric." In time however, even Bain became Tommy's friend.

When Tommy first stumbled through the front door of the YP, he had just moved with Sally and their six-year-old son, Buddy, into a lovely house that Sally's father had bought for her on Tennyson Avenue. For the past three years, Tommy, Sally, and Buddy had been living in Brinklow, a nearby village best known for the ruined Norman castle that stood atop an ancient burial mound. Although Tommy and Sally had done their best to fit in with the local citizenry, they were both still using and drinking heavily and were often unable to pay their electric bill, much less deal with the debt collectors who came around regularly. As a child in Brinklow, Buddy's breakfast often consisted of toast cooked over an open fire.

After having gone through a hospital program to withdraw from drugs, Sally was now clean. The same could not be said for Tommy. No longer injecting heroin, he was, in Jake's words, "buying morphine sulfate in pill form from junkies who were on methadone and doubling and tripling up his doses and going out and buying smack, which he was probably snorting, because he wouldn't want to waste any by smoking it. With the morphine sulfate, he would take these really powerful painkiller pills. I once took a quarter of one, and I was bedridden for two days. One of my friends took a whole one, and he was out for a week. Tom would take six at a time."

By then, Tommy had already tried his hand at a variety of jobs. Thanks to Charley, who had bought him a Volkswagen transit van, Tommy ran a small transport company for a while. The business ended when he crashed the van. He had studied database management at East Warwickshire College, edited the Rugby community database from a local library, and gone on the road to sell the *Encyclopedia Britannica* before becoming the gardener at the downtown shopping mall.

During the course of a typical day on the job, Tommy would sit in a pub all day long until his boss came around to make sure he was working. Once his boss had left, Tommy would return to the pub. As Prince soon discovered, Tommy was also growing cannabis plants on a balcony in the mall where the plants could only be seen by those who knew where to look for them. For Tommy, growing dope at the mall was not so much a money-making proposition as, in Prince's words, "a way to put his own twist on it, just as Tommy always did."

In Pete Prince, who was half Jewish and half Romany, Tommy found a younger, sweeter version of his old pal Taffy, who was eventually found dead under suspicious circumstances. Although Prince was nearly thirty years younger than Tommy, the two soon became best friends. Which did not mean that they did not also have their differences. As part of the YP's role as the center of everything hip in Rugby, those who ran the facility used some extra funding to persuade David "Honeyboy" Edwards, a seventy-seven-year-old black Mississippi blues man who was then touring England and claimed to have known the legendary Robert Johnson, to play there on November 3, 1992.

Assigned the job of looking after Honeyboy, Prince picked up the blues man at the train station and took him to his hotel. Intent on partying with the aged musician, Tommy turned up at two in the afternoon with a bottle of whiskey in his hand. Terrified that Honeyboy would be in no shape to perform if he began drinking with Tommy, Honeyboy's manager did his best to persuade Tommy to leave. When he refused to do so, the manager instructed Prince to throw Tommy out of the room.

Trying to reason with Tommy, Prince told him the cops would soon be there if he did not leave. When that did no good, Prince grabbed Tommy by the scruff of the neck and dragged him out into the street. Becoming "a bit impertinent," Tommy said, "Princie! You're such a fucking peasant, man!" As Prince later recalled, "So I just went *bang!* and hit him on the chin, and he sat down in the middle of the road. And I said, 'I might be a peasant. But you don't have to fucking tell me so.' He apologized later, and I didn't really hurt him. Just enough to knock him down."

While this might have been more than enough to keep a lesser man from having anything more to do with Honeyboy Edwards or his gig at the YP, that man would not have been Tommy. As Honeyboy was about to begin performing on a makeshift stage in a tiny room at the YP into which a hundred people had somehow managed to cram themselves, Tommy threw open the front door of the building and let it slam loudly behind him. In a voice everyone recognized and no one could ignore, Tommy began shouting, "Ho-ney . . . *Boy*! Ho-ney Boy, Can-dy . . . *Man*! Sugar Boy's here!"

"At this point," Prince said, "the tears were running down my face. Tommy was completely pissed, and he burst into the room where the gig was happening, and we had to wrestle him back out again because he was so excited the guy had turned up that he couldn't control himself. We shut him up in another room so the gig could go on, but every now and then, we would hear him in the background going, 'Ho-ney . . . *Boy*! Can-dy . . . *Man*! It's Tom . . . *mee*!' It was just hilarious."

Despite his antics, Tommy eventually became one of the general managers of the YP. During his tenure, a well-funded local Boy's Club donated its beat-up old minibus to the YP. Christening it "the Magic Bus" after the Who song of the same name, Tommy, in Prince's words, "became the Magic Bus Driver, and of course, he drove the bus just like he had driven his racing car, and we started going off to see all these odd, weird bands. Everyone who worked there would get in the bus at the end of work, and we would all drive to the gig, have a ball, and then drive back again."

One night in March 1995, Tommy decided to take everyone to see Bob Dylan at the Brixton Academy in London. "Dylan came on," Prince said, "and he [Dylan] was sort of whining and the people down front were transfixed and the people halfway back were mumbling and the people at the back were angry." Before anyone could stop him, Tommy pushed his way through the crowd. Stopping directly in front of the stage, Tommy shouted, "Bob! Bob! Bob! It's *Tommy*! You sound *shit*, man! Get it together!"

As Prince would later say, "Dylan definitely heard him. Because it was virtually silent at the time. And then the show got better. I'm sure Tom wouldn't have known Dylan back in the day. I'm sure he had never, ever met him. What Dylan did know was that one person had the bollocks to stand up and say, 'Man, I paid for this. You better get it together!' And he even had the decency to tell his name before he said so."

The single greatest scam Tommy pulled in Rugby occurred after the YP had shut its doors in 1994, when central funding for the project was withdrawn. By then, the widespread use of ecstasy as a party drug had brought about what became known as the Second Summer of Love in England. In the huge concrete bunker built as a nuclear fallout shelter on Lawford Heath, a bleak, rundown vista just outside town, as many as eighty people, all of them out of their heads on "e," would regularly gather for impromptu all-night raves. When the cops came by at three in the morning to break up the party, those inside would shout, "What are you going to do? Put your shoulder to the door and break it down?" Safely ensconced in the impenetrable bunker, everyone would then go right on raving.

When the property came up for sale in 1995, Tommy decided to buy it lock, stock, and barrel. His plan was to transform the former Royal Observer Corps Headquarters building on the heath into a new home for the collection of twentieth-century English art that was then languishing in a basement at nearby Warwick University. As Tommy wrote in a curriculum vitae that was itself a minor masterpiece of fiction, the nuclear bunker would be maintained as a "permanent monument to and reminder of the Coventry Blitz and its aftermath, for it was from this control centre . . . that the air defences of the city should have been marshalled. Instead, orders were given that led to the city of Coventry being sacrificed, apparently to disguise the ENIGMA code breakthrough."

Tommy then went on to explain that the reason Rugby owed this gesture to its neighbors in Coventry was because "Rugby was never seriously bombed—apparently because Adolf Hitler had a girlfriend from his Liverpool days living in Hillmorton, so Rugby was under Hitler's protection and therefore was spared from his own Luftwaffe, throughout the war!" Resurrecting his failed plans for Lundy Island and Radio Rolling Stone, Tommy also proposed to build a community FM radio station on the site that would serve both Coventry and Birmingham.

In truth, Tommy intended to convert the bunker into a club where he could hold massive raves on the weekend and that would also serve as a huge indoor marijuana plantation. Prince accompanied Tommy to the Lawford Heath auction: "We went, and nobody was there. Me and him, suited and booted, and about three or four other people, and he bought it for about nine or ten thousand quid [about fifteen thousand dollars]. He had no money at all, but he had this big story that these investors were going to put money into it."

After he had made the winning bid, Tommy was unable to come up with the money to close the deal. After the botched sale became a continuing story in the local newspapers, Lawford Heath went back on auction. Although the bunker eventually did become a place where raves were held, Tommy had nothing to do with it and "was completely gutted" when the deal fell through. Despite the willingness he expressed in his curriculum vitae to take on any kind of job, Tommy never worked again after the YP shut its doors.

Although Tommy and Sally continued to see one another on a regular basis, Tommy moved out of her house on Tennyson Avenue in 1994 and went to live in a council flat at 220 Parkfield Avenue in Newbold so that he could be near his son Buddy, who was then attending the Stowe School. On the day Buddy was to be presented with an award at the school, Tommy persuaded Prince to drive him to the ceremony. On the way, he asked Prince to stop the car so he could get something from a shop. Emerging with a bottle of brandy, Tommy began to drink from it. Asking Prince to stop again, Tommy then bought a bottle of champagne. When Prince ordered him to stop drinking because "You're going to turn up booted, and your son's going to be really pissed off," the two began to argue.

As they made their way across the school grounds to the awards ceremony, both Prince and Tommy realized they were not really suitably attired for an occasion attended "by all these well-dressed, quiet-spoken people who were clapping" for their sons and daughters. Suddenly, Tommy caught sight of his son on stage being given the award. Knowing that Tommy was about to begin shouting out Buddy's name, Prince "rugby tackled him, and he went down and we wrestled a bit, and I said, 'Look, man, you're not doing this. I'm sorry. I'm keeping you right here.' Buddy knew we had been there, but Tom was drunk and it was beyond the pale."

While living in Newbold, Tommy acquired "this weird little Fiat car" that he called "the Bubble." So he could fit more people inside and because "he reckoned it went faster without the weight," Tommy removed all the seats but his own from the vehicle, which he always drove at an incredible speed without either insurance or a license.

Stopped more than once by the police while he and Tommy were in the car, Pete Prince would watch in wonder as Tommy, "who could speak like the lord mayor of London," would politely inform the officer that he had made an awful mistake by pulling them over as Tommy himself was just on his way back home. Tommy would then drive off without presenting any of the official documents he did not have. "Because he had the right voice and that aura about him, like Alec Guinness in *Star Wars*," Prince later said, "nobody could deny him."

Despite Tommy's lack of regular income during this period, he could still pull off the grand gesture with great style. "He didn't want to be wealthy," Prince said. "He once got a payment of about two hundred quid into his bank account, and he went into the worst pub in town, which was full of all the single mothers with their children rolling about on the floor and cigarette ends. He walked around the room, gave it all away to them, and walked back out."

Although Tommy and Sally were no longer lovers, he continued doing all he could to persuade her to renew their relationship. One night in December 1997, after Tommy had drunk an entire bottle of brandy in her house, the two of them argued and she told him to go home. With the Fiat now a thing of the past, Tommy hopped onto his Winton bicycle, went flying down the steep, icy hill outside her house, put his legs up in the air as he rounded a corner, and came flying off. "He thought he was racing again," his son Buddy recalled. "He was a bit drunk and trying to hit the apex of this curve and bank it over, and he got it all wrong and slammed into a curb and fractured his femur in a couple of places."

While breaking bones was nothing new for Tommy, he had for the first time seriously damaged the virtually indestructible body that had enabled him to survive for so long. Because one of the fractures was in the ball of his femur, surgeons had to insert a steel rod into his left leg to secure it. Although Tommy's doctors had prescribed opiates for the pain, nurses at the hospital refused to administer them to him because of his long record of addiction. Feeling as though he was being made to withdraw cold turkey, Tommy angrily discharged himself from the hospital two days after the operation and made Buddy drive him home. Heeding Buddy's advice, Tommy then returned to the hospital. Later, he told his son, "I'm glad you did that. I wouldn't be alive if you hadn't."

A year after the initial operation, Tommy's doctors discovered that the bone around the rod they had inserted was deteriorating and so were forced to operate again. After the surgery, Tommy's left leg, in Buddy's words, "shrunk two or three inches, so he was hobbling about." Tommy's disability profoundly affected his life. "Before that," Prince said later, "there wasn't a gig in Rugby he wasn't at. There wasn't a Saturday night when he wouldn't drink at the pub. He was out all the time and always involved with what was going on. Breaking his hip really messed him up because he was then stuck in the flat. I think that was when it all started to change for him."

Leaving Newbold, Tommy moved into a flat at 108 Deetmore Road, where he lived with a junkie friend in a scene that was "manic." Prince recalled watching Tommy take five tabs of ecstasy at once there: "That was when he really got fucked up and started doing loads of gear. He was hanging out with this family of junkies, and they were all mad for crack, smack, and Caramac [a caramel-flavored candy bar made by Nestlé]. They were going round there and getting him to buy stuff so they could all do it as well. He was going through a hell of a lot of money, and he really, really deteriorated quickly. I had to stop going there, because it got too heavy."

During this period, one of Tommy's junkie friends drove him to London, where Tommy was interviewed on camera for a BBC documentary about Jimi Hendrix. Looking more than slightly out of it in a loose, yellow turtleneck sweater beneath a red velvet jacket, his face lined and weathered but with his hair still somehow blonde at the age of sixty, Tommy can be seen in the documentary telling a rambling, disjointed story about an epic contest between himself and Hendrix to swallow as many drops of LSD as possible to ensure they would both get high. Prince later said, "He looked so bad at that point, I thought he was going to die."

In 1998, Tommy, who had not seen his half-sister Lulu in many years, went to visit her in Bali. Charley, now thirty-three years old, accompanied him on the trip. Bearing a distinct resemblance to Eric Clapton, Charley had worked all over the world as a film and video editor. He had organized the first techno-musical festival in Istanbul, where he had also managed a nightclub and fallen in love with and married a woman of Kurdish descent. In time, they divorced and Charley married another Turkish girl.

A talented musician who had played the drums before switching to guitar, Charley also began writing and recording his own songs. Moving constantly, he would eventually live in New York, Los Angeles, Edinburgh, Istanbul, Berlin, and Montreal before returning to England. In Jake's words, Charley was "a highwayman like Tommy, but he's not blond."

After arriving in Bali with Tommy, Charley learned to his great horror that Tommy had brought morphine pills with him to Indonesia, where, in Charley's words, "You get put away for life if you're carrying." While the two of them were staying with Lulu and her family, Tommy would sometimes wake up and have a beer for breakfast. During his visit, he flew to Australia, where his mother was then living, and the two of them reconciled.

After Tommy returned to Bali from Australia with a large supply of opium, he and Charley had a serious falling out. When Charley told his father how badly he missed his wife, Tommy said,

"Charley, fucking grow up." "And that was it," Charley said. "I took this motorbike helmet and threw it at him, and they had to pull me off him. I had hit him once before, but this was when I lost it. When people say something like that, there's more truth than you know behind it. Because he had never grown up, and he was also talking to himself."

During his stay in Bali, Tommy also suffered two minor heart attacks, about which he chose to tell no one at the time. "While he was here," his half-sister Lulu would later say, "we both took a Breath of Life course from a Russian scientist who had studied the terminally ill and determined that when they were about to die, they began to hyperventilate. By giving them little spurts of breath, they normalized and lived. Tommy practiced this technique during the attacks, and it saved him twice."

Although Lulu loved Tommy "desperately and wanted him to be around us, he would become so insane after a few days that all you could think about was how to get rid of him. I had to throw him out of my house in Bali. I literally had to put him on a plane and get him out of there, because he was a risk to our safety in Indonesia. One time, he was lying under the car with no clothes on, screaming his head off, and all my kids were freaking out. He even accused the maids of having taken his lump of opium. Actually, the dog had eaten it and was lying on his back for three days with very dreamy eyes."

In Bali, as in Rugby, Tommy had demonstrated the basic paradox that was the core of his personality. When he was loaded, Tommy could became so obnoxious that it was impossible be around him for long. Yet he could also still sometimes charm the birds out of the trees while seeming more vibrant and vital than those half his age. It was a quality that had attracted Keith Richards to him nearly a quarter of a century earlier. Unlike Richards, who also continued living on the edge, Tommy was trying to maintain a rock-star lifestyle without any real means of support.

After Tommy returned to Rugby, Jake and Charley continued doing all they could to help their father. After graduating from Middlebury College in Vermont, Jake had attended the Julliard School in New York City and then begun working steadily as an actor in theater, television, and films. In 2000, at the age of thirty-seven, he had "impulsively married" a woman he had only known for a few months.

When the marriage ended in divorce two years later, it was, in Jake's words, "a watershed. I went into a sort of spiral and have been in pretty intensive therapy ever since. From growing up in such perilous places and dangerous situations, I have a very highly developed fight-or-flight syndrome. My journey has been to feel safe and love someone in a relationship. Which can be pretty hard when the person I loved more than anyone was suicidal and schizophrenic and killed herself." In 1993, Jake had a featured role in *The Pelican Brief*, which starred Julia Roberts, Denzel Washington, and Sam Shepard. Five years later, he appeared with Brad Pitt and Anthony Hopkins in *Meet Joe Black*.

Two years later, Tommy stumbled into a windfall. Although he never found the hundreds of hours of performances by other bands he had shot as a rock 'n' roll film producer, Tommy did finally manage to locate the footage of Jimi Hendrix, Traffic, and Eric Burdon and the New Animals performing at the Kensington Olympia on December 22, 1967, that had been part of "Watch Out for Your Ears." The Hendrix footage was so rare that a private collector paid more than two hundred thousand dollars to acquire it.

What for anyone else would have been an unexpected stroke of tremendous good fortune became for Tommy simply a means of survival. Jake, who by then was living in Los Angeles, used the money to establish the Tommy Weber Trust and sent Tommy "a couple of hundred quid [about four hundred dollars] a week and a thousand whenever he needed it." Although the division of the proceeds from the sale of the Hendrix footage caused a long and contentious wrangle between Jake and Charley, the brothers eventually managed to resolve their differences. When the money from the trust ran out five years layer, Jake again began supporting his father.

In 2001, Jake came to Rugby to help move Tommy from his dire, drug-ridden flat on Deetmore Road to a warden-controlled housing unit at 6 Harold Cox Place. Considered a disabled person because the surgery on his leg had made it so difficult for him to walk, Tommy was given a small council flat consisting of a kitchenette, a bedroom, a living room, and a bathroom. Equipped with central heating and a brand new refrigerator-freezer that Jake and Charley bought him, the unit also had a panic button so Tommy could summon an ambulance if he was ever in distress. Because Tommy now had to use a motorized disability scooter to get around, the unit was located on the ground floor.

"The place was a wreck," Pete Prince said. "I used to go over and tidy it, and then Tommy got some girl to come round and clean for him, who he called 'the Char.' I think she was the daughter of one of his drug dealers, and she used to go through his pockets and take his money and drugs as well." Tommy, who had suffered an epileptic seizure shortly before his bicycle accident, was now also suffering from hepatitis C as well as what may have been cirrhosis of the liver.

Although his world had shrunk to the confines of his immediate neighborhood, Tommy would go each day on his scooter to the Sainsbury's market on Dumchurch Road, where everybody knew him, to buy champagne. Still moving as fast as humanly possible, he often slammed into the side of his front door as he went full throttle into his flat on his scooter.

In 2002, Tommy again went to Bali to see Lulu on his way to Australia to visit his mother. When Pamela died at the age of eighty-seven in 2004, she left him seventy thousand pounds (about $122,000). Although Tommy himself was then once again broke, he refused to keep any of the money and instead divided the sum equally among his three sons, Jake, Charley, and Buddy, each of whom he adored to the end of his days.

During that same year, Charley, recording as We Are Juan, released *Road 2 Reach You*, a CD of his own songs that Tommy listened to over and over. In Buddy's words, Tommy would "sometimes physically weep when he heard it. He was immensely proud of both Jake and Charley."

While on his way to the 2004 Cannes Film Festival, where *Dawn of the Dead*, an acclaimed remake of the 1978 George Romero–directed cult classic in which he appeared was to be screened, Jake began interviewing his father as well as many of those who had known his parents for a video documentary about his mother. Charley would eventually edit the documentary. A few months after he returned from Cannes, Jake was cast in the role of Joe DuBois, Patricia Arquette's husband on the long-running NBC television series *Medium*.

Although Jake and Charley remained in contact, they continued as adults to be as different from one another as they had been as children. In Jake's words, "We've always had a confrontational relationship, but if someone picked on me as a kid, Charley would come barreling in. He always had my back. We are close emotionally, but we have radically different tastes and world views. In many ways, we are as different as two brothers could possibly be."

One day, when Charley came to visit at Harold Cox Place, Tommy was leaning on his crutches when he saw a flock of birds come to roost on a huge tree across the way. "Look at that, Charley," he said. "Do you get it? Isn't it fantastic!" In Charley's words, "The girl who lived across the way would see him on this little triangle of grass by the side of his front door, and he'd be in a collapsible chair with a bottle of champagne and he'd give her a glass and say, 'Life is too short. You should drink champagne every day.'"

On March 24, 2006, Jake's companion Liz Carey, a former model who had been married to the drummer in the English rock band Oasis and now designs high-end women's handbags while also doing sketch comedy and appearing in films, gave birth to their son, Waylon. "Unlike the rest of my family," Jake said, "I didn't have a kid for a long time. I was forty-three when Waylon was born, and he definitely gave my life a context and took away a lot of the ambient noise. His birth also made me furious at my parents for what they missed. I remembered all the terrible things my father used to say to me and how my mother had checked out. I still carry a lot of emotional baggage with me, but I'm working on it and trying not to be a prisoner of my past, and my son is helping me."

"The first time I saw Waylon," Charley said, "I had just been around the world again, and there was a breaking of the waves, a parting of the waters. It felt like there was a connection between Jake and I again, and it was peaceful. Before then, Jake and I had hit cool running waters. I had been getting much happier by trying to understand my family members from different points of view—aspects of them I had never understood—and it became silly to blame people. We had a distant relationship for a long time. But now it's kind of healed over, and Jake and I have slipped back into the relationship we had when we were young."

By then, Charley, who is currently working as a Web developer in England while feeling "happier and more stable" than ever before, had come to understand that his father was much like an old wolf Charley had encountered while recording on a ranch in Los Angeles. "You could love him but only on his own terms, and you shouldn't ever expect to change him, because you probably wouldn't want to."

Four months after Tommy's grandson Waylon was born, Tommy left Rugby for a short road trip with an acquaintance from the YP to see his old friend Frank Duggan, whom he thought was dying. Along the way, they visited a racecourse where Tommy had driven and an air field where he claimed to have flown for the RAF. On the night of September 21, 2006, Pete Prince took Tommy out for a drink at a quiet, country pub that he liked, where nobody knew him and "he could have a laugh."

Although the doctors who had examined him six months earlier had found no traces of the disease, Tommy told Prince he had cancer. "I was saying, 'No, Tommy, don't say stuff like that. You're just going to freak yourself out.' Because he could wind himself up in the same way he could wind everyone else up to have an amazing night. He could also wind himself up to freak out." While Tommy never conveyed this information to his sons, he had already told Sally and Lulu that "he felt he didn't have much time."

Whether or not Tommy knew he was dying, those closest to him had already noticed a distinct change in his personality—a change that Jake would later call his father's "moment of grace." As Charley said, "He now felt he had paid his debt for whatever he had done. Somehow, he had come to terms with the fact that he had made choices that were very dangerous and very harmful. And probably irresponsible." Sally said, "I think he did come to some peace of mind at the end. He got incredibly nice and caring to the people he loved."

After returning home from the pub with Prince that night, Tommy was taken to the hospital at one-thirty in the morning in a great deal of pain with what was later diagnosed as an abscessed tumor on his liver. Because Tommy's level of drug tolerance was off the charts, the morphine he was given did little to help ease his pain. When Sally persuaded his doctor to administer something stronger, Tommy winked at her. With all the veins in his arms having long since collapsed from intravenous drug use, the drug had to be injected into his groin and through the soles of his feet.

Buddy, who had not seen his father in three weeks and was working in France, talked to him at about five-thirty in the morning. "I could hear the equipment pinging on and off, and he was struggling to speak, and they were talking to him as though he was fairly incoherent, so I knew this was very serious. He said, 'I'm pretty ill.' He died an hour after I spoke to him."

Jake flew from California to England for the funeral, which was attended by about forty people, among them Jenny Ponte, Mary's daughter, Pete Prince, and many of the regulars from the YP. Jake, Charley and his son Beau, and Buddy carried the casket into a room on which a large photograph of Tommy sat before a large wooden cross on a table bedecked with flowers. "Kinder Days," a song Charley had written with the lyrics "But don't it feel like somebody nearby is / Guiding you through light to kinder days" was played as they brought Tommy into the room.

Jake spoke first. Charley followed. Buddy then talked about his father as a fragile star. Pete Bain spoke about Tommy's days at the YP. And then Tommy, who had always said that after he died, he wanted to be pushed out to sea in a flaming ship like the Viking warrior he was meant to be, was cremated. Had he lived until his birthday in December, he would have been sixty-seven years old.

After the ceremony, Pete Prince recalled, "Everyone said, 'Oh, let's go back to the office at the YP, where we all used to get booted together and get booted and watch him on the video.' So we all got booted and put on the video of him on television talking about Hendrix. After it finished and he said the last word, we just all stood up and walked out, because he looked worse on it than when he died."

Thirty-five years after Puss had killed herself in a hotel room in Paddington and long after most of those who knew him had expected it to happen, Tommy Weber's life was over. To the very end, he had remained true to himself. Not for Tommy the path of rehabilitation or the kind of moderation that passed for socially acceptable behavior. Like so many of his generation who defied all the rules, his greatest fault had also been the foundation of his character. Despite how stoned he had been throughout his life, Tommy had lived it fully and on the only terms he had ever understood—his own.

epilogue: another day in the life, ardeley, december 2007

Beyond Stevenage, the fields on both sides of the road suddenly open up into endless vistas, revealing rolling green ridges across which ribbons of frost gleam like diamond necklaces in the brilliant winter sunshine. Behind thick, verdant hedges that frame the village green, large whitewashed country cottages with thatched roofs dotted with patches of pale green moss stand around an open-air pavilion that houses an ancient wooden wagon with rusted gears.

Down the road from the school and the Church of St. Lawrence, hefty black pigs grunt and bellow in a muddy field. A huge barn is filled with spotted cows. In the Rabbit's Foot, the local public house, gourmet meals are served and dogs are welcome. In its entirety, this is the village of Ardeley in the parish of St. Albans in Hertfordshire.

The church itself is ancient, made of rough stone set in mortar and framed with timbers reinforced with sandstone and Portland cement. Above its buttresses and crenellated tower, a shiny brass rooster on a weather vane turns in golden sunlight. From the narrow road on which no cars pass, a gravel path leads the visitor through a swinging wooden gate beneath a vaulted wooden arch to the side of the church where songbirds trill from the branches of holly trees heavy with red fruit and a great, towering pine. There is no other sound.

In a field of tilting stones below a weathered gray Gothic arch fashioned by James Pepper of Hitchin, a nearby market town, Puss lies beneath the inscription, "In Loving Memory, Susan Weber 1943–1971." Above the words, a cross is etched in stone. Although she was not born in Ardeley nor is this where she chose to end her life, her final resting place seems entirely in keeping with the England in which both she and Tommy were reared.

In this silent, green country churchyard, something more than just Puss' mortal remains have been interred. What also lies buried with her is the spirit of an age now long since gone, a moment in time when those engaged in a grand social experiment did everything they could to break free from all constraints. Shattering every rule of conventional behavior, none of them gave much thought to the consequences of their actions. Nor would they have believed how that experiment would end.

Whether it is better to have burned out or to just fade away, no one can say for sure. And while the story of Puss and Tommy's lives may be one of failed promise and great expectations that went sadly unfulfilled, it is hard not to wonder where all that youth and grace and joy and beauty have gone. Consumed by the madness of their age as well as their own needs and desires, they have both now been reduced to dust and ashes.

Born to privilege, Puss and Tommy threw away opportunities that others never had. How their lives as well as those of their sons might have turned out if Puss had not killed herself at the age of twenty-seven, no one will ever know. And while it is not fair to claim that Puss and Tommy are now together again at last, it is hard not to believe that his spirit is here as well.

That Puss and Tommy shared a mighty love, there can be no doubt. That the choices they made led them both to tragic ends is also clear. Because this is real life and not a movie, what can be learned from their story is more difficult to say. On what is just another day in the life in Ardeley, the best anyone can offer is the hope they have both found the kind of peace in death that they never knew in life.

acknowledgments

First and foremost, I would like to thank Jake and Charley Weber for their unending support in helping me put this book together. Without their open-hearted cooperation, it would not exist. In London, Andrew and Angela Bailey were kind enough to open up their home to me so I could the visit the places where Puss and Tommy had been. Jeff Dexter, the first man ever to dance the Twist in England, drove me to Ardeley to visit Puss' grave and put up with innumerable e-mail inquiries, shedding light on an era he knows as well as anyone on the planet.

At what is now known as Whatley Manor, an extraordinary world-class spa hotel in Wiltshire, the incredibly gracious Peter Egli provided me with chocolate torte, an extensive tour of the house and the grounds, and the amazing Reg Wood. At Haileybury, Val Proctor, Roger Woodburn, and Toby Parker made it possible for me to journey through Tommy's schoolboy past. I would also like to thank Toby for providing me with photographs of Tommy at Haileybury as well as all the priceless information about R. E. Weber.

In north London, Edda Tasiemka allowed me access to the Hans Tasiemka Archives, an astonishing one-of-a-kind collection of newspaper clippings. She also gave me tea. Thanks to David Robson for introducing me to her. Richard Jones allowed me to comb through the extensive Associated Newspapers morgue. I am indebted to him for all his help.

In Rugby, Pete (who is a) Prince picked me up at the train station and walked me through Tommy's haunts, the YP foremost among them. I want to thank Amy Whittern Hardy for providing me with digital scans of many of the photographs in this book as well as those she took that appear in her own memorial book for Tommy, who, in her words, "loved all things bright and beautiful." My thanks to Paul and Katie Conroy, and not just for the Adventures in Music cap. And, a shout-out to my longtime "boys" in London, the eminent Robert Allan and the always gracious Andrew Hodgkinson. Greetings as well to longtime fellow traveler Harriet Brand in Hampstead.

Via e-mail, people I have never met in person provided me with information I could not have found anywhere else. Although the Perse School lost most of its records when it was bombed during World War II, Jennie Wallis supplied me with invaluable assistance concerning the time that Percy and Harold Coriat spent there. Pauline McCausland, the former secretary at St. Edmund's School in Hindhead, Surrey, was kind enough to send me photos and postcards of the school as it was when Tommy was there. Christopher Coriat sent me Puss' childhood poem and a copy of the astonishing Cecil Beaton photograph of his mother. David Marks provided me with a copy of Tommy's appearance on the BBC. Thanks to Mary Keil for her interview with Charley Weber.

Martin Hadwen at the British Motor Racing Archive researched Tommy's racing career. J. N. Houterman advised me on British military matters. Thanks to Abigail Humphries and Sir Stirling Moss (who himself went to Haileybury) for replying to my questions about Tommy's racing career. On more subjects than I can name, Nik Douglas was an endless font of priceless information.

My heartfelt thanks to Raj Prem in London and the indefatigable David Tillier in Paris. Merci beaucoup to mon vieux Dominique Tarle for the stunning photographs of that endless summer at Villa Nellcote.

I would like to thank Mike McInnerney for his description of the creation of the Flying Dragon as well as the photograph of it that he sent me. My thanks to Vic Singh for setting me straight on what really happened the night the Beatles finished recording "A Day in the Life." Thanks as well to Alan Ponte for answering my e-mail questions about events long past.

Ben Schafer, my long-suffering editor of long standing at Da Capo Press, always believed in this book. For that, as well as his work on the manuscript, I thank him. For finding what has come to be known as "the famous lost chapter" and for being so responsive to all my requests concerning the style of this book, I would like to thank Collin Tracy. Thanks to Patricia Boyd, who did such a fantastic job of copyediting that all the remaining errors are entirely mine. Thanks as well to Paul Bresnick and Brian Lipson. I especially want to extend my most sincere gratitude to all those who allowed me to interview them at length for this book and for having the courage to speak openly about matters that were still painful for some of them to discuss even now. Without Jenny Ponte and Lulu, I could never have clarified certain issues.

Closer to home, I want to thank Karin Perling-Mayeri, translator par excellence and my expert on all things Danish. Thanks as well to Chris Cochran, a technical wizard of infinite proportions, for keeping me up and running as well as for the digital scans. Much love to Janice and Brian for always checking in and for providing me with a second home in Los Angeles. As always, Donna, who right from the start insisted this would be a good idea for a book, deserves a special prize for putting up with all the insanity. I also owe a debt of gratitude to Sandy and Anna for letting me be myself again.

Had I not found myself sitting on the back steps of Villa Nell-cote reading the day-old English newspapers alongside Tommy Weber in June 1971 as his two sons scuttled about before us in the brilliant sunshine, I might never have been fortunate enough to write this book. But then, as Tommy himself might have said, if you roll those tumbling dice long enough, sometimes you just get lucky.

sources

1. hald hovedgaard

Page 1   **Hald** *Wikipedia, the Free Encyclopedia*, s.v. "Hald Hovedgärd," http://da.wikipedia.org/wiki/Hald_Hovedgärd; and Worldonline, Danish Web site on Hald Hovegärd, http://home.worldonline.dk/wildau/Hald.htm.

Page 1   **Pamela** Fairlie "Lulu" Mackenzie-Kerr (hereinafter referred to as Lulu), interview with author, October 10, 2007.

Page 2   **Lionel Boyd** J. N. Houterman, e-mail to author, November 15, 2007.

Page 2   **Joyce Boyd** Joyce Boyd, *My Farm in Lion Country* (New York: Fredrick A. Stokes Company, 1933).

Page 2   **Joyce Boyd and Karen Blixen** Lulu, interview with author, October 10, 2007.

Page 3   **"just used people all his life"** Reginald Arkner, interview with author, September 14, 2007.

Page 3   **Poul Arkner** Reginald Arkner, e-mail to author, February 6, 2008.

Page 3   **Poul Arkner and French Foreign Legion** Reginald Arkner, interview with author, September 14, 2007.

Page 4   **Hald** Lulu, interview with author, October 11, 2007.

Page 5   **"That was the last I saw of him"** Tommy Weber, videotape interview by Jake Weber, May 2004.

Page 6   **"I wouldn't say he was anti-Semitic"** Reginald Arkner, interview with author, September 14, 2007.

Page 6   **Union Jack Flags affixed to their bicycles** Tommy Weber, videotape interview by Jake Weber, May 2004.

Page 7   **Poul Arkner and Pamela** Lulu, interview with author, October 10, 2007.

Page 7   **"I don't blame her for leaving him"** Reginald Arkner, interview with author, September 14, 2007.

Page 7   **Going underground** Tommy Weber, videotape interview by Jake Weber, May 2004; and Lulu, interview with author, October 10, 2007.

Page 7   **"I pissed in his pumps"** Tommy Weber, videotape interview by Jake Weber, May 2004.

Page 8   **As she neared the end of her life** Lulu, interview with author, October 11, 2007.

Page 8   **"very easy going"** Tommy Weber, videotape interview by Jake Weber, May 2004.

Page 8   **Coming home from school** Reginald Arkner, interview with author, September 14, 2007; and Reginald Arkner, e-mails to author, February 6, 7, 8, 2008.

Page 9   **Hamish Mackenzie-Kerr** Lulu, interview with author, October 11, 2007.

Page 9   **Fantasie Impromptu** Tommy Weber, videotape interview by Jake Weber, May 2004.

Page 10   **"No, no, no"** Lulu, interview with author, October 11, 2007.

Page 10   **"We were a pair, the two of us"** Anders Reginald Arkner, interview with author, September 14, 2007.

Page 10   **"literally captured and kidnapped"** Tommy Weber, videotape interview by Jake Weber, May 2004.

2. *twatley manor*

Page 13   **They called her Puss** Jenny Ponte, interview with author, October 18, 2007.

Page 13   **In 1871, at the age of sixteen** Sue Cook, "Sir John Blundell Maple: Victorian Furniture Entrepreneur," BBC Making History series, www.bbc.co.uk/radio4/history/making_history/makhist10_prog 13b.shtml.

Page 14   **"even if it meant carrying the grand piano"** Ibid.

Page 14   **valued at more than £2.1 million** "Millionaire's Daughter," *Evening Standard*, August 1, 1956.

Page 14   **von Eckardstein, a Prussian nobleman who served for ten years** Roderick R. McLean, *Royalty and Diplomacy in Europe, 1890–1914* (Cambridge: Cambridge University Press, 2007).

Page 14   **a decree rarely granted** Mary Keen, interview with author, September 19, 2007.

Page 14   Sorely disappointed by the failure of his daughter's marriage "Romance of £1,500,000 Heiress," *Daily Mail*, May 6 1935.

Page 14   On August 16, 1910, Grace "Weigall, Sir William Ernest George Archibald (1874–1952)," Australian Dictionary of Biography Online, www.adb.online.anu.edu.au/biogs/A120485b.htm.

Page 15   "a complete charmer and a lovely man" Jenny Ponte, interview with author, October 17, 2007.

Page 15   she once carefully arranged herself at the bottom Jenny Ponte, interview with author, January 29, 2008.

Page 15   wore her dyed blonde hair to the very end of her days Reg Wood, interview with author, December 5, 2007.

Page 15   great walled garden . . . "She was an absolute old tart" Jenny Ponte, interview with author, October 17, 2007.

Page 15   arches of pink and white Dorothy Perkin roses *Daily Mail*, May 19, 1914.

Page 16   Petwood, the oversized Tudor cottage Keith Parkins, "Petwood Hotel," http://home.clara.net/heureka/lincolnshire/petwood-hotel.htm.

Page 16   "the soiree may be too grown up a function for her" "To Meet the Princess," *Daily Mail*, July 3, 1925.

Page 16   "Who will be the prettiest debutante" "My Selection," *Daily Mail*, January 11, 1932.

Page 16   Englemere, an imposing white mansion Englemere Web site, www.englemere.co.uk.

Page 16   "The lovely young Weigall daughter" "A Debutante at Home," *Daily News*, May 11, 1932.

Page 17   the only girl to have both of her parents "Presentation Rehearsal," *Daily News*, June 15, 1932.

Page 17   "marked the beginning of the 'Season'" Gerard O'Donovan, "Last Dance of the Debutantes," *Daily Telegraph*, December 14, 2007.

Page 17   she stands with arms akimbo Cecil Beaton photo, supplied by Christopher Coriat.

Page 17   "that fashionably, kind of shot-at-dawn, gloomy" Mary Keen, interview with author, September 17, 2007.

Page 17   "In the small hours of the morning" *Evening News*, July 13, 1932.

Page 18   "midnight bathing in the swimming pool" "A June Ball and Bathing," *Daily News*, March 22, 1933.

Page 18   Six months later "Autumn Plans Already," *Daily Telegraph*, January 16, 1934.

Page 18   she was feted with a tea and party "Miss Priscilla Weigall's Birthday," *MP*, April 18, 1935.

Page 18   **a trust fund of a million pounds** "Me and My Million Pounds—by an Ex-Viscountess," *Daily Mirror*, October 25, 1956.

Page 18   **In May 1935** "Romance of £1,500,000 Heiress," *Daily Mail*, May 6 1935.

Page 18   **after having being fined several times for speeding** Earl Howe obituary, *Times* (London), July 27, 1964.

Page 18   **"David Niven was quite in love"** Jenny Ponte, interview with author, January 29, 2008.

Page 18   **On July 12, 1935** "Lord Curzon and Miss Weigall," *Times* (London), July 24, 1935.

Page 19   **honeymoon plans had to be curtailed** "Lady Curzon," *Daily Telegraph*, August 18, 1935.

Page 19   Gopsall Hall, a beautiful house on a family estate *Wikipedia, the Free Encyclopedia*, s.v. "Gopsall," http://en.wikipedia.org/wiki/Gopsall _park.

Page 19   **various tints of apricot, peach, and buff** "Apricot Buff Scheme," *Daily Telegraph*, March 25, 1936.

Page 20   **"some of the year's most interesting young-marrieds"** "A New Hostess," *Daily Telegraph*, January 18, 1936.

Page 20   **"Ideal New Hostess"** "Ideal New Hostess," *Daily Mail*, April 2, 1936.

Page 20   **"Fortunately, speaking comes easily to her"** "Lady Curzon's Election Work," *Daily Sun*, February 27, 1937.

Page 20   **was so run-down that only Priscilla** Christopher Coriat, interview with author, February 21, 2008.

Page 20   **mullioned windows, stone-flagged floors** "Furnishing Old Family Seat in Modern Country House Manner," *Daily Telegraph*, January 16, 1939.

Page 20   **As Priscilla herself would later confirm** Ibid.

Page 20   **Lady Priscilla Mary Rose Curzon and Lady Jennifer** Darryl Lundy, compiler, "Person Page 5006," www.thepeerage.com/p5006.htm.

Page 21   **Perse School in Cambridge** Jennie Wallis, Perse School Application Officer, e-mail to author, February 14, 2008.

Page 21   **walked overland from Great Britain** *Wikipedia, the Free Encyclopedia*, s.v. "Thomas Coryat," http://en.wikipedia.org/wiki/Thomas_Coryate.

Page 21   **Thomas Coryate himself was never married** Dom Moraes and Sarayu Srivatsa, *The Long Strider: How Thomas Coryate Walked from England to India in the Year 1613* (New Delhi: Penguin Books India, 2003).

Page 21   **Nor did he have any siblings** Juzer Mohammed Husain, e-mail to the author, February 1, 2008. Husain is a researcher cited in Moraes and Srivatsa, *The Long Strider*.

Page 21 **Born on February 13, 1904** *Rex v. Coriat*, trial record, July 15, 1941, National Archive, United Kingdom.

Page 21 **Now called Essaouira** *Wikipedia, the Free Encyclopedia*, s.v. "Essaouira," http://en.wikipedia.org/wiki/Essaouira.

Page 21 **five rabbis bearing the Coriat name** World Sephardic Heritage Center, "Spanish: Moroccan Heritage," Sephardic Library Web page, www.wslibrary.com/wsl/doc.php?id=57&lang=EN.

Page 21 **Unlike his father** http://familytreemaker.genealogy.com/users.

Page 22 **On February 28, 1898, Flora gave birth** Christopher Coriat, interview with author, February 21, 2008.

Page 22 **In 1910, when Harold was six years old** *Rex v. Coriat.*

Page 22 **(later nicknamed "Cory" at school)** Christopher Coriat, e-mail to author, February 21, 2008.

Page 22 **known as Hillel House** Jennie Wallis, Perse School Application Officer, e-mail to author, February 14, 2008.

Page 22 **In 1924, twenty-year-old Harold Coriat** British National Archives, www.nationalarchives.gov.uk.

Page 22 **In February of that year** *Rex v. Coriat.*

Page 23 **Robert Coryat, as Harold** Ibid.

Page 23 **"the obtaining from any other person"** *Encyclopedia Britannica: A Dictionary of Arts.*

Page 23 **Colin Coryton was sentenced** *Rex v. Coriat.*

Page 23 **he married a twenty-nine-year-old** Ibid.

Page 24 **"independent means"** Ibid.

Page 25 **"Yes, I understand"** Ibid.

Page 25 **"subject to circumstances"** Ibid.

Page 26 **Priscilla visited his wife** "Lady Curzon in Divorce Suit," *Daily Mail*, April 18, 1942.

Page 26 **Less than three months later** "Decree Nisi for Viscount Curzon," *Times* (London), July 16, 1942.

Page 26 **her former husband burned everything** Mary Keen, interview with author, September 19, 2007.

Page 27 **to the wet lea** Mary Keen, e-mail to author, December 18, 2007.

Page 27 **"He used to hunt"** Jenny Ponte, interview with author, October 17, 2007.

Page 27 **the Beaufort Hunt** *Wikipedia, the Free Encyclopedia*, s.v. "Duke of Beaufort's Hunt," http://en.wikipedia.org/wiki/Beaufort_hunt.

Page 28 **"It was absolutely incredible"** Jenny Ponte, interview with author, October 17, 2007.

Page 29 **embraced the values of the Victorian era** Christopher Coriat, interview with author, February 21, 2008.

Page 29   **"We barely saw them as children"** Mary Keen, interview with author, September 17, 2007.

Page 29   **"a bit snooty"** Reg Wood, interview with author, December 5, 2007.

Page 30   **"We had sort of a horse governess"** Mary Keen, interview with author, September 19, 2007.

Page 30   **"There is nothing to do"** Susan Coriat, "There Is Nothing to Do," poem written by Coriat at age eight, Twatley Manor, 1952. Poem obtained courtesy of Christopher Coriat.

Page 31   **"My mother did love him"** Mary Keen, interview with author, September 19, 2007.

Page 31   **"the cameelious hump"** Rudyard Kipling, "How the Camel Got His Hump," in *Just So Stories* (London: MacMillan, 1902).

Page 31   **"I think it came from when he went to prep school"** Jenny Ponte, interview with author, October 17, 2007.

Page 31   **Christopher tells yet another version** Christopher Coriat, interview with author, February 21, 2008.

Page 31   **"very, very amused"** Mary Keen, interview with author, September 17, 2007.

Page 32   **After falling in love with a brand-new Rolls Royce** Reg Wood, interview with author, December 5, 2007.

Page 32   **After deciding one day she wanted fresh salmon** Ibid.

Page 33   **"Now, how much did we spend today, dear?"** Ibid.

Page 33   **"He was an absolutely appalling womanizer"** Jenny Ponte, interview with author, September 17, 2007.

Page 34   **"We've got a son!"** Reg Wood, interview with author, December 5, 2007.

Page 34   **"the crown prince"** Christopher Coriat, interview with author, February 21, 2008.

Page 34   **"You can grow some more next year"** Reg Wood, interview with author, December 5, 2007.

Page 35   **"due to two things"** "Heiress Tells 'Where My Money Went'—Order Against Woman Who Inherited One Million Pounds," *Daily Express*, August 2, 1956.

Page 35   **"When my mother started making settlements"** "Ex-Viscountess Owes 35,872 Pounds for Death Duties—Mother Settled One Million Pounds on Her at 21," *Evening Standard*, August 17, 1956.

Page 36   **"Sometimes I wonder"** "10,000 Pound a Year Heiress 'Ruined by Tax'—AND NOW SHE IS LIVING IN SERVANTS' ROOMS," *Daily Express*, August 18, 1956.

Page 36   **"That is the thing"** "Me and My Million Pounds—by an ex-Vicountess," *Daily Mirror*, October 25, 1956.

Page 37   **"Let My Children Pay"** "Let My Children Pay, Says Woman Who Spent Million," *Daily Mail*, October 25, 1956.

Page 37   **"My wife was jolly well off"** "10,000 Pound a Year Heiress."

Page 37   **"I was brought up in a very extravagant way"** "Me and My Million Pounds."

Page 38   **sold at auction** Christopher Coriat, interview with author, February 21, 2008.

3. new barn farm and haileybury

Page 39   **speak it reasonably well within three weeks' time** Tommy Weber, videotape interview by Jake Weber, May 2004.

Page 39   **blue shirt, a pair of gray trousers** Pauline McCausland, interview with author, March 6, 2008.

Page 40   **"I was considered a Nazi when I came in there"** Tommy Weber, videotape interview by Jake Weber, May 2004.

Page 40   **Tommy boxed without much success** Pauline McCausland, interview with author, March 6, 2008.

Page 40   **"absolutely gorgeous"** Lulu, e-mails to author, October 20, 2007, and March 3, 2008.

Page 41   **"My dad shot at Tommy"** Lulu, e-mail to author, October 16, 2008.

Page 41   **Armstrong Siddeley Sapphire saloon cars** Charley Weber, e-mail to author, January 6, 2009.

Page 41   **a house near the sea** Lulu, e-mail to author, March 15, 2008.

Page 41   **After attending Haileybury College** Toby Parker, e-mail to author, January 31, 2008.

Page 42   **stored along the Thames from the Tower of London** Tommy Weber, videotaped interview by Jake Weber, May 2004.

Page 42   **Married twice, he had numerous mistresses** Lulu, e-mail to author, November 19, 2007.

Page 42   **"My grandfather's sister, Audrey"** Lulu, e-mail to author, October 12, 2008.

Page 43   **Designed by William Wilkins** Imogen Thomas, *Haileybury 1806– 1987* (Hertford: Haileybury Society, 1987).

Page 43   **a majestic tree that had continued to grow** Ibid.

Page 44   **"Haileybury then was a very hard place"** Richard Rhodes James, interview with author, November 26, 2007.

Page 44   **a cipher offer with a British army special forces** Why? Clublet, "Richard Rhodes James," http://clublet.com/c/c/why?RichardRhodes James; and Tony Gould, *Imperial Warriors: Britain and the Gurkhas* (London: Granta Press, 1999).

Page 44   **"At Haileybury, where life for us"** "Extracts from the Memoirs of
            Peter Townshend," www.archivist.f2s.com/cpa/biogs/ptownshened
            .htm.

Page 44   **looked much like a British army barracks** Photo, Haileybury Col-
            lege, supplied by Roger Woodbourn.

Page 45   **"It was cold baths every morning"** Tommy Weber, videotaped in-
            terview by Jake Weber, May 2004.

Page 45   **Tommy attended classes from nine until one** Richard Rhodes
            James, interview with author, November 26, 2007.

Page 46   **"consistent anti-social behavior"** Hugh Ramsbotham, e-mail to
            author, March 14, 2008.

Page 46   **"For the victim"** "Extracts from the Memoirs of Peter Townshend."

Page 46   **"you rose with all the dignity"** Ibid.

Page 46   **On Sunday evenings, at the chime** Thomas, *Haileybury 1806–1987.*

Page 47   **In the first photograph** Photo, Haileybury College Archive, sup-
            plied by Toby Parker.

Page 47   **as a British army general in Northern Ireland** *Wikipedia, the Free
            Encyclopedia,* s.v. "David Ramsbotham," http://en.wikipedia.org/
            wiki/David_Ramsbotham.

Page 47   **"Tom and I went to"** Hugh Ramsbotham, interview with author,
            November 27, 2007.

Page 47   **"Being dyslexic, I couldn't"** Tommy Weber, videotaped interview
            by Jake Weber, May 2004.

Page 47   **"really sensible, but casual"** ledger book, Haileybury College
            Archive, supplied by Toby Parker.

Page 48   **a top speed of more than five hundred miles** *Wikipedia, the Free
            Encyclopedia,* s.v. "de Havilland Vampire," http://en.wikipedia.org/
            wiki/De_Havilland_Vampire.

Page 48   **His ruse came to an end when an officer asked** Charley Weber, in-
            terview with author, April 23, 2007.

Page 48   **would somehow manage to fake** Reginald Arkner, interview with
            author, September 14, 2007.

Page 48   **"Tom was color blind"** Hugh Ramsbotham, interview with author,
            November 27, 2007.

Page 48   **"land girls"** Tommy Weber, videotaped interview by Jake Weber,
            May 2004.

Page 49   **"Something for the weekend, sir"** Ibid.

Page 49   **"traditionally the butt of sexual banter"** Hugh Ramsbotham,
            e-mail to author, March 14, 2008.

Page 49   **Tommy, clad in yet another tweed suit** Photo, Haileybury College
            Archive, supplied by Toby Parker.

Page 50   "If this trend can continue" Tommy Weber, Melvill House Records, March 11, 1956.

Page 50   "go fuck himself" Jake Weber, interview with author, January 28, 2008.

Page 50   "very ungrateful bastard" Ibid.

Page 50   died suddenly on May 9, 1956 Toby Parker, e-mail to author, January 31, 2008.

Page 50   was found clasping Tommy's letter in his hand Pete Prince, e-mail to author, January 23, 2008.

Page 50   In her brand new Jaguar Lulu, interview with author, October 11, 2007.

Page 51   "In a boys' school" Hugh Ramsbotham, interview with author, November 27, 2007.

Page 51   "If you were part of the fifteen" Toby Parker, interview with author, December 4, 2007.

Page 51   Tommy can be seen in a team photograph Photo, Haileybury College Archive, supplied by Toby Parker.

Page 51   Tommy stands at attention Ibid.

Page 52   "in some way off-sets the above bloomer" Neil W. Smyth, Melvill House Records, Easter term, 1956, Haileybury College Archive.

Page 52   "That in the opinion of this house" Neil W. Smyth, Melvill House Records, 192nd House Meeting, November 1, 1956, Haileybury College Archive.

Page 52   "To love driving is to want to" T. E. Weber, Haileybury College Student Magazine, 1956, pp. 11–13.

Page 53   "it was a scandal" Tommy Weber, videotaped interview by Jake Weber, May 2004.

Page 53   two A-levels in Medieval English Ibid.

Page 53   "Gone into business" Ledger book, Haileybury College Archive, supplied by Toby Parker.

4. *lilliesden and cambridge*

Page 55   "very recherché" Jenny Ponte, interview with author, March 24, 2008.

Page 55   Because Miss Winifred Barrows, Worcestershire Archive, August, 3, 2001, www.worcesternews.co.uk.

Page 55   "Greek dancing and verse speaking" Jenny Ponte, interview with author, March 24, 2008.

Page 55   "All I can remember" Jenny Ponte, interview with author, October 17, 2007.

Page 55   **Puss herself would later tell a friend** Juliet Harmer, interview with author, October 16, 2007.

Page 56   **"local bicycle"** Jenny Ponte, interview with author, October 17, 2007.

Page 56   **"a fantastic story"** Ibid.

Page 56   **"My parents were hauled off"** Ibid.

Page 56   **"incredibly naughty"** Jenny Ponte, videotaped interview by Jake Weber, date unknown.

Page 56   **"a step down from Lawnside"** Jenny Ponte, interview with author, October 17, 2007.

Page 56   **"practically nothing"** Christopher Coriat, interview with author, February 21, 2008.

Page 57   **"Puss was sort of a honey pot at age fourteen"** Mary Keen, videotaped interview by Jake Weber, date unknown.

Page 57   **"The relationship between Puss and Camel"** Jenny Ponte, interview with author, October 17, 2007.

Page 57   **"There was always a sense of drama about her"** Jenny Ponte, videotaped interview by Jake Weber, date unknown.

Page 57   **a Victorian farmhouse surrounded** Parks and Gardens Data Services, "Lilliesden," www.parksandgardens.ac.uk/component/option ,com_parksandgardens/task,site/id,2063/Itemid,292.

Page 57   **"a ghastly little tunic"** Juliet Harmer, October 16, 2007.

Page 57   **"palled up"** Ibid.

Page 58   **"Which one of us is going"** Ibid.

Page 58   **"was not stupid by any means"** Jenny Ponte, October 17, 2007.

Page 58   **"kicked out for not doing"** Mary Keen, September 19, 2007.

Page 59   **"It was absolutely brilliant"** Juliet Harmer, October 16, 2007.

Page 59   **"We went out with"** Ibid.

Page 60   **"They were called the Ice Cream Boys"** Jenny Ponte, March 24, 2008.

Page 60   **"the most beautiful man"** Jenny Ponte, interview with author, October 17, 2007.

Page 60   **Captain Leo Ponte** Alan Ponte, e-mail to author, February 7, 2008.

Page 60   **"gallant young undergraduate"** Alan Ponte, videotaped interview by Jake Weber, date unknown.

Page 61   **"so struck by her"** Alan Ponte, e-mail to author, March 26, 2008.

Page 61   **"my feet were cold"** Jenny Ponte, interview with author, March 24, 2008.

Page 61   **"We disliked each other on sight"** Alan Ponte, e-mail to author, March 26, 2008.

Page 61   **"much preferred Puss"** Alan Ponte, videotaped interview by Jake Weber, date unknown.

Page 61   **"I'm going to marry one"** Juliet Harmer, interview with author, October 16, 2007.

Page 62   **where his pet elephant** Lynn Yaeger, "A Koda Moment," *Travel and Leisure*, May 2004, www.travelandleisure.com/articles/a-koda -moment.

Page 62   **"had a bath in the kitchen"** Jenny Ponte, videotaped interview by Jake Weber, date unknown.

5. *pont street*

Page 65   **saluted him** Tommy Weber, videotaped interview by Jake Weber, May 2004.

Page 65   **striped red-and-black Melvill House tie did look** Richard Rhodes James, interview with author, November 26, 2007.

Page 65   **food rationing had only recently ended** *Microsoft Encarta Online Encyclopedia 2008*, s.v. "post-war Britain," http://uk.encarta.msn .com/encyclopedia_781539317/post-war_britain.html.

Page 66   **"In those days"** John Green, videotaped interview by Jake Weber, date unknown.

Page 66   **"this tall, gorgeous looking man"** Ibid.

Page 66   **"Tom was a gaming person"** Michael Taylor, interview with author, October 29, 2007.

Page 67   **forced to sell all the furniture** Jake Weber, interview with author, November 11, 2006.

Page 67   **Pamela, who had been brought up to believe** Lulu, interview with author, October 11, 2007.

Page 67   **"I remember him coming"** Ibid.

Page 67   **In several photographs** Photos supplied by Jake Weber.

Page 67   **"They all thought"** Tommy Weber, videotaped interview by Jake Weber, May 2004.

Page 68   **had been asked to join Team Lotus** British Racing Drivers' Club Archive, s.v. "Taylor, Michael," www.brdc.co.uk/brdcarchive.cfm/ flag/2/member_id/121.

Page 68   **"Tommy was pretty wild in a car"** Michael Taylor, interview with author, October 29, 2007.

Page 68   **he would walk into a flat for sale** John Green, videotaped interview by Jake Weber, May 2004.

Page 68   **"Deb-of-the-Year"** *Daily Mail*, June 16, 1959.

Page 69   **"I was the deb's delight"** Tommy Weber, videotaped interview by Jake Weber, May 2004.

Page 69   **"He beat me by twenty seconds"** John Green, videotaped interview by Jake Weber, date unknown.

Page 69   **"*Reckless* is the word that describes him"** Michael Taylor, interview with author, October 29, 2007.

Page 70   **was born in East Prussia** "Elisabeth Furse," obituary, *Times* (London), October 15, 2002.

Page 70   **in condoms hidden** Nicholas de Jongh, "Elisabeth Furse, " obituary, *Guardian*, October 16, 2002.

Page 70   **"young men on the verge of making it"** Elisabeth Furse," obituary, *Times* (London), October 15, 2002.

Page 70   **"a club hideaway"** Peter Jenkins, as quoted in ibid.

Page 70   **"all sorts of luscious goodies"** Tommy Weber, videotaped interview by Jake Weber, May 2004.

Page 71   **"It was the voice that did it"** Ibid.

Page 71   **"A lot of the people"** Juliet Harmer, interview with author, October 16, 2007.

Page 71   **"the obligatory bottle of wine"** Tommy Weber, videotaped interview by Jake Weber, May 2004.

Page 71   **"It was love at first sight"** Ibid.

6. *holy trinity church*

Page 73   **"He felt very strongly that"** Ibid.

Page 74   **"Mary and I had inherited much more"** Jenny Ponte, interview with author, October 17, 2007.

Page 74   **"He was always trying to get money"** Mary Keen, interview with author, September 19, 2007.

Page 74   **"My mother was hopelessly in love"** Jenny Ponte, videotaped interview by Jake Weber, date unknown.

Page 74   **"He did a lot of research into me"** Tommy Weber, videotaped interview by Jake Weber, May 2004.

Page 74   **"She wanted to learn how to look out"** Ibid.

Page 75   **"Funnily enough"** Lulu, interview with author, October 11, 2007.

Page 75   **"Tommy had to convince them"** John Green, videotaped interview by Jake Weber, date unknown.

Page 75   **"rubbish"** Alan Ponte, videotaped interview by Jake Weber, date unknown.

Page 75   **a sheep farmer who had lived one valley over** Charley Weber, e-mail to author, October 20, 2008.

Page 75   "The irony was that" Jenny Ponte, interview with author, October 17, 2007.

Page 76   "Puss was found to be pregnant" Tommy Weber, videotaped interview by Jake Weber, May 2004.

Page 76   "Heiress Engaged" *Evening News*, July 24, 1962.

Page 76   After seeing Tommy drive Tommy Weber, videotaped interview by Jake Weber, May 2004.

Page 76   "they had to make sure" *Daily Mail*, July 25, 1962.

Page 77   "to apply to the trustee every time" Ibid.

Page 77   "left-handed drive so" Jenny Ponte, interview with author, March 24, 2008.

Page 78   "Church of the Holy Trinity on Sloane Street" Peyton Skipworth, *Holy Trinity Sloane Street London* (London: Trinity Arts & Crafts Guild, 2002).

Page 78   "a swinging affair" *Daily Sun*, August 31, 1962.

Page 78   Tommy did decide Charles Greville, "100,000 Pound Brides!" *Daily Mail*, September 7, 1962.

Page 78   "big banking job" "Says Sister Susan: Share My Wedding," *Daily Express*, September 6, 1962.

Page 78   "We got married on the same day" Jenny Ponte, interview with author, January 28, 2008.

Page 79   "larking about in this rented house" Tommy Weber, videotaped interview by Jake Weber, May 2004.

Page 79   bought so many Bentley Continentals Rolls Royce Enthusiasts Club, Web page, www.rrec.org.uk/website/public/thecars.

Page 79   "looking glamorous in" Mary Keen, interview with author, September 19, 2007.

Page 80   "Three-year-old Cathryn Harrison" Charles Greville, *Daily Mail*, September 7, 1962.

Page 80   "what I think was" Tommy Weber, videotaped interview by Jake Weber, May 2004.

Page 80   "Puss looked very beautiful" Jenny Ponte, videotaped interview by Jake Weber, date unknown.

Page 81   "She did actually express feelings of regret" Jenny Ponte, interview with author, January 29, 2008.

Page 81   "blew the whole lot on flowers" Jenny Ponte, videotaped interview by Jake Weber, date unknown.

Page 82   "100,000 Pound Brides!" Charles Greville, *Daily Mail*, September 7, 1962.

Page 82   around the square again and again Lulu, videotaped interview by Jake Weber, date unknown.

Page 82   **Because Tommy did not own** Michael Taylor, videotaped interview by Jake Weber, date unknown.

Page 82   **"We spent most of our time down"** Tommy Weber, videotaped interview by Jake Weber, May 2004.

Page 82   **"I don't know who paid the bill"** Juliet Harmer, interview with author, October 16, 2007.

Page 83   **"We were having a very lovely time"** Tommy Weber, videotaped interview by Jake Weber, May 2004.

7. cambridge street

Page 85   **Six months after they were married** Tommy Weber, interview with author, March 20, 2006.

Page 86   **"She liked the letter J"** Jenny Ponte, videotaped interview by Jake Weber, date unknown.

Page 86   **"It was a joy to have a child"** Tommy Weber, videotaped interview by Jake Weber, May 2004.

Page 86   **"They were both so proud of him"** Jenny Ponte, videotaped interview by Jake Weber, date unknown.

Page 86   **"the most glamorous couple in London"** Juliet Harmer, interview with author, October 16, 2007.

Page 86   **"one of those little streets in Pimlico"** *Tatler*, date unknown.

Page 86   **"They had an extraordinary flat"** Juliet Harmer, interview with author, October 16, 2007.

Page 87   **"going to Cambridge Street"** Christopher Coriat, interview with author, February 21, 2008.

Page 88   **"To keep the racing team in funds"** Tommy Weber, videotaped interview by Jake Weber, May 2004.

Page 88   **"The motor racing was hard for her to take"** Ibid.

Page 88   **"greatest and most challenging race circuit in the world"** Jackie Stewart, quoted in Ben Lovejoy's Nürburgring Web site, www.nurburgring .org.uk.

Page 88   **"that got lost in the clouds"** Tommy Weber, videotaped interview by Jake Weber, May 2004.

Page 88   **"I had gone out a week early"** Ibid.

Page 88   **"Tommy was crammed into"** Jenny Ponte, videotaped interview by Jake Weber, date unknown.

Page 89   **"with a picnic basket filled"** Lulu, videotaped interview by Jake Weber, date unknown.

Page 89   **"He was so angry"** Lulu, e-mail to author, October 12, 2008.

Page 89   **"He was very fearless"** Michael Taylor, interview with author, October 29, 2007.

Page 89   **turning the fastest lap at Snetterton** Martin Hadwen, Tommy Weber Results Sheet, British Motor Racing Archive, December 14, 2007.

Page 90   **"That was the last time"** Tommy Weber, videotaped interview by Jake Weber, May 2004.

Page 90   **"He was selling land"** Jake Weber, interview with author, November 11, 2006.

Page 90   **"If things were successful"** Frank Duggan, videotaped interview by Jake Weber, date unknown.

Page 90   **"beaten up quite badly"** John Green, videotaped interview by Jake Weber, date unknown.

Page 90   **"Tommy had lots of racing car debts"** Jenny Ponte, videotaped interview by Jake Weber, date unknown.

Page 90   **"discovered at a happening"** Ibid.

Page 91   **"not content to stay at home"** "Ambitious," *Evening Standard*, undated.

Page 91   **"Tommy went to see the play"** Jenny Ponte, videotaped interview by Jake Weber, date unknown.

Page 91   **"shouting instructions to everybody"** Ibid.

Page 92   **"Puss was always hopeless with money"** Ibid.

Page 92   **"nearly died"** Charley Weber, e-mail to author, July 7, 2008.

Page 92   **"virtually a blue baby"** Ibid.

Page 92   **"She decided to get both of her boys"** Jenny Ponte, videotaped interview by Jake Weber, date unknown.

Page 92   **"My mother said it was"** Ibid.

Page 93   **"the Biba of Brompton Road"** emmapeelplants, Vintage Fashion Guild, www.vintagefashionguild.org.

Page 93   **"There were so few people"** Juliet Harmer, interview with author, October 16, 2007.

Page 93   **"through Puss while she was at the BBC"** Tommy Weber, interview with author, March 20, 2006.

Page 93   **"lethal Lotus BRM"** Ibid.

Page 93   **Snetterton, Goodwood, Brands Hatch** Martin Hadwen, Tommy Weber Results Sheet, British Motor Racing Archive, December 14, 2007.

Page 93   **"To start with"** Tommy Weber, videotaped interview by Jake Weber, May 2004.

Page 94   **"foreplay was lacking"** Tommy Weber, videotaped interview by Jake Weber, date unknown.

Page 94   **"very strange conversation"** Tommy Weber, videotaped interview by Jake Weber, May 2004.

Page 94   "Puss had a life of her own" Ibid.
Page 94   "By then, there was a change happening" Alan Ponte, videotaped
             interview by Jake Weber, date unknown.
Page 95   "Peace, peace." . . . fuck off Ibid.
Page 95   cruised on up the path Jenny Ponte, videotaped interview by Jake
             Weber, date unknown.

8. the flying dragon

Page 97   two contact sheets of black-and-white photographs Contact sheets
             courtesy of Jake Weber, from Jenny Ponte, photographer unknown.
Page 98   "experienced" Jimi Hendrix Experience, "Are You Experienced?"
             from the album of the same name, August 1967.
Page 98   "She was one of the first" Tommy Weber, videotaped interview by
             Jake Weber, May 2004.
Page 98   "took to acid like a duck to water" Harriet Vyner, *Groovy Bob: The
             Life and Times of Robert Fraser* (London: Faber and Faber, 1999).
Page 98   Gibbs was first given LSD by Michael Hollingshead Robert Green-
             field, *Timothy Leary: A Biography* (New York: Harcourt, 2006).
Page 98   "psychedelic jamboree" Ibid.
Page 99   "toffs" Douglas Harper, "Toffs," Online Etymology Dictionary,
             www.etymonline.com/index.php?term=toff.
Page 99   "The center of it was Robert Fraser" Nik Douglas, interview with
             author, October 13, 2007.
Page 99   soon turned Rolling Stones founder Brian Jones Robert Green-
             field, *Exile On Main St.: A Season in Hell with the Rolling Stones*
             (New York: Da Capo Press, 2007).
Page 100   "a reaction to the era of austerity and war" Nigel Waymouth, in-
             terview with author, October 24, 2007.
Page 100   "We came out of a Victorian England" Michael Rainey, interview
             with author, November 5, 2007.
Page 100   "A lot of it was aesthetics" Nigel Waymouth, interview with author,
             October 24, 2007.
Page 100   "away a lot" Tommy Weber, videotaped interview by Jake Weber,
             May 2004.
Page 101   "Both Puss and Tommy were highly sexually" Juliet Harmer,
             videotaped interview by Jake Weber, date unknown.
Page 101   "She was the one who started it" Tommy Weber, videotaped inter-
             view by Jake Weber, May 2004.
Page 102   "By the time Jake got to be about three or four" Juliet Harmer,
             videotaped interview by Jake Weber, date unknown.
Page 102   "She asked me" Ibid.

Page 102   **"a music film"** Vic Singh, e-mail to author, May 5, 2008.

Page 102   **"out of the blue"** Ibid.

Page 102   **"quite a far-out idea"** Ibid.

Page 103   **"accommodate up to a thousand musicians"** Bob Spitz, *The Beatles: The Biography* (New York: Little, Brown and Company, 2005).

Page 103   **"tricked out in a wildly flamboyant, neon-rainbow wardrobe"** Ibid.

Page 103   **"orchestral orgasm"** Ibid.

Page 103   **"I didn't know who the Beatles were"** Tommy Weber, videotaped interview by Jake Weber, May 2004.

Page 104   **"out of focus or very shaky"** Vic Singh, e-mail to author, May 5, 2008.

Page 104   **fueled by their own supply of pure Owsley acid** Robert Greenfield, "The LSD King," *Rolling Stone*, July 12–16, 2007.

Page 104   **"the most expensive home movie ever"** Spitz, *The Beatles*.

Page 105   **"The next thing we heard"** Vic Singh, e-mail from author, May 5, 2008.

Page 105   **"And I said, 'I'd like to make"** Tommy Weber, videotaped interview by Jake Weber, May 2004.

Page 106   **the group's investment of £100,000** *John Lennon: The Life*, Phillip Norman (New York: Ecco, 2008).

Page 106   **"an injunction against all four"** "Court Move to Stop a Beatle Film," *Daily Sun*, November 21, 1967.

Page 106   **"We went to court to get an injunction"** Tommy Weber, videotaped interview by Jake Weber, May 2004.

Page 107   **"Christmas on Earth Continued" concert** Jeff Dexter, e-mail to author, April 8, 2008.

Page 107   **sparsely attended** Ibid.

Page 107   **Clad in full "Foxy Lady" gear in a brocaded orange red** Tommy Weber, producer, *Watch Out for Your Ears*.

Page 108   **"I had the first real video studio in London"** Tommy Weber, videotaped interview by Jake Weber, May 2004.

Page 109   **"Their values were very much the same"** Charley Weber, interview with author, April 23, 2007.

Page 109   **"the last-stop watering hole on a medieval cart track leading west"** World's End Camden Web page, www.theworldsend.co.uk.

Page 109   **"Historically"** Nigel Waymouth, interview with author, October 24, 2007.

Page 109   **"shifted her plans towards a tea house serving light healthy meals"** Mike McInnerney, e-mail to author, October 15, 2007.

Page 110   **"Flying dragon in the heavens"** Richard Wilhelm translator, *The I Ching, or Book of Changes* (Princeton, N.J.: Princeton University Press, 1950).

Page 110   "Things that accord in tone vibrate together" Ibid.

Page 110   "As I got to know Puss" Mike McInnerney, e-mail to author, October 15, 2007.

Page 110   "the heavenly dragon descended to earth" Ibid.

Page 111   "A moving cloud effect was created" Ibid.

Page 111   "Cambridge Street was getting out of control" Juliet Harmer, videotaped interview by Jake Weber, date unknown.

Page 111   "a growing group of people" Mike McInnerney, e-mail to author, October 15, 2007.

Page 111   "Compassionate Father" *Wikipedia, the Free Encyclopedia*, s.v. "Meher Baba," www.wikipedia.org/wiki.Meher_Baba.

Page 112   "own solutions to the great questions" Kid Glove Enterprises, review of *Who Came First*, by Pete Townsend, on "Hittin' the Note" Web site, www.hittinthenote.com/PeteTownsend_feature.asp.

Page 112   "For a while" Mike McInnerney, e-mail to author, October 15, 2007.

Page 112   "smoked joints and dropped Mandrax" Nigel Waymouth, interview with author, October 24, 2007.

Page 112   "It was my local, as it were" Christopher Gibbs, videotaped interview by Jake Weber, date unknown.

Page 113   "I went to the Dragon one day to have lunch with Puss" Juliet Harmer, interview with author, October 16, 2007.

Page 113   "I only went in there twice" Tommy Weber, videotaped interview by Jake Weber, May 2004.

Page 113   "It's so peaceful here" "Future Among the Tea Leaves," *Daily Express*, March 12, 1968.

Page 113   "a regular hangout for a particular hippie crowd" Mike McInnerney, e-mail to author, October 15, 2007.

Page 114   "purchasing provisions for the tea house" Ibid.

9. *glastonbury and hugh street*

Page 115   **King Arthur and Queen Guinevere** Ellie Crystal, "Glastonbury Tor, Chalice Hill, King Arthur, Giants," Crystalinks, www.crystalinks.com/glastonburytor.html.

Page 115   **Joseph of Arimathea** Ibid.

Page 115   "triangle with the enormous stone" Ibid.

Page 115   "hypothetical alignments of" *Wikipedia, the Free Encyclopedia*, s.v. "ley line," http://en.wikipedia.org/wiki/ Ley_line.

Page 116   "zodiac signs appear" Crystal, "Glastonbury Tor."

Page 116   "It followed the idea" Andy Roberts, "A Saucerful of Secrets," Fortean Times, October 2007, www.forteantimes.com/features/articles.

Page 116   "The King's Road led straight" Barry Miles, quoted in ibid.

Page 116   "John Michell was the first" Michael Rainey, interview with author, November 5, 2007.

Page 117   "often camped near the Tor" Roberts, "A Saucerful of Secrets."

Page 117   "My Darling Tommy" Susan Weber, letter to Tommy Weber, no date, courtesy of Jake Weber.

Page 120   "She wasn't a very stable girl" Michael Rainey, interview with author, November 5, 2007.

Page 120   "The beauty of your mother" Christopher Gibbs, videotaped interview by Jake Weber, date unknown.

Page 120   "speak easy, drink easy, and pull easy" Jeff Dexter, e-mail to author, April 12, 2008.

Page 120   "There was this gorgeous little American girl" Tommy Weber videotaped interview by Jake Weber, date unknown.

Page 121   "Puss walked in on me" Ibid.

Page 121   "It's my main interest now" "Future Among the Tea Leaves," *Daily Express*, March 12, 1968.

Page 121   "standing on the steps" Tommy Weber videotaped interview by Jake Weber, date unknown.

Page 122   uncredited part as a water skier *Wikipedia, the Free Encyclopedia*, s.v. "Charlotte Rampling," http://en.wikipedia.org/wiki/Charlotte _Rampling.

Page 122   "a very outrageous, rebellious character" Charlotte Rampling, interview with Peter Cowie, in "Charlotte Rampling: I Have to Work With a Lot of Love," Berlinale Talent Campus, www.berlinale-talent campus.de/story/85/1785.html.

Page 122   she never employed a press agent Charlotte Rampling, interview with author, December 19, 2007.

Page 122   "The law" "Actress Charley Arrested—and Her Dog Goes Too," *Daily Express*, September 5, 1967.

Page 123   Godfrey Lionel Rampling *Wikipedia, the Free Encyclopedia*, s.v. "Godfrey Rampling," http://en.wikipedia.org/wiki/Godfrey_Rampling.

Page 123   he never discussed it Bryan Appleyard, "On the Road Back from a Lonely Place," May 9, 2004, http://entertainment.timesonline .co.uk.

Page 123   "a crippling perfectionist" Ibid.

Page 123   the thirty-seven-year old actor "'A Bit Difficult,' Says Charlotte," *Sunday Express*, April 21, 1968.

Page 123   **a hospital so understaffed** Roderick Mann, "Miss Rampling Talks of Youth, Love, and Tragedy," *Sunday Express*, September 29, 1968.

Page 123   **"The death was what the French"** Appleyard, "On the Road Back."

Page 124   **"the Chelsea Girl"** Mann, "Miss Rampling Talks of Youth."

Page 124   **"a high-ceilinged, barn-like room"** Paul Errol, "Miss Rampling Only Wants Peace and Love," *Sunday Express*, January 5, 1969.

Page 124   **"I haven't been away on holiday"** "Lying on Beaches Is Moronic" *Observer*, August 25, 1968.

Page 124   **"At Hugh Street"** Charlotte Rampling, interview with author, December 19, 2007.

Page 124   **"Poor Puss took the brunt of it"** Tommy Weber, videotaped interview by Jake Weber, date unknown.

Page 125   **"At that time"** Charlotte Rampling, interview with author, December 19, 2007.

Page 125   **"the longest continually inhabited dwelling"** *Wikipedia, the Free Encyclopedia*, s.v. "Port Eliot," en.wikipedia.org/wiki/Port_Eliot.

Page 126   **Obby Oss Festival** BBC, "About Cornwall: Obby Oss Day," www.bbc.co.uk/cornwall/content/articles/2007/04/11/padstow_obbyoss_feature.shtml.

Page 126   **"the crops to grow and the hours"** Cornwall in Focus, "Padstow," www.cornwallinfocus.co.uk/leisure/padstow.php.

Page 126   **"a great hoop of kind of tarred canvas"** Christopher Gibbs, videotaped interview by Jake Weber, date unknown.

Page 126   **"a special padded stick"** www.shimbo.co.uk.

Page 126   **"Unite and unite and let us all unite"** BBC, "About Cornwall: Obby Oss Day."

Page 126   **"One of the things"** Christopher Gibbs, videotaped interview by Jake Weber, date unknown.

Page 127   **"Jake and I went down there"** Charley Weber, interview with author, April 23, 2007.

10. london to sydney

Page 129   **As each actor spoke the lines** Charlotte Rampling, interview with Peter Cowie, February 16, 2006, Berlinale Talent Campus Web page, www.berlinale-talentcampus.de/story/85/1785.html.

Page 129   **"We gypsied around in the car"** Charlotte Rampling, interview with author, December 19, 2007.

Page 130   **Unable to have dinner with him** James Salter, *Burning the Days* (New York: Random House, 1997).

Page 130   a forty-four-year-old West Point *Wikipedia, the Free Encyclopedia*, s.v. "James Salter," http://en.wikipedia.org/wiki/James_Salter.

Page 130   "chewed wads of gum" Salter, *Burning the Days.*

Page 130   "soiled clothes piled in corners" Ibid.

Page 131   "unless her salary" Ibid.

Page 131   "mutiny," he "found it hard" Ibid.

Page 132   Innes Ireland and Andrew Hedges in car 26 "Welcome to the 1968 London-Sydney Marathon," Web page dedicated to the 1968 marathon, http://marathon68.homestead.com.

Page 132   "raise the country's spirits" *Wikipedia, the Free Encyclopedia*, s.v. "London-Sydney Marathon," http://en.wikipedia.org/wiki/London -Sydney_Marathon.

Page 132   "as a showcase for British engineering" Ibid.

Page 132   "the shorter, but more treacherous" Ibid.

Page 132   who braved snow Alan Sawyer, http://marathon68.homestead.com.

Page 133   "Why did I begin smuggling?" Tommy Weber, videotaped interview by Jake Weber, date unknown.

Page 133   a generic and somewhat derogatory name Francis Grose, *Lexicon Balatronicum, or Dictionary for Jesters* (1811), s.v. "taffy," www.from oldbooks.org/Grose-VulgarTongue/t/taffy.html.

Page 133   "Taffy was a Welshman" *Wikipedia, the Free Encyclopedia*, s.v. "Taffy was a Welshman," http://en.wikipedia.org/wiki/Taffy_was_a _Welshman; and Tommy Weber, videotaped interview by Jake Weber, date unknown.

Page 133   "By then" Lulu, interview with author, October 11, 2007.

Page 133   A rugged-looking character Photos supplied by Lulu.

Page 133   "actually slept with one eye open" Lulu, interview with author, October 11, 2007

Page 133   "everything from cheese to the crown jewels" Jake Weber, e-mail to author, October 27, 2007.

Page 133   "The best one" Lulu, interview with author, October 11, 2007.

Page 134   "famous spy" Ibid.

Page 134   "We have our weekends away" "Lying on Beaches Is Moronic," *Observer* (London), August 25, 1968.

Page 135   car 35, a Mercedes 280 "Welcome to the 1968 London-Sydney Marathon," Web page dedicated to the 1968 marathon, http://marathon68 .homestead.com.

Page 135   chatting up a girl Tommy Weber, videotaped interview by Jake Weber, date unknown

Page 135   "caught the clap off this girl" Ibid.

Page 135   "**What happened**" Charlotte Rampling, interview with author, December 19, 2007.

Page 136   **Mohammed Zahir Shah** *Wikipedia, the Free Encyclopedia*, s.v. "Mohammed Zahir Shah," http://en.wikipedia.org/wiki/Mohammed_Zahir_Shah.

Page 136   **Hyatullah Tokhi** Robert Greenfield, *Timothy Leary: A Biography* (New York: Harcourt, 2006).

Page 136   "**all over the Mercedes**" Tommy Weber, videotaped interview by Jake Weber, date unknown.

Page 137   **who was quite sure**" Ibid.

Page 138   "**I knew there were two gas tanks**" Charlotte Rampling, interview with author, December 19, 2007.

Page 138   "**There was a new system**" Tommy Weber, videotaped interview by Jake Weber, date unknown.

Page 138   "**And this bloody engine**" Ibid.

Page 139   "**bags and camel bags and robes**" Ibid.

Page 139   **Malana Cream** *Wikipedia, the Free Encyclopedia*, s.v. "Malana Cream," http://en.wikipedia.org/wiki/Malana.

Page 139   "**When we arrived at airport**" Tommy Weber, videotaped interview by Jake Weber, date unknown.

Page 139   "**sort of his version of the Jedi mind trick**" Pete Prince, interview with author, November 2, 2007.

Page 139   "'**Here you go**" Tommy Weber, videotaped interview by Jake Weber, date unknown.

Page 139   "**I didn't see Taffy again**" Ibid.

Page 140   "**For Tommy, it was all**" Charlotte Rampling, interview with author, December 19, 2007.

11. samye ling and lundy island

Page 141   "**charismatic and unusual**" Nik Douglas, e-mail to author, October 27, 2007.

Page 141   **a Spaulding scholarship** Naropa University main Web page, www.naropa.edu.

Page 142   "**Trungpa liked his ladies**" Nik Douglas, interview with author, October 20, 2007.

Page 142   **married a sixteen-year-old English girl** Robert Greenfield, *The Spiritual Supermarket* (New York: E. P. Dutton & Co., 1975).

Page 142   **died of cardiac arrest** *Wikipedia, the Free Encyclopedia*, s.v. "Chögyam Trungpa," http://en.wikipedia.org/wiki/Chogyam_Trungpa.

Page 142   **"a popular place for people"** Nik Douglas, e-mail to author, October 27, 2007.

Page 142   **"where all the upper class rich girls"** Michael Rainey, interview with author, November 5, 2007.

Page 142   **"Taliesen" and "Hercules"** Susan Weber, letter to Jake and Charley Weber, no date, courtesy of Jake Weber.

Page 143   **"My Darling Tommy"** Susan Weber, letter to Tommy Weber, no date, courtesy of Jake Weber.

Page 145   **the Orthon Cult** Willy Wegner, "The Orthon Cult: Doomsday in Denmark 1967," Skeptic Report Web page, www.skepticreport.com/ufo/orthon.htm.

Page 145   **"Honey. Bio Strath"** Susan Weber, letter to V. J. Birt, Esq., January 8, 1969, courtesy of Jake Weber.

Page 147   **"Somehow"** Jenny Ponte, videotaped interview by Jake Weber, date unknown.

Page 147   **"She'd had a death wish forever"** Jake Weber, interview with author, January 28, 2008.

Page 148   **"We were at the back of the Albert Hall"** Charley Weber, interview with author, April 23, 2007.

Page 149   **"always hated conflict"** Charley Weber, e-mail to author, July 7, 2008.

Page 149   **"cool"** Ibid.

Page 149   **"You were always the extrovert"** Ibid.

Page 149   **"Jake always had this little observing face"** Charlotte Rampling, interview with author, December 19, 2007.

Page 149   **"One was this huge needle"** Charley Weber, interview with author, April 23, 2007.

Page 149   **"stop the car"** Jake Weber, interview with author, January 28, 2008.

Page 150   **descended from the Duke of Buckingham** Nik Douglas, interview with author, October 20, 2007.

Page 150   **in India, Sri Lanka, Nepal, Sikkim, Thailand** Tantra Works, "About Nik Douglas," www.tantraworks.com/bionik.html.

Page 150   **his mother and father had met there** Nik Douglas, e-mail to author, October 25, 2007.

Page 150   **Granted to the Knights Templar** *Wikipedia, the Free Encyclopedia*, s.v. "Lundy," http://en.wikipedia.org/wiki/Lundy.

Page 150   **free island** Ibid.

Page 151   **Broadcasting from a ship** *Wikipedia, the Free Encyclopedia*, s.v. "Radio Caroline," en.wikipedia.org/wiki/Radio_Caroline.

Page 151   **one of Sweden's leading fashion models,** Nik Douglas, October 13, 2007.

Page 151   **"small screw-top jars of pure"** Nik Douglas, e-mail to author, October 14, 2007.

Page 151   **"scoping out the place"** Nik Douglas, e-mail to author, October 27, 2007.

Page 152   **"Tommy and I had this flash idea"** Ibid.; and Nik Douglas, e-mail to author, April 25, 2008.

Page 152   **Trungpa had blacked out** Greenfield, *The Spiritual Supermarket.*

Page 152   **"He was quite badly hurt"** Nik Douglas, e-mail to author, October 27, 2007.

Page 152   **"a private arrangement"** Ibid.

Page 153   **"and then donate it"** Ibid.

Page 153   **"to commit some funds to the project"** Ibid.

Page 153   **the scion of an old English banking family** *Wikipedia, the Free Encyclopedia,* s.v. "John Smith (Conservative politician)," http://en .wikipedia.org/wiki/John_Smith_(Conservative_politician).

Page 153   **"all coked up"** Nik Douglas, e-mail to author, October 27, 2007.

Page 153   **"if the Landmark people wouldn't step aside"** Ibid.

Page 154   **"driving the wrong way up a narrow street"** Ibid.

Page 154   **£150,000** "Tycoon's 150,000 Pounds Buys Lundy," *Daily Express,* May 23, 1969.

Page 154   **"the Lundy debacle"** Nik Douglas, interview with author, October 20, 2007.

Page 154   **"Tommy never closed"** Charlotte Rampling, December 19, 2007.

12. chester square

Page 155   **"It was a huge mansion"** Tommy Weber, interview with author, March 20, 2006.

Page 156   **"In Hugh Street"** Charlotte Rampling, interview with author, December 19, 2007.

Page 156   **Jimi Hendrix stayed** Nik Douglas, interview with author, October 13, 2007.

Page 156   **Steve Winwood** Tommy Weber, interview with author, March 20, 2006.

Page 156   **Stash Klossowski** Ibid.

Page 156   **On alternate nights** Lulu, interview with author, October 11, 2007.

Page 156   **Helmut Berger** Lulu, e-mail to author, April 28, 2008.

Page 156   **George Lazenby** Lulu, interview with author, October 11, 2007.

Page 156   **Roman Polanski** Lulu, e-mail to author, April 28, 2008.

Page 156   **Douglas Fairbanks, Jr.** Lulu, interview with author, October 11, 2007.

Page 157   "We didn't have a manager," Teddy Osei, interview with author, December 7, 2007.

Page 157   "That was a wicked idea, actually" Ibid.

Page 157   "He must have nicked it" Ibid.

Page 158   "Tommy's manic-depressive condition" Charlotte Rampling, interview with author, December 19, 2007.

Page 158   "Tommy loved us very much" Teddy Osei, interview with author, December 7, 2007.

Page 159   "I think Puss had a real thirst" Christopher Gibbs, videotaped interview by Jake Weber, date unknown.

Page 159   "I knew him when he first" Nik Douglas, interview with author, October 13, 2007.

Page 159   "was a white elephant" Nigel Waymouth, interview with author, October 24, 2007.

Page 159   "a terrible story about him" Jenny Ponte, videotaped interview by Jake Weber, date unknown.

Page 160   "a bit of a Machiavellian character" Nik Douglas, interview with author, October 13, 2007.

Page 160   "a wheeler dealer" Ibid.

Page 160   "very serious about him" Jenny Ponte, videotaped interview by Jake Weber, date unknown.

Page 160   "We were having a big party at Chester Square" Tommy Weber, videotaped interview by Jake Weber, date unknown.

Page 161   on May 28, 1969 "Heiress Seeks Divorce Decree," *Evening Standard*, May 28, 1969.

Page 161   "In order for us to take Jake and Charley" Tommy Weber, videotaped interview by Jake Weber, date unknown.

Page 161   July 9, 1969 "Divorce Decreed for Maple Heiress," *Daily Telegraph*, July 9, 1969.

Page 161   "nervous as hell" Tommy Weber, videotaped interview by Jake Weber, date unknown.

Page 161   did appoint the official solicitor "Divorce Decreed for Maple Heiress."

Page 161   Then the young lord wrote Tommy letter to Tommy Weber, no date, courtesy of Jake Weber.

Page 161   sitting down to breakfast Charlotte Rampling, interview with author, December 19, 2007.

13. almora

Page 163   "suitably dramatic" Christopher Coriat, interview with author, February 21, 2008.

Page 164   "the Royal Military Academy at Sandhurst" "Christopher Coriat," LinkedIn Web page, www.linkedin.com/in/coriat.

Page 164   "I distinctly remember that" Christopher Coriat, interview with author, February 21, 2008.

Page 164   "shot down over the North Sea" Ibid.

Page 164   "unrelentingly faithful" Ibid.

Page 165   "put LSD powder in" Jenny Ponte, videotaped interview by Jake Weber, date unknown.

Page 165   "had been always a most generous" Priscilla Coriat, letter to Tommy Weber, December 6, 1968, courtesy of Jake Weber.

Page 165   "Naturally we long" Ibid.

Page 165   "She became quite active" Christopher Coriat, interview with author, February 21, 2008.

Page 166   the two of them were so happy Ibid.

Page 166   "It was a crippling blow." Tommy Weber, videotaped interview by Jake Weber, date unknown.

Page 166   "go out of their bodies" Nik Douglas, interview with author, October 13, 2007.

Page 167   "find a house in Turkey" Susan Weber, letter to Jake and Charley Weber from Rabat, Morocco, no date, courtesy of Jake Weber.

Page 167   "an Indian sunrise" Susan Weber, letter to Tommy Weber from Bombay, no date, courtesy of Jake Weber.

Page 167   "Very blue without" Ibid.

Page 168   "in the mirror far too often" Susan Weber, letter to Jake and Charley from Bombay, no date, courtesy of Jake Weber.

Page 168   one of the many opium dens David Tomory, *A Season in Heaven* (New York: HarperCollins, 1996).

Page 169   "I met her when" Susan Weber, letter to Jake and Charley from Bombay, no date, courtesy of Jake Weber.

Page 169   "steamy honking teeming seething" Susan Weber, letter to Tommy Weber from Bombay, no date, courtesy of Jake Weber.

Page 169   "ancient buses that made a lot of noise" Nik Douglas, interview with author, October 13, 2007.

Page 169   "an old Nepali town" Ibid.

Page 170   Ambassador Hotel, a dark inn Robert Greenfield, *Timothy Leary: A Biography* (New York: Harcourt, 2006).

Page 170   "The girls are moving in circles" Susan Weber, aerogramme to Taliesen Weber, March 8, 1970, courtesy of Jake Weber.

Page 170   "typical Brahmin house" Nik Douglas, interview with author, October 13, 2007.

Page 171   "We spend most of the time listening" Susan Weber, aerogramme to Taliesen Weber, March 8, 1970, courtesy of Jake Weber.

Page 171   "He wasn't trying to transform lead" Nik Douglas, interview with author, October 13, 2007.

Page 172   "Bindu was a very open-minded guy" Ibid.

Page 172   "would not have gone down well with Bindu" Ibid.

Page 172   "You could eat that all day" Ibid.

Page 172   "Ruby's Groovy" Susan Weber, aerogramme to les Pomfretz de Ruby Hercule et Taliesin, March 25, 1970, courtesy of Jake Weber.

Page 173   "painting prolifically" Susan Weber, aerogramme to Tommy Weber, March 30, 1970, courtesy of Jake Weber.

Page 173   "a whole box of lovely pastels" Tommy Weber, videotaped interview by Jake Weber, date unknown.

Page 173   "veins" Tommy Weber, interview with author, March 22, 2006.

Page 174   "Looking back" Charley Weber, interview with author, April 23, 2007.

Page 174   "charged" Nik Douglas, interview with author, October 13, 2007.

Page 174   "very beautiful kids" Ibid.

Page 174   "I think she took off" Ibid.

Page 174   "that everyone was" Jake Weber, interview with author, May 2, 2008.

Page 175   "conservative" Nik Douglas, interview with author, October 13, 2007.

Page 175   "particularly susceptible, having been" Susan Weber, letter to Tommy Weber from Turkey, May 2, 1970, courtesy of Jake Weber.

Page 175   "In Bindu's words" Nik Douglas, e-mail to author, October 14, 2007.

Page 175   "disowned responsibility" Nik and Eva Douglas, letter to Tommy Weber, May 25, 1970, courtesy of Jake Weber.

Page 175   "He turned up on my doorstep" confidential source, interview with author, November 5, 2007.

14. on the way home

Page 177   "wanted to be beside the sea & see Lulu" Susan Weber, letter to Tommy Weber from Turkey, May 2, 1970.

Page 177   "unobtainable" Ibid.

Page 177   "the sweet tea and the pistachios" Charley Weber, interview with author, April 23, 2007.

Page 178   "lovely old hotel" Susan Weber, letter to Tommy Weber from Turkey, May 2, 1970.

Page 179　**"Look, we're not in a"**　Tommy Weber, videotaped interview by Jake Weber, date unknown.

Page 179　**"There are horse drawn carriages"**　Susan Weber, letter to Tommy Weber from Turkey, May 2, 1970.

Page 179　**"a Turkish bloke who"**　Charley Weber, interview with author, April 23, 2007.

Page 180　**"papers drawn up there"**　Tommy Weber, videotaped interview by Jake Weber, date unknown.

Page 180　**"becoming a lot sicker"**　Jake Weber, interview with author, November 11, 2006.

Page 180　**"bloody sick of it all"**　Ibid.

Page 180　**"You're embarrassing yourself and us"**　Ibid.

Page 181　**"Older brothers always see"**　Charley Weber, e-mail to author, September 22, 2008.

Page 182　**"bleeding and a little shaky"**　Charley Weber, interview with author, April 23, 2007.

Page 182　**"As she came"**　Jake Weber, interview with author, November 11, 2006.

Page 182　**"Okay"**　Charley Weber, interview with author, April 23, 2007.

Page 183　**"It was just so awful"**　Mary Keen, videotaped interview by Jake Weber, date unknown.

Page 183　**Jake and Charley had been "put to stay"**　Juliet Harmer, interview with author, October 16, 2007.

Page 183　**"in which she wanted to live"**　Mary Keen, videotaped interview by Jake Weber, date unknown.

Page 184　**"He was a terribly nice man"**　Ibid.

Page 184　**"informal patient"**　Health Records Manager, Oxford and Buckinghamshire Mental Health Partnership, e-mail to author, January 7, 2008.

Page 184　**"certified" or "sectioned"**　*Wikipedia, the Free Encyclopedia*, s.v. "Mental Health Act 1983," http://en.wikipedia.org/wiki/Mental _Health_Act_1983.

15. warneford and bowden house

Page 185　**"to recreate the atmosphere of a gentleman's country house"**　"Warneford Hospital, Warneford Lane," Headington, Oxford, Web page, www.headington.org.uk/history/listed_buildings/warneford .htm.

Page 185　**"for the accommodation of lunatics"**　Ibid.

Page 185   **"very strange people who were nodding"** Tommy Weber, video-taped interview by Jake Weber, date unknown.

Page 185   **"I went to see her"**   Jenny Ponte, interview with author, October 17, 2007.

Page 185   **"She was mad as a hatter"** Jenny Ponte, interview with author, May 12, 2008.

Page 186   **"They say of the Warneford"** Alan Ponte, videotaped interview by Jake Weber, date unknown.

Page 186   **"beloved pomfrets"** Susan Weber, letter to Jake and Charley Weber from Warneford Hospital, July 23, 1970.   •

Page 186   **"reams"** Mary Keen, videotaped interview by Jake Weber, date unknown.

Page 187   **to determine the exact nature** Health Records Manager, Oxford and Buckinghamshire Mental Health Partnership, e-mail to author, January 7, 2008.

Page 187   **"I just wanted to get her"** Tommy Weber, videotaped interview by Jake Weber, date unknown.

Page 187   **"He turned up in my"** Mary Keen, videotaped interview by Jake Weber, date unknown.

Page 188   **In photographs taken in the south** Photos courtesy of Jake Weber.

Page 188   **"terrible things were going to happen"** Mary Keen, videotaped interview by Jake Weber, date unknown.

Page 188   **"He was so threatening"** Ibid.

Page 189   **Modecate** Health Records Manager, Oxford and Buckinghamshire Mental Health Partnership, e-mail to author, January 7, 2008.

Page 189   **"shaking, stiffness, and facial tics"** Alex Berenson, "Daring to Think Differently About Schizophrenia," *New York Times*, January 24, 2008.

Page 189   **"robotic and compliant"** Dr. Ronald Weinberg, interview with author, May 13, 2008.

Page 189   **"a sort of halfway house"** Mary Keen, interview with author, September 19, 2007.

Page 189   **"rode in like a knight"** Mary Keen, videotaped interview by Jake Weber, date unknown.

Page 189   **"To some extent"** Alan Ponte, videotaped interview by Jake Weber, date unknown.

Page 190   **"a private nursing home in Harrow"** Tommy Weber, videotaped interview by Jake Weber, date unknown.

Page 191   **"the dealer by appointment"** Marianne Faithful with David Dalton, *Faithfull* (New York: Little, Brown, and Company, 1994).

Page 191   **thereby causing her doctor** Robert Greenfield, *Exile On Main St.: A Season in Hell with the Rolling Stones* (New York: Da Capo Press, 2006).

Page 191   **as Tommy later confirmed** Tommy Weber, interview with author, March 22, 2006.

Page 191   **while leafing through a fashion magazine** Andy Johns, interview with author, November 15, 2006.

Page 192   **"Puss was not nearly as ill as Anita"** Tommy Weber, videotaped interview by Jake Weber, date unknown.

Page 192   **"He was getting high every day"** Charlotte Rampling, interview with author, December 19, 2007.

Page 193   **"going off and was controlling"** Ibid.

Page 193   **"one of the top girls in the world"** Tommy Weber, interview with author, March 22, 2006.

Page 194   **"Bowden House was a very strange scene"** Charley Weber, interview with author, April 23, 2007.

Page 194   **Electrodes were then placed** *Wikipedia, the Free Encyclopedia*, s.v. "Electroconvulsive therapy," http://en.wikipedia.org/wiki/Electro convulsive_therapy.

Page 195   **225 to 450 volts of electricity** Gina Castellano, "Voltage of Electroshock Therapy," The Physics Factbook, http://hypertextbook .com/facts/2005/GinaCastellano.shtml.

Page 195   **Known side effects** Ibid.

Page 195   **"Puss was terrified"** Jenny Ponte, videotaped interview by Jake Weber, date unknown.

Page 195   **"Anita said she came back"** Jake Weber, interview with author, January 28, 2008.

Page 195   **"We visited her at Ardeley"** Ibid.

Page 195   **from London to Ireland** Tommy Weber, interview with author, March 22, 2006.

Page 196   **"Dad was so busy"** Jake Weber, interview with author, November 11, 2006.

16. ardeley

Page 197   **a sixteenth-century redbrick mansion** Chris Reynolds, "Towns and Villages in Herts: Ardeley, or Yardeley," Genealogy of Hertfordshire, www.hertfordshire-genealogy.co.uk/data/places/ardeley.htm.

Page 197   **"a fairy-tale castle."** Jenny Ponte, videotaped interview by Jake Weber, date unknown.

Page 197   **"pretty mad"** Jenny Ponte, interview with author, October 17, 2007.

Page 197   **"Gothic castle"** Alan Ponte, videotaped interview by Jake Weber, date unknown.

Page 198   **Although Alan was so angry** Ibid.

Page 198   **"thrilled to bits"** Jenny Ponte, interview with author, October 17, 2007.

Page 198   **"I am a mother"** Juliet Harmer, letter to author, October 17, 2007.

Page 198   **"may is the most beautiful"** Susan Weber, letter to Jake and Charley Weber, May 1971.

Page 199   **"Now more than ever"** John Keats, "Ode to a Nightingale" in *The Complete Poems of John Keats* (Ware, Hertfordshire: Wordsworth Editions, Ltd., 1998).

Page 199   **"I am very happy"** Susan Weber, letter to Jake and Charley Weber, May 1971.

Page 200   **"Do take care of yourself"** Jenny Ponte, videotaped interview by Jake Weber, date unknown.

Page 200   **After getting the prescription** Alan Ponte, videotaped interview by Jake Weber, date unknown.

Page 201   **a pack of hot dogs** Jake Weber, interview with author, November 11, 2006.

Page 201   **a half bottle of whiskey** Alan Ponte, videotaped interview by Jake Weber, date unknown.

Page 201   **"To Jake and Charley"** Jenny Ponte, videotaped interview by Jake Weber, date unknown.

Page 201   **"where men sit and hear"** Keats, "Ode to a Nightingale."

Page 201   **it was not as though they could** Alan Ponte, videotaped interview by Jake Weber, date unknown.

Page 201   **"Jenny, you're wanted"** Jenny Ponte, videotaped interview by Jake Weber, date unknown.

Page 201   **even in death** Alan Ponte, videotaped interview by Jake Weber, date unknown.

Page 202   **"Thomas Weber, a Company Director"** Death certificate of Susan Ann Caroline Weber, June 15, 1971.

Page 202   **"the most beautiful summer's day"** Jenny Ponte, videotaped interview by Jake Weber, date unknown.

Page 202   **"millions of lilies sent"** Ibid.

Page 202   **"Puss had gotten on very well"** Jenny Ponte, interview with author, October 17, 2007.

Page 202   **who had a beautiful voice** Alan Ponte, videotaped interview by Jake Weber, date unknown.

Page 202   "It was absolutely the worst" Jenny Ponte, videotaped interview by
             Jake Weber, date unknown.
Page 203   "I'm sure it was Puss" Ibid.

17. *villa nellcote*

Page 205   flew to Ireland Tommy Weber, interview with author, March 22, 2006.
Page 205   Covering his tracks Tommy Weber, videotaped interview by Jake
             Weber, date unknown.
Page 205   "It was more than a pound" Jake Weber, interview with author,
             June 19, 2008.
Page 206   "All smugglers have tape issues" Charley Weber, interview with au-
             thor, April 23, 2007.
Page 206   "knew what was happening" Tommy Weber, videotaped interview
             by Jake Weber, date unknown.
Page 206   "There was no voting" Ibid.
Page 206   "Aren't you going to search us?" Ibid.
Page 207   "The difference between Jake" Charley Weber, interview with au-
             thor, April 23, 2007.
Page 207   "Because it was much too much" Tommy Weber, interview with
             author, March 22, 2006.
Page 207   "I know a lot of people" Charley Weber, interview with author,
             April 23, 2007.
Page 207   "If the plane had gone down" Greenfield, *Exile on Main St.*
Page 208   "The wedding was very funny" Charley Weber, interview with au-
             thor, April 23, 2007.
Page 208   "clucking" Tommy Weber, interview with author, March 22, 2006.
Page 208   "Christ, you can't leave him" Ibid.
Page 209   "It was the same film crew" Tommy Weber, videotaped interview
             by Jake Weber, date unknown.
Page 210   "old Etonian" Tony Sanchez, *Up and Down with the Rolling Stones*
             (New York: William Morrow and Company, 1979).
Page 210   "to unwind by gulping down" Ibid.
Page 211   "whispers and faint gigglings" Ibid.
Page 211   "The reason I was able to" Tommy Weber, interview with author,
             March 22, 2006.
Page 211   "We are not old men" Richard Edmondson, "Keith Richards: Arise,
             Sir Keef," *The Independent on Sunday*, December 14, 2003.
Page 211   "a liberty" Sanchez, *Up and Down.*
Page 211   "a shower of warm summer rain" Ibid.

Page 212   "having a lovely time" Tommy Weber, interview with author, March 22, 2006.

Page 212   "clean the place up before" Ibid.

Page 213   "feel important" Ibid.

Page 213   "Marlon was also a bit wild" Charley Weber, interview with author, April 23, 2007.

Page 213   "the Rollies" Ibid.

Page 213   "We could roll a long one" Ibid.

Page 214   "backup copies" Tommy Weber, interview with author, March 22, 2006.

Page 214   "Look, I've got some" Ibid.

Page 214   "There was no way" Tommy Weber, videotaped interview by Jake Weber, date unknown.

Page 214   "Boys, I've got some terrible" Jake Weber, interview with author, January 29, 2008.

Page 214   "breaking into pathetic sobs" Charley Weber, interview with author, April 23, 2007.

Page 215   "I went immediately" Jake Weber, interview with author, January 29, 2008.

Page 215   "It was weird because" Charley Weber, interview with author, April 23, 2007.

Page 215   "saying how much she" Tommy Weber, videotaped interview by Jake Weber, date unknown.

18. on the riviera

Page 217   "I don't know why you say" Tommy Weber, videotaped interview by Jake Weber, date unknown.

Page 217   "It all started with the go-kart accident" Tommy Weber, interview with author, March 22, 2006.

Page 218   "torn all the skin from his back" Bill Wyman with Richard Havers, *Rolling with the Stones* (London: DK Publishing, 2003).

Page 218   "Now's the time" Tommy Weber, videotaped interview by Jake Weber, date unknown.

Page 218   "It was something I hadn't" Tommy Weber, interview with author, March 22, 2006.

Page 218   "I don't know if Keith had any real friends" Andy Johns, interview with author, April 4, 2005.

Page 219   just had it off with Errol Flynn's daughter Greenfield, *Exile on Main St.*

Page 219　　"**built on a slab on the side**" Tommy Weber, interview with author, March 22, 2006.

Page 221　　"**a girl with big tits**" Jake Weber, interview with author, March 15, 2006.

Page 221　　"**when one of these huge liners**" Tommy Weber, interview with author, March 22, 2006.

Page 221　　"**weird mechanics**" Charley Weber, e-mail to author, July 7, 2008.

Page 222　　"**Keith really loved Charley**" Jake Weber, interview with author, September 25, 2008.

Page 222　　"**There was I sitting**" Tommy Weber, interview with author, March 22, 2006.

Page 222　　"**You've got to see this**" Ibid.

Page 224　　"**That's it**" Ibid.

Page 224　　"**and I would come down once**" Tommy Weber, videotaped interview by Jake Weber, date unknown.

Page 225　　"**Come on, we're off**" Tommy Weber, interview with author, March 22, 2006.

Page 225　　**one year suspended sentences** Greenfield, *Exile on Main St.*

Page 225　　"**Eventually, they all got off**" Tommy Weber, interview with author, March 22, 2006.

19. on the road

Page 227　　"**a Janis Joplin-type**" Jake Weber, interview with author, November 11, 2006.

Page 228　　"**Coco was so vicious**" Jake Weber, interview with author, October 10, 2008.

Page 228　　"**directing her energy**" Ibid.

Page 228　　"**a loose sort of relationship**" Charley Weber, interview with author, April 23, 2007.

Page 228　　"**He slashed his wrists**" Jake Weber, interview with author, November 11, 2006.

Page 228　　"**hard-core bender**" Jake Weber, interview with author, May 27, 2008.

Page 228　　"**There were maybe five**" Charley Weber, interview with author, April 23, 2007.

Page 229　　"**a partner in crime**" Ibid.

Page 229　　"**ballistic**" Jake Weber, interview with author, November 11, 2006.

Page 229　　"**Black and blue all over**" Charley Weber, interview with author, April 23, 2007.

Page 229   **"It was not in the house"** Jake Weber, interview with author, July, 2008.

Page 229   **"some kind of royalty"** Charley Weber, interview with author, April 23, 2007.

Page 230   **"a 21st century fox"** Timothy Leary, *What Does WoMan Want?* (Los Angeles: 88 Books, 1976).

Page 230   **"a beautiful house in Marbella"** Joanna Harcourt-Smith, interview with author, December 7, 1996.

Page 230   **"this beautiful creature sailed"** Ibid.

Page 231   **"sort of a gangster"** Ibid.

Page 231   **"very sedate"** Charley Weber, interview with author, April 23, 2007.

Page 231   **"Look, I've got this guy"** Tommy Weber, interview with author, March 22, 2006.

Page 232   **"the most dangerous man in the world"** Greenfield, *Timothy Leary*.

Page 232   **"Washington was great"** Charley Weber, interview with author, April 23, 2007.

Page 233   **"lounging around on a mink blanket"** Joanna Harcourt-Smith, interview with author, December 7, 1996.

Page 233   **"either seeing Michel Hauchard"** Charley Weber, interview with author, April 23, 2007.

Page 233   **"We rang the doorbell"** Joanna Harcourt-Smith, interview with author, December 7, 1996.

Page 233   **"The problem was"** Tommy Weber, interview with author, March 22, 2006.

Page 234   **"Tom passed me a joint"** Charley Weber, July 7, 2008.

Page 234   **"willing to do anything"** Tommy Weber, interview with author, March 22, 2006

Page 234   **"I was actually"** Ibid.

Page 234   **"Oh, he's an old"** Lulu, interview with author, October 11, 2007.

Page 235   **"We would do an"** Joanna Harcourt-Smith, interview with author, December 7, 1996.

Page 235   **"One day, Peter said"** Charley Weber, interview with author, April 23, 2007.

Page 235   **"hysterical"** Tommy Weber, interview with author, March 22, 2006.

Page 236   **"perfect love"** Greenfield, *Timothy Leary*.

Page 236   **"fantastic"** Charley Weber, interview with author, April 23, 2007.

Page 236   **"Dad went into a dark place"** Jake Weber, interview with author, November 11, 2006.

Page 236   **"They took one look"** Jake Weber, interview with author, May 27, 2008.

Page 237   "We were all saying" Teddy Osei, interview with author, December 7, 2007.

Page 237   "nostalgic feelings for" Jake Weber, interview with author, November 11, 2006.

Page 237   "Skunk weed were sold" *Wikipedia, the Free Encyclopedia*, s.v. "Freetown Christiana," http://en.wikipedia.org/wiki/Freetown_Christiana.

Page 237   "I know we arrived" Jake Weber, interview with author, May 27, 2008.

Page 238   "play Chopin" Charley Weber, interview with author, April 23, 2007.

Page 238   "a ghostly figure" Ibid.

Page 239   "At this point" Jake Weber, interview with author, November 11, 2006.

Page 240   "When on alcohol" Charley Weber, interview with author, July 7, 2008.

Page 240   "in reduced circumstances" Jake Weber, interview with author, November 11, 2006.

Page 240   "bloody disinherited me" Reginald Arkner, interview with author, September 14, 2007.

Page 241   "It was very awkward" Jake Weber, interview with author, November 11, 2006.

Page 241   "bad-mannered, difficult brat" Charley Weber, e-mail to author, July 7, 2008.

Page 241   "There was a lot of screaming" Jake Weber, interview with author, November 11, 2007.

Page 241   "This little nebbishy guy" Jake Weber, interview with author, November 11, 2006.

Page 242   "got busted by the" Ibid.

Page 242   "It was the size" Charley Weber, interview with author, April 23, 2007.

Page 242   "I drove back" Lulu, interview with author, October 11, 2007.

Page 242   "had shot up the cat" Charley Weber, interview with author, April 23, 2007.

Page 242   "he looked like a cat" Jake Weber, interview with author, June 19, 2008.

Page 243   "was loaded" Charley Weber, interview with author, April 23, 2007.

Page 243   "Dad had all these blank airlines" Jake Weber, interview with author, June 19, 2008.

20. st. ann's villas

Page 245   "We got back to England" Jake Weber, interview with author, November 11, 2006.

Page 245   "smaller than a living" Ibid.

Page 246   "I thought he was pretty tasty" Sally, interview with author, October 23, 2007.

Page 246   "smoking and eating" Ibid.

Page 246   "They were so strung out" Jake Weber, interview with author, November 11, 2006.

Page 247   "We were both really" Ibid.

Page 247   "We were strung out" Sally, interview with author, October 23, 2007.

Page 247   "It was the ultimate betrayal" Jake Weber, interview with author, November 11, 2006.

Page 248   "they didn't have any food" Ibid.

Page 249   "There were no uniforms" Charley Weber, interview with author, April 23, 2007.

Page 249   "Jake did a little better" Charley Weber, e-mail to author, July 7, 2008.

Page 249   "mortified every time he did so" Jake Weber, interview with author, October 10, 2008.

Page 249   "always grim" Jake Weber, interview with author, November 11, 2006.

Page 250   "because there was no" Ibid.

Page 250   "Tommy would set up" Charley Weber, interview with author, April 23, 2007.

Page 250   "He kept hitting Tommy" Jake Weber, interview with author, June 19, 2008.

Page 251   "Tommy took the guy" Jake Weber, interview with author, November 11, 2006.

Page 251   "Well, I'm sitting in" Tommy Weber, letter to Jake and Charley Weber, July 3, 1979, courtesy of Jake Weber.

Page 252   "He saved me" Jake Weber, interview with author, November 11, 2006.

Page 252   "The whole thing about" Charley Weber, interview with author, April 23, 2007.

Page 252   "It was insanity cubed" Ibid.

Page 253   "twenty-nine and super beautiful" Ibid.

Page 253   "shot about seventy-five music" Charley Weber, e-mail to author, July 7, 2008.

Page 253   "I'd seen that sort" Charley Weber, interview with author, April 23, 2007.

Page 254   "It is never summer" Miles Cookman, interview with author, December 13, 2007.

Page 254   "the Scrubs, that's hard time" Harriet Vyner, *Groovy Bob: The Life and Times of Robert Fraser* (London: Faber and Faber, 1999).

Page 254   **"I was only in there"** Adam Higginbotham, "Dear Superstar: Keith Richards," *Blender Magazine*, May 2008.

Page 254   **"some traces of smack"** Tommy Weber, letter to Jake Weber, June 28, 1982.

Page 255   **"strung out"** Ibid.

Page 255   **"Hi Jake, hope"** Ibid.

Page 256   **"Your bounty astonishes"** Tommy Weber, letter to Jake Weber, June 27, 1982.

Page 257   **"I remember walking"** Buddy (Tommy's son), October 20, 2007.

Page 257   **"There is a very important secret"** Tommy Weber, letter to Jake Weber, June 28, 1982.

Page 258   **"been quite a long struggle"** Tommy Weber, letter to Jake Weber, July 27, 1982.

Page 258   **"go around the world"** Sally, interview with author, October 23, 2007.

21. *rugby*

Page 259   **"oppressive market town"** Pete Prince, interview with author, November 2, 2007.

Page 259   **"no money at all"** Ibid.

Page 261   **"He never brandished"** Ibid.

Page 261   **"He threw pills at people"** Pete Bain, interview with author, December 6, 2007.

Page 262   **"buying morphine sulphate"** Jake Weber, interview with author, January 28, 2008.

Page 262   **"to put his own twist,"** Pete Prince, interview with author, November 2, 2007.

Page 263   **"a bit impertinent"** Ibid.

Page 263   **"Ho-ney . . . *Boy*!"** Ibid.

Page 265   **"What are you going to do?"** Ibid.

Page 265   **"permanent monument to"** Tommy Weber CV, May 1995, courtesy of Jake Weber.

Page 265   **"We went"** Pete Prince, interview with author, November 2, 2007.

Page 266   **"was completely gutted"** Ibid.

Page 267   **"this weird little Fiat car"** Ibid.

Page 267   **"Because he had the right"** Ibid.

Page 267   **"He didn't want to be wealthy"** Ibid.

Page 267   **"He thought he was racing again"** Buddy, interview with author, October 20, 2007.

Page 268   **"I'm glad you did that"** Ibid.

Page 268   "shrunk two or three" Ibid.

Page 268   "Before that" Pete Prince, interview with author, November 2, 2007.

Page 268   "manic" Sally, interview with author, October 23, 2007.

Page 268   "That was when" Pete Prince, interview with author, November 2, 2007.

Page 269   "He looked so bad" Ibid.

Page 269   "a highwayman like Tommy" Jake Weber, interview with author, May 23, 2006.

Page 269   "you get put away for life" Charley Weber, interview with author, April 23, 2007.

Page 270   "Charley, fucking grow up" Ibid.

Page 270   "And that was it" Ibid.

Page 270   "While he was here" Lulu, e-mail to author, September 26, 2008.

Page 270   "desperately and wanted" Lulu, interview with author, October 11, 2007.

Page 271   "impulsively married" Jake Weber, interview with author, September 25, 2008.

Page 271   "a couple of hundred quid" Jake Weber, interview with author, June 19, 2008.

Page 272   "The place was a wreck" Pete Prince, interview with author, November 2, 2007.

Page 273   "sometimes physically weep" Buddy, interview with author, October 20, 2007.

Page 273   "We've always had a confrontational relationship" Jake Weber, interview with author, May 27, 2008.

Page 273   "Look at that, Charley" Charley Weber, interview with author, April 23, 2007.

Page 273   "The girl who lived" Ibid.

Page 274   "Unlike the rest of my family" Jake Weber, interview with author, September 25, 2008.

Page 274   "The first time I saw Waylon" Charley Weber, interview by Mary Keil, February 13, 16, 2007.

Page 274   "happier and more stable" Charley Weber, interview with author, October 21, 2008.

Page 275   "he could have a laugh" Pete Prince, interview with author, November 2, 2007.

Page 275   "he felt he didn't have much time" Lulu, interview with author, October 11, 2007.

Page 275   "he had paid his debt" Charley Weber, interview with author, April 23, 2007.

Page 275   "**moment of grace**" Jake Weber, interview with author, June 19, 2008.

Page 275   "**I think he did come**" Sally, interview with author, October 23, 2007.

Page 275   "**I could hear the equipment**" Buddy, interview with author, October 20, 2007.

Page 276   "**But don't it feel like somebody nearby**" We Are Juan, "Kinder Days," on *Road 2 Reach You*, Mary Keil Productions, 2004.

Page 276   "**Everyone said, 'Oh, let's'**" Pete Prince, interview with author, November 2, 2007.

Index

"A Day in the Life" (song), 102, 104, 105
Afghanistan
  hashish smuggling and, 108, 133, 135–137
  Puss in, 148
Aitken, Max, 132
Allen, Barbara, 112, 113
Allen, Field Marshall Viscount, 43
Almora, 169–176
Altamont Speedway concert, 162
"Ambitious" (article), 91
Anderson, Poul, 3
Anderson, Poul Christian. *See* Arkner, Poul Christian
Anger, Kenneth, 150
Anna Cat (boutique), 93
Antonioni, Michelangelo, 97
Ardeley, 277–278
Arkner, Anders Reginald, 4, 8–9, 10, 48, 240
Arkner, Pamela Joyce (Weber). *See* Weber, Pamela Joyce
Arkner, Poul Christian, 1, 3–4
  Finnish military service and, 5, 6–7
  reunion with son Tommy, 240–241
  transfer of Tommy to mother, 10

Arkner, Thomas Ejnar. *See* Weber, Thomas Evelyn (Thomas Ejnar Arkner)
Artane, 189
Arthurian legend, 115–116
Atlee, Clement, 41
Auden, W. H., 40
Avengers, The (television show), 101, 122
Ayurvedic medicine, 171
Aznavour, Charles, 230

Baba, Meher, 111–112
Bacall, Lauren, 230
Baghdad House, 112
Bain, Pete, 261, 276
Barbarella (film), 190
Bardot, Brigitte, 230
Barrett, Syd, 187
Barrows, Winifred, 55
Baxter, Raymond, 88
Beatles, the, 102–107, 108
Beaton Cecil, 17
Beaufort Hunt, 27–28
Bell College of Languages, 58, 61
Benson, Bobby, 236–237
Berger, Helmut, 129, 156
Betjeman, John, 78